DZOGCHEN

The Heart Essence of the Great Perfection

DZOGCHEN

The Heart Essence of the Great Perfection

Dzogchen Teachings
given in the West

by

HIS HOLINESS THE DALAI LAMA

Translated by
Geshe Thupten Jinpa
and
Richard Barron (Chökyi Nyima)

Edited by Patrick Gaffney

Snow Lion Publications
Ithaca, NY USA

Snow Lion Publications
P.O. Box 6483
Ithaca, New York 14851 U.S.A
Telephone: +1 607-273-8519

www.snowlionpub.com

Printed in Canada on acid-free recycled paper.

Library of Congress Cataloging-in-Publication Data
Bstan-dzin-rgya-mtsho, Dalai lama XIV, 1935–
Dzogchen: The heart Essence of the Great Perfection
p. cm.
Includes biliographical references
ISBN 1-55939-157-x
1. Rdzogs-chen (Rñiṅ-ma-pa) I. Thupten Jinpa.
II. Nyima, Chökyi, 1951–
III. Gaffney, Patrick. IV. Title.
BQ7662.4 .B783 2000
294.3'420423--dc21   00-010505

CONTENTS

FOREWORD

BY
SOGYAL RINPOCHE

His Holiness the Dalai Lama is the supreme head of Tibetan Buddhism, an exceptional Buddhist master. For the Tibetan people, he has been their guiding light through half a century of struggle, and for countless others around the world, the compassionate apostle of peace whose message brings such solace and inspiration. His achievements have been many and great, but one of the most far-reaching, I believe, is what he has achieved for the Buddhist tradition of Tibet. How differently it would have turned out, I sometimes think, had he not been there, with his courage, patience and vision, to protect the continuity of Tibetan Buddhism during such a precarious period in its history, and so give it the integrity and vigour it possesses today.

Through his teachings and his writings, the Dalai Lama has also taken on an ever more important role for those practising and studying Buddhism in the west. Having received and studied teachings of all the Buddhist schools of Tibet, His Holiness is an authority on the whole range of teaching and practice within the different traditions. On four occasions during his tours of the west, he has taught on Dzogchen, the innermost teachings treasured at the heart of the ancient Nyingma order of Tibetan Buddhism, and these occasions are recorded here in this book. To receive such teachings from His Holiness is, I feel, something quite extraordinary, and the fact that he has given these Dzogchen teachings, choosing as well to grant the empowerment of Padmasambhava from the pure visions of the fifth Dalai Lama, not only counts as a wonderful blessing but contains, I believe, a very deep significance. In Paris in 1982, conferring this empowerment for the first time in the west, he made a point of expressing his delight at how auspicious it had been. When he gave it again in San Jose in 1989 in the context of his Dzogchen teachings, history itself lent the whole event an altogether special meaning, with the announcement that he had been awarded the Nobel Peace Prize.

With his knowledge, his learning and his experience, His Holiness brings to his explanation of Dzogchen a perspective and breadth which are unique. Of course, one of his characteristics has always been his all-embracing attitude towards all Buddhist traditions, indeed towards all faiths. When I think of His Holiness's open-minded and unbiased vision of the Dharma, I cannot help but remember my master Jamyang Khyentse Chökyi Lodrö, whose whole life was lived in the spirit of Ri-mé, the ecumenical or non-partisan movement that had been nurtured with such care by his predecessor Jamyang Khyentse Wangpo and the lamas of the nineteenth century. I can never forget the day in 1955 when I went with my master to meet His Holiness for the very first time. Earlier that year, Jamyang Khyentse had decided to leave his monastery in Dzongsar in Kham, as conditions in East Tibet were deteriorating rapidly, and we had travelled slowly on horseback to Central Tibet, visiting the great holy sites of Tibetan Buddhism on the way. When we arrived in Lhasa, Jamyang Khyentse was invited to meet His Holiness almost at once. I still remember the awe and excitement that filled me as we climbed the steps of the Potala Palace, gazing about me and catching my breath at every turn.

My master had requested a particular empowerment of Avalokiteśvara, and we were led to a room where a small throne had been prepared for Jamyang Khyentse in front of His Holiness's own throne. There was a young incarnate lama from the Geluk tradition who had been waiting for a long time to see His Holiness, and he and I were seated on small carpets to the right and left of my master. Now and again during the lengthy empowerment and teaching that followed, His Holiness would catch my eye and give me a smile which was utterly disarming. I sat there transfixed by his presence, smiling back at him. He was twenty years old then, and there are two things I can remember which struck me: his sparkling alertness and intelligence, and the warmth and compassion of that smile.

My master was invited to see His Holiness in private, and at the end of the teaching they retired together into the Dalai Lama's private quarters. I was waiting on a balcony, lost in my thoughts and looking out over Lhasa, when His Holiness's principal bodyguard, a tall, thickset monk with an imposing presence, came out to get me. I joined my master inside, and as we were served tea, His Holiness asked me my name and my age. He then held me in a piercing gaze and told me pointedly to make sure I studied hard. It was a moment I have always remembered, for it was probably one of the most important of my entire life.

I did not know it then, but Jamyang Khyentse had been unanimously chosen and requested to transmit to the Dalai Lama the teachings of the Nyingma, Sakya, and Kagyü traditions. Yet that was never to happen. My master passed away in Sikkim in 1959, just months after His Holiness went into exile in India. In fact it was many of Jamyang Khyentse's own disciples who passed on the different lineages to the Dalai Lama, and especially Kyabjé Dilgo Khyentse Rinpoche, who offered him Nyingma and Dzogchen teachings and become one of His Holiness's main teachers.

The years during which His Holiness gave the teachings in this book were also a time when truly great exponents of Dzogpachenpo were still among us, masters born in the early part of the last century, whose soaring realization embodied the full force of the wisdom and mystery of the Dzogchen teachings. I think of Dudjom Rinpoche, Dilgo Khyentse Rinpoche, Tulku Urgyen Rinpoche and Nyoshul Khenpo Jamyang Dorje. They are gone now, though of course their presence is always with us, and their wisdom lives on, in the disciples they cared for with such compassion. These extraordinary masters had been instrumental in establishing these teachings in the west, so enacting all those prophecies that the practice of Dzogchen would take root here. And as they left this world, I am sure that as they prayed for the teachings of Buddha to benefit countless beings, they will have invested those prayers, and all their aspirations, in His Holiness the Dalai Lama. For now that this generation of masters is no more, a teacher like His Holiness becomes even more precious, his role in securing the future of the teachings and their authenticity of even more vital and urgent significance.

To Rigpa and to me fell the great privilege of inviting His Holiness to teach on Dzogchen in Paris in 1982, in London in 1984, and in San Jose, California, in 1989. In this book, for the sake of completeness, another teaching he gave on Dzogchen in Finland in 1988 has been included, and, as an afterword, a teaching given spontaneously by Nyoshul Khen Rinpoche during the Dalai Lama's programme in 1989. As you will see, what comes through in these historic teachings are His Holiness's vast knowledge of the Buddhist traditions of Tibet, his passionate interest in that ultimate point where they all converge, and his profound respect for the Dzogchen teachings and their realized practitioners and masters.

These teachings weave together in fact so many elements and figures of crucial importance for the Nyingma and Dzogchen tradition: the first human Dzogchen master, the vidyādhara Garab Dorje; the incomparable Longchen Rabjam; the 'Great Fifth' Dalai Lama and his pure visions; the extraordinary teaching of Patrul Rinpoche, master of the Longchen Nyingtik and the oral lineage of Dzogchen pith instructions; and the writings of the third Dodrupchen, Jikmé Tenpé Nyima. And the presence that shines through them all, like a great sun, majestic and sublime, is Padmasambhava, the Precious Guru and father of Tibetan Buddhism.

Here then is His Holiness in one of his many aspects—as great Buddhist master speaking from the innermost reaches of his tradition. There are many other Dalai Lamas: spokesman for non-violence, human rights and the unprotected; defender of the environment;

leader of a threatened people; and, increasingly, a world leader to whom people in their millions turn instinctively, as a repository of their dreams and hopes. For so many, it must be said, His Holiness is a living metaphor for all they hold true and sacred, an axis around which they can centre their vision of humanity. In him the history of Tibet and the destiny of the world are tantalizingly bound together.

It is a tremendous honour and blessing to introduce this book. At the end of his teachings in San Jose in 1989, His Holiness suggested to me that we compile the teachings he had given on Dzogchen in Europe and the United States into one book, and I am delighted that we have been able to fulfil his wish. Let us hope that His Holiness will consider that by giving these teachings he has created a certain understanding, and so will feel inspired to continue to expand on his teachings of Dzogchen in the west.

As I write this, in the millennial year, His Holiness is visiting southern France to teach on 'The Path to Enlightenment' at the request of a group of Buddhist centres in the Golfe du Lyon region, of which Lerab Ling, Rigpa's main retreat centre, is one of the members. At Lerab Ling, he will confer the empowerment of Vajrakīlaya, according to the terma revelation of Tertön Sogyal, Lerab Lingpa. This great light of the teaching of Buddha, friend to each and every human being, continues to give of himself tirelessly in his extraordinary mission of wisdom and compassion. And I pray, I know along with countless others, that he lives long and that every one of his aspirations be fulfilled.

Sogyal Rinpoche
Lerab Ling, 6 July 2000

PREFACE

The teachings gathered in this book all took place between 1982 and 1989. They spanned almost a decade, one which changed beyond recognition the degree to which people in the west took an active interest in Buddhism and Tibet. For the Tibetans, striving to capture the attention of the world, the early years of the 1980s were often a bleak and uphill struggle. Yet by the end of the decade, organizations of every kind had sprung up, driven by an irresistible wave of interest in Tibet, its culture and its Buddhist traditions. In 1989 came a climax and a turning point, when His Holiness the Dalai Lama was awarded the Nobel Peace Prize.

All through the 1980s, His Holiness visited different countries around the world, to give Buddhist teachings and spread his philosophy of peace. His first, historic, journey to the west had been in 1973, when he travelled to Italy, the Vatican, Switzerland, Holland, Belgium, Ireland, Norway, Sweden, Denmark and the United Kingdom. But it was only after 1979 and his first visit to the United States that he began to travel more often and more widely. On four occasions during these visits to the west, His Holiness accepted invitations to teach on Dzogchen or 'The Great Perfection', the ultimate teachings at the heart of the ancient Nyingma school of Tibetan Buddhism.

The first of these occasions was in Paris, at the Pagode de Vincennes in 1982, when he conferred the empowerment of Guru

Padmasambhava and his Eight Manifestations from the *Sangwa Gyachen* visionary teachings of the 'Great Fifth' Dalai Lama. Speaking about the process of empowerment in general, he then outlined the ground, path and fruition of Dzogchen. Next, in the summer of 1984, during a two week tour of England and Scotland, His Holiness dedicated a one day teaching to Dzogchen, following a two and a half day seminar on Buddhist philosophy in London. Granting a blessing of 'Liberation upon Contact', he gave a commentary on the heart of Dzogchen practice, 'Hitting the Essence in Three Words', from a famous and much loved teaching by the great nineteenth century master, Patrul Rinpoche.

In 1988, at the request of one of the organizers of his visit to Finland, the Dalai Lama gave a public teaching entitled 'Dzogchen' in Helsinki. There he set the practice of Dzogchen within a context of the the Four Noble Truths and the Four Seals of Buddhism. The following year, in October 1989, His Holiness made his longest presentation on Dzogchen in the west, in a two day teaching in San Jose, California. This event was made all the more historic and auspicious as it took place only three days after the dramatic announcement that he had been awarded the Nobel Peace Prize. Basing his teaching on Longchenpa's *The Treasury of the Dharmadhātu*, and drawing inspiration from the writings of Dodrupchen Jikmé Tenpé Nyima, His Holiness concluded with the empowerment of Guru Padmasambhava and his Eight Manifestations from the fifth Dalai Lama's pure visions.

Included in this book is also a teaching by Nyoshul Khen Rinpoche, 'A Gift to the World', which he gave one evening in San Jose in 1989 after His Holiness had taught. Khen Rinpoche was one of the foremost authorities on Dzogchen of his time, and a teacher for whom His Holiness had the highest respect. Speaking on the essence of Buddhadharma, he captured the effortless depth and ease of Dzogpachenpo, which he embodied with such perfect completeness.

To these teachings, His Holiness brings all those qualities which are so uniquely his—the accumulated knowledge of years of study, his incisive insight, his curiosity, humour and compassion, and his seemingly infinite subtlety of mind. During the teachings, there were moments of infectious hilarity, when His Holiness would burst out into peals of laughter, whether it was while speculating on an unorthodox use for the vajra and bell, or at the protracted convolutions of a Finnish translator grappling with his words. There were moments of humility, as he played down his own understanding and grasp of the teachings, moments of reflection, of intense concentration and of a transcendent, transparent stillness. And as always with His Holiness, there were moments of heart-stopping warmth and tenderness.

In these teachings, we find a number of themes recur. His Holiness explains why it is that Dzogchen is called 'the pinnacle of all vehicles', while at the same time the final teachings in all the Buddhist traditions of Tibet lead to the same ultimate point: the clear light. This is a subject, His Holiness admits, which fires his interest like few others, and a theme throughout these teachings, as he reveals the subtle affinities and differences between Dzogchen and the teachings and practices of the other schools of Tibetan Buddhism.

His Holiness seems moved by a concern to dispel the kind of misunderstandings that could come from a facile comparison of one tradition with another. During his teachings in London in 1984, he quoted a remarkable statement by Jamyang Khyentse Chökyi Lodrö (1893-1959), which throws light on the particular character of the teachings of the different schools:

> As is said in an oral transmission by the great lama Jamyang Khyentse Chökyi Lodrö, when the great Nyingmapa adept Longchen Rabjam gives a presentation of the ground, path and fruit, he does so mainly from the perspective of the enlightened state of a Buddha, whereas the Sakyapa presentation is mainly from the perspective of the spiritual experience of a yogi on the path, and the Gelukpa presentation is mainly from the perspective of how phenomena

appear to ordinary sentient beings. His statement
appears to be worthy of considerable reflection;
through it many misunderstandings can be removed.[1]

Naturally, in many places in these teachings, His Holiness speaks
about the pure, pristine awareness of rigpa. As Dodrupchen Jikmé
Tenpé Nyima explains: "Generally speaking, in the instructions on
Dzogchen, profound and special aspects are endless. The key point,
however, is the differentiation between the ordinary mind and rigpa.
As Jikmé Lingpa puts it in his *Treasury of Enlightened Attributes*:

> Rigpa, which transcends the ordinary mind,
> Is the special feature of the natural Dzogpachenpo".[2]

One factor to which His Holiness returns again and again here is
the importance, for a practitioner, of a wider knowledge of the
whole structure of the Buddhist teaching. Hand in hand with this,
he underlines the need to learn how to interpret the specific
terminology used in the different schools and strata of Buddhism.
And at the same time as he insists on a more rigorous approach to
studying the sources of Buddhism, His Holiness loses no
opportunity to provide clues and instructions on how to apply
specific points to the everyday business of living. In giving teachings
such as these, it becomes clear that His Holiness's aim is to
strengthen the bases of Buddhadharma among practitioners in the
west, by clarifying and deepening their understanding, and with an
eye to the future stability and authenticity of the Dharma here.

In this book, His Holiness's teachings appear in chronological
order. Each one is prefaced by a brief sketch of the background to
the teachings, allowing the reader to locate them in time and place,
and also opening a window onto His Holiness's interests and life.
For these teachings and the events that took place around them are,
in a very real sense, part of the Dalai Lama's biography. Some of the
important sources or masters to whom His Holiness refers are
noted, although there is no need to dwell on the lives of the masters

of the Dzogchen lineage mentioned here—Garab Dorje, Guru Padmasambhava, Longchen Rabjam, Jikmé Lingpa, Jikmé Gyalwé Nyugu, Patrul Rinpoche, Dodrupchen Jikmé Tenpé Nyima, Jamyang Khyentse Chökyi Lodrö and Dilgo Khyentse Rinpoche— when they have been recounted so authentically and with such beauty by Tulku Thondup Rinpoche in his *Masters of Meditation and Miracles.*

The teachings in 1988 and 1989 were translated by Geshe Thupten Jinpa, and those from 1982 and 1984 by Richard Barron (Chökyi Nyima). The overall process of producing this book entailed returning to original audio cassettes and Tibetan transcripts of His Holiness's words, and several layers of revision ensued. Since the teachings in 1982, 1984 and 1989 were given at the request of Rigpa and Sogyal Rinpoche, the great blessing of compiling and editing all these teachings into one book, as suggested by His Holiness, devolved onto members of Rigpa.

The translation of *The Special Teaching of the Wise and Glorious King* included here is based on one made by Sogyal Rinpoche during a retreat at Loch Lomond in Scotland in 1984, but includes a number of clarifications by Alak Zenkar Rinpoche, and insights gleaned from several excellent translations of this text, by Tulku Thondup Rinpoche, Sarah Harding, Erik Pema Kunsang, John Reynolds and Richard Barron.

On a linguistic note, as this volume represents the work of more than one translator, and involved an extensive editing process, there have been alternative translations for certain terms, and these are often reflected in the glossary. At the same time an effort has been made towards consistency and towards following the choice of terminology which has been used for some time to translate His Holiness's teachings.

PART ONE

GROUND, PATH AND FRUITION

Paris, 1982

GROUND, PATH AND FRUITION

THE BACKGROUND

In the chilly, wet October of 1982, His Holiness the Dalai Lama visited France for the first time. Over twelve days, in Paris, Strasbourg, Toulouse and Digne, he gave Buddhist teachings and interviews, met dignitaries of every description, and touched on all the points of contact between France and Tibetan culture, in what was becoming a blueprint for his visits to different countries. The France he encountered in 1982 was one gripped by uncertainty, with a new socialist government, terrorist attacks in Paris, and bread, petrol and public transport all rising in price. Yet this was also a France with a deep and serious interest in all things Tibetan, and where the public response to His Holiness's visit was tumultuous. Three articles splashed across the pages of *Le Monde*, excited yet baffled at discovering his "disconcerting, engaging personality", "disarming" and "always joyful". At his public talk in Paris, 'Universal Compassion and the World Crisis', a vast, ebullient crowd unable to gain entry to the hall spilled out onto the pavement in their hundreds, milling around in noisy abandon, as the police attempted to disembroil them.

The Pagode de Vincennes in the far south-east corner of Paris was the setting for the empowerment which His Holiness granted at the invitation of Rigpa and Sogyal Rinpoche. This exotic building dates back to 1931 and the Colonial Exhibition, held to celebrate the civilizing virtues of France's colonial past in Asia, Africa and Oceania. The Cameroon and Togo pavilion was designed as a replica of a tribal hut, but at sixty metres square and some twenty-two metres high and with a roof formed of 180,000 chestnut tiles, it was a lot more ambitious than its original model. After serving for forty years as a museum of wood, it lay empty till 1977, when Jean Sainteny, former French representative in Cambodia, requested it from the city of Paris as a site for an International Institute that would cater for all the ethnic Buddhist groups in France. A competition was launched for a large international looking statue of Buddha, which was won by a Yugoslav sculptor, François Mozes. His Buddha, crafted in the workshop of the Catalan surrealist painter Joan Miró, is made of fibreglass covered with twenty-three carat gold, and bears a face which is regarded as distinctly European. Inaugurated in October 1977 by Jacques Chirac, then Mayor of Paris, the Pagode has ever since remained a unique and important venue for major Buddhist gatherings. By 1982, large teachings and empowerments had already been given there by masters such as Kyabjé Dudjom Rinpoche, Kyabjé Dilgo Khyentse Rinpoche and Kyabjé Kalu Rinpoche. And it was here that, at 2pm on Thursday 7 October, hundreds gathered to receive His Holiness's empowerment and teaching.

THE FIFTH DALAI LAMA

As he explains, His Holiness chose to give the empowerment of Padmasambhava and his Eight Manifestations from the cycle of profound pure visions of the 'Great Fifth' Dalai Lama, Ngawang Lobsang Gyatso. Born in 1617 to descendants of the royal house of Zahor, the fifth Dalai Lama was one of the most dynamic, skilful and influential figures in Tibetan history. Out of the chaos of seventeenth century Central Asia, he emerged in 1642 with the whole land of Tibet from Ladakh to Tachienlu under his rule. Ten years later he was invited to Beijing by the emperor Shun-chih, where he was treated as an equal and offered an imperial proclamation inscribed in gold, calling him 'Dalai Lama, Vajra Holder and Master of the Teaching'.

The fifth Dalai Lama constructed the Potala Palace, pioneered the dual system of spiritual and temporal governance of Tibet, and is credited with establishing a national health system and educational programme. He was a prolific writer, his historical and autobiographical writings supplying a crucial source for historians of the period. He passed away in his sixty-sixth year in 1682 in the Potala Palace, while absorbed in meditation on Kurukullā, a deity associated with power and magnetizing. This was read as an auspicious sign of the power of his enlightened activity in the future.

Ngawang Lobsang Gyatso occupies an important place in the transmission of the Nyingma teachings, and is included by Dudjom Rinpoche in his famous 'History of the Nyingmapas' among the biographies of the tertöns.[3] This is particularly on account of his revelation of the 'pure visions' of the *Gyachen Nyer Nga*—'Twenty-five Sealed Teachings'. The fifth Dalai Lama was prophesied in certain termas as an emanation of the enlightened activity of King Trisong Detsen. He felt a deep connection with the Nyingma tradition of Guru Padmasambhava, and had a number of important Nyingma teachers, such as Zurchen Chöying Rangdrol, Khöntön Paljor Lhundrup, and Terdak Lingpa, Minling Terchen Gyurmé Dorje.[4] He was particularly close to the masters of the 'Northern Treasure' lineage of Rigdzin Gödem, who appear frequently in his visions. In his autobiography he also speaks of Pema Rigdzin, the first Dzogchen Rinpoche, whom he urged to found the Dzogchen monastery in Kham; he calls him "the great Dzogchenpa who has totally understood the Nyingtik". Dudjom Rinpoche writes:

> Of particular interest is the manner in which the Dalai Lama received the teachings contained in the 'Profound Pure Visions', which was foretold in a prophecy in the termas of the glorious Tashi Topgyal: [5]

> > You who are now king of the black-headed race,
> > Through pure aspirations, your fifth incarnation will reveal
> > 'Twenty-five'—with five special mind treasures.

In fact, when the fifth Dalai Lama went to glorious Samyé, the auspicious conditions arose for him to reveal actual termas. However, on account of the time, the place and the situation, he did not take possession of them. Later on, when the infinite deities of the three roots actually appeared to him in visions, according to the prophecies and empowerments he received, he wrote down the twenty-five sections of teaching called *Sangwa Gyachen*—'Bearing the Seal of Secrecy'. Along with his orally composed additional commentary, they amount to two volumes. He bestowed the empowerments and instructions of all of them on a gathering of supreme beings, principally the holders of the tradition of the ancient translation school such as the sovereign of the dharma Terdak Lingpa and the vidyādhara Pema Trinlé. As a result, they came to spread far and wide, and their lineage has continued, unimpaired, up until the present day.[6]

From the age of six, the fifth Dalai Lama began to experience a stream of visions which continued, almost uninterrupted, throughout his entire life. They are chronicled in his autobiographical writings.[7] In the seventh month of the fire monkey year, 1656, at the age of forty, the Dalai Lama prepared to celebrate the tenth day offerings to Padmasambhava by collecting together an extraordinary group of nine terma images of Guru Padmasambhava, discovered by Nyangral Nyima Özer, Guru Chöwang, Sangyé Lingpa, Ratna Lingpa, Kunkyong Lingpa and Trango Sherab Özer. Not long after he had started the practice, along with the monks of the Namgyal College, a vision began to materialize, in which Guru Rinpoche appeared and conferred empowerment on him. He witnessed all the eight manifestations of Padmasambhava dancing in the maṇḍala, and then dissolving into him. Yeshé Tsogyal appeared and led him to meet the Great Guru in his palace, surrounded by the eight manifestations. This was the vision that was the source of the empowerment which His Holiness the Dalai Lama would give in Paris.

As His Holiness explains in his introduction, the empowerment of Padmasambhava and his Eight Manifestations[8] is the sādhana of the guru—*ladrup*—from the *Sangwa Gyachen* cycle. This was the first time His Holiness had given this empowerment in the west, and he was to give it again in 1989 in California. In January 1992, at the request of the seventh Dzogchen Rinpoche, he began to transmit the complete cycle of empowerments from the *Sangwa Gyachen* on the occasion of the inauguration of the new Dzogchen monastery in Kollegal, South India. He gave the empowerments of Kagyé and Dorje Drolö, during which he made this fascinating personal reflection:

> I was quite young when I received the complete teachings of the secret visions of the fifth Dalai Lama. Although I did not pay too much attention at the time, I remember that I did have a number of very good dreams, and so it appears we have a special connection. Later, in Lhasa, I found the works of the fifth Dalai Lama, which had been preserved mainly, I believe, by the later Dalai Lamas. Among them are the very secret teachings which exist in the form of illustrated manuscripts. . . Later, in India I obtained these scriptures and spent a few months in retreat, practising Kagyé, Hayagrīva, Avalokiteśvara and others. On my side, I feel that I am very fortunate: right from the fifth Dalai Lama, because of aspirations and prayers, I have been in the long line of those who hold the name of Lotus Holder. And it seems there is some particularly special connection with the fifth Dalai Lama.

Before beginning the empowerment at Vincennes in 1982, His Holiness explained the meaning of empowerment and then gave an outline of ground, path and fruition in Dzogchen.[9] Here he unveiled a theme which appears throughout all these teachings: the affinities, differences and ultimate oneness, of the view and practice of the Highest Yoga Tantra in the new translation schools, and the ancient tradition of Dzogchen. He also underlined the importance of the introduction to the pure awareness of rigpa, preparing, in a way, for the teachings in 1984 and 1989.

His Holiness sat directly in front of the great golden figure of
Lord Buddha, before him the crowded pagoda, and lamas repres-
enting all of the Buddhist traditions: Nyoshul Khen Rinpoche,
Lama Yeshé, founder of the FPMT, Dagpo Rinpoche, Taklung
Tsetrul Pema Wangyal Rinpoche, Sogyal Rinpoche and geshes and
lamas from all the Buddhist centres in France. Two days later, His
Holiness returned to the Pagode to give a brief teaching for the
Buddhist community. Then, in the centre of the front row, sat
Jacques Chirac. At the end of the session, His Holiness leant down
and quietly asked him never to forget to care for the people of Paris.

HIS HOLINESS THE DALAI LAMA

THE PURE VISIONS

The empowerment I am going to give today is in response to a
request I received some time ago from Sogyal Rinpoche. He asked
that when I came to Europe I might consider visiting some of his
centers to give empowerments, particularly from the cycle known
as *Sangwa Gyachen*—'Bearing the Seal of Secrecy'—and I agreed that
I would, as long as time permitted. Now, since my travels have
brought me to Europe and to France, I have been invited once again
by Sogyal Rinpoche to teach in Paris. From all the possible empowerments within the Sangwa Gyachen cycle, I have decided to
bestow the empowerment for the "mind sādhana" known in Tibetan
as *Tukdrup Yang Nying Kundü*—'The Union of All the Innermost
Essences', as I think this will be the most appropriate of them all.

As many of you know, this Sangwa Gyachen cycle forms part
of a larger tradition, the Secret Mantra teachings of the Nyingma
or Ancient school of Tibetan Buddhism. The rituals and practices
of this school are transmitted in three ways—the extensive lineage
of *kama*, the shorter lineage of *terma*, and the profound transmission
through pure visions—*dak nang*. The Sangwa Gyachen cycle consists

of transmissions which have their origin in these pure visions.

Now pure visions can be considered from two points of view. First, there are meditative experiences of a more ephemeral kind, known in Tibetan as *nyam*. Then there are the pure visions in which a master actually experiences receiving the transmission from a deity in a pure realm, and this is considered to be quite different from a meditative experience. This cycle of pure visions of Sangwa Gyachen comes down to us from the fifth Dalai Lama. What is remarkable about these visions is that, far from being simply meditative experiences that arose during practice, they were received on occasions when the fifth Dalai Lama actually went to pure wisdom realms, and was given the transmissions encoded in these empowerments. To a yogin of his stature, who is able to perceive directly enlightened forms or kāyas, and realms of wisdom, the pure visions that occur will naturally belong to this category.

In the case of the 'Great Fifth' Dalai Lama, the predispositions from his previous lifetimes awakened in him at a very early age, and this allowed him to experience any number of such pure visions throughout his life. The most extraordinary of these are contained in the Sangwa Gyachen cycle, which is composed of twenty-five sections dealing with distinct visions. The accounts of the pure visions experienced by the fifth Dalai Lama can be found in his secret autobiography.

Among these twenty-five sections, the principal one focuses on the *Kagyé*, or 'Eight Commands', where all the deities appear in a single mandala. Individual practices also exist for each of these deities. The whole cycle of Sangwa Gyachen contains a number of empowerments, blessings, and permission ceremonies for different deities, both peaceful and wrathful, out of which I have chosen today to perform the empowerment of 'The Union of All the Innermost Essences'. This empowerment is based on the mandala of the guru as the vidyādhara. It is an empowerment which is easy to perform, and yet which at the same time transmits enormous blessing and the potential for great spiritual attainment. Generally speaking, very profound teachings can often take a considerable amount of time for a teacher to confer and for students to assimilate. The advantage here is that this empowerment is quite short and easy to transmit, and yet it does possess that profound depth. But even in saying that, I am aware of the fact that normally it would take some three or four hours to perform, if we had the time. This afternoon we only have an hour or so available, so we will be going even faster than would normally be the case.

The master from whom I received the transmission for this extraordinary Sangwa Gyachen cycle was Taktra Rinpoche.[10] The main sādhana from this cycle that I have practised myself is the one associated with the maṇḍala which unifies the eight deities of the Kagyé. I have also focused on several of the other practices to a certain extent, such as Vajrakīlaya, Hayagrīva, and Avalokiteśvara. Generally speaking, if you are going to transmit empowerments for a given cycle of teachings in the Nyingma tradition, you should ideally have completed retreats on all the deities of the three roots for that cycle. However when I received these empowerments from my teacher, I also received permission from him to give them to others if there was benefit for them in my doing so. In addition, it was explained to me that the Kagyé practice is the principal focus of all the twenty-five sections of the Sangwa Gyachen cycle, and so to complete a full retreat on this particular practice constitutes the minimum requirement for a vajra master to confer the empowerments on others. So, while I have not had the opportunity to accomplish a more thorough practice of the other sections of this cycle, I have completed the Kagyé section and am therefore in a position to offer the empowerments of Sangwa Gyachen.

THE MEANING OF EMPOWERMENT

As for empowerment in general, what does the term *wang*, or empowerment, signify? To begin with, our fundamental nature— what we term 'the buddha nature', or *tathāgatagarbha*, the very nature of our mind, is inherently present within us as a natural attribute. This mind of ours, the subject at hand, has been going on through-out beginningless time, and so has the more subtle nature of that mind. On the basis of the continuity of that subtle nature of our mind rests the capacity we have to attain enlightenment. This potential is what we call 'the seed of buddhahood', 'buddha nature', 'the fundamental nature', or 'tathāgatagarbha'. We all have this buddha nature, each and every one of us. For example, this beautiful statue of Lord Buddha here, in the presence of which we are now sitting, is a representation that honours someone who attained buddhahood. He awakened into that state of enlightenment because his nature was the buddha nature. Ours is as well, and just as the Buddha attained enlightenment in the past, so in the future we can become buddhas too.

When, at some future point, we do attain buddhahood, that subtle continuum of our awareness will awaken to a state of omniscience called *dharmakāya*. The nature of mind at that point is what we term *svābhāvikakāya*. The fact that it is totally pure by its very nature is one aspect of the svābhāvikakāya—that of total and natural purity. The fact that adventitious obscurations have been removed and no longer obscure that true nature of mind is another aspect of the svābhāvikakāya—that of being purified of adventitious obscurations.[11]

In any case, there dwells within us all this potential which allows us to awaken into buddhahood and attain omniscience. The empowerment process draws that potential out, and allows it to express itself more fully. When an empowerment is conferred on you, it is the nature of your mind—the buddha nature—that provides a basis upon which the empowerment can ripen you. Through the empowerment, you are empowered into the essence of the buddhas of the five families. In particular, you are 'ripened' within that particular family through which it is your personal predisposition to attain buddhahood.

So, with these auspicious circumstances established in your mindstream, and when you reflect on what is taking place and maintain the various visualizations, the conditions are right for the essence of the empowerment to awaken within you, as a state of wisdom which is blissful yet empty—a very special state that is the inseparability of basic space and awareness. As you focus your devotion in this way, it allows this special quality of mind, this new capability, as it were, to awaken. There are three circumstantial factors that support this—the ritual objects that are employed on the outer level, the mantras that are repeated by the vajra master, and the vajra master's own *samādhi*, or meditative absorption. When these three factors come together, they form a basis on which the mind can focus, and so become ripened.

As these three factors are so important, we should examine them a little more closely. The outer ritual objects, such as the vase and so forth, have already been arranged on the shrine, and are all in place. As for the mantras, while I cannot claim to have read them all in pure Sanskrit, I have done my best while reading and reciting them. So what is most important during the remainder of the empowerment is meditative absorption. For my part, I will be doing what I can to maintain a state of samādhi, and so at the same time each of you should focus your minds, step by step, on the explanations I will give, and rest, as much as possible, in a similar state of samādhi meditation.

THE GROUND, PATH AND FRUITION OF DZOGCHEN

Let us now consider the teachings particular to the Secret Mantra Vehicle of the early transmission school of the Nyingma tradition, and what these teachings say about the three phases of ground, path, and fruition. The way in which the *ground* of being abides, as this is definitively understood and described in the Nyingma teachings, entails its essence, its nature, and its energy, or responsiveness. In particular, the first two aspects define the ground for the Nyingma school, its essence being primordial purity or *kadak*, and its nature being spontaneous presence or *lhundrup*.

Nāgārjuna, in his *Fundamental Treatise on the Middle Way, called 'Wisdom'*,[12] states:

> The dharma that is taught by the buddhas,
> Relies completely upon two levels of truth:

> The worldly conventional level of truth,
> And the ultimate level of truth.

All that is knowable—all phenomena and all that is comprised within an individual's mind and body—is contained within these two levels of truth, conventional and ultimate. In the Dzogchen context, the explanation given would be in terms of primordial purity and spontaneous presence, and this is analogous to a passage in the scriptures:

> It is mind itself that sets in place the myriad array
> Of beings in the world, and the world that contains them.[13]

That is to say, if we consider the agent responsible for creating saṃsāra and nirvāṇa, it comes down to mind. *The Sutra on the Ten Grounds* states, "These three realms are mind only". In his commentary to his own work, *Entering the Middle Way*[14] Candrakīrti elaborates on this quotation, stating that there is no other creative agent apart from mind.

When mind is explained from the point of view of the Highest Yoga Tantra teachings and the path of mantra, we find that many different levels or aspects of mind are discussed, some coarser and some more subtle. But at the very root, the most fundamental level embraced by these teachings is mind as the fundamental, innate nature of mind. This is where we come to the distinction between the word *sem* in Tibetan, meaning 'ordinary mind' and the word *rigpa* signifying 'pure awareness'. Generally speaking, when we use the word sem, we are referring to mind when it is temporarily obscured and distorted by thoughts based upon the dualistic perceptions of subject and object. When we are discussing pure awareness, genuine consciousness or awareness free of such distorting thought patterns, then the term rigpa is employed. The teaching known as the 'Four Reliances' states: "Do not rely upon ordinary consciousness, but rely upon wisdom".[15] Here the term *namshé*, or ordinary consciousness, refers to mind involved with dualistic perceptions. *Yeshé*, or wisdom, refers to mind free from dualistic perceptions. It is on this basis that the distinction can be made between ordinary mind and pure awareness.

When we say that 'mind' is the agent responsible for bringing the universe into being, we are talking about mind in the sense of rigpa, and specifically its quality of spontaneous presence. At the same time, the very essence of that spontaneously present rigpa is timelessly empty, and primordially pure—totally pure by its very nature—so there is a unity of primordial purity and spontaneous presence. The Nyingma school distinguishes between the ground itself, and the ground manifesting as appearances through the 'eight doorways of spontaneous presence', and this is how this school accounts for all of the perceptions, whether pure or impure, that arise within the mind. Without ever deviating from basic space, these manifestations and the perceptions of them, pure or impure, arise in all their variety. That is the situation concerning the ground, from the point of view of the Nyingma school.

On the basis of that key point, when we talk about the *path*, and if we use the special vocabulary of the Dzogchen tradition and refer to its own extraordinary practices, the path is twofold, that of *trekchö* and *tögal*. The trekchö approach is based upon the primordial purity of mind, kadak, while the tögal approach is based upon its spontaneous presence, lhundrup. This is the equivalent in the Dzogchen tradition of what is more commonly referred to as the path that is the union of skilful means and wisdom.

When the *fruition* is attained through relying on this twofold path of trekchö and tögal, the 'inner lucidity' of primordial purity leads to dharmakāya, while the 'outer lucidity' of spontaneous presence leads to the rūpakāya. This is the equivalent of the usual description of dharmakāya as the benefit that accrues to oneself and the rūpakāya as the benefit that comes to others. The terminology is different, but the understanding of what the terms signify is parallel. When the latent, inner state of buddhahood becomes fully evident for the practitioner him or herself, this is referred to as 'inner lucidity' and is the state of primordial purity, which is dharmakāya. When the natural radiance of mind becomes manifest for the benefit of others, its responsiveness accounts for the entire array of form manifestations, whether pure or impure, and this is referred to as 'outer lucidity', the state of spontaneous presence which comprises the rūpakāya.

In the context of the path, then, this explanation of primordial purity and spontaneous presence, and what is discussed in the newer schools of Highest Yoga Tantra both come down to the same ultimate point: the fundamental innate mind of clear light.

What, then, is the profound and special feature of the Dzogchen teachings? According to the more recent traditions of Tibetan Buddhism, collectively known as the *Sarma* schools of the Secret Mantra Vehicle, in order for this fundamental innate mind of clear light to become fully evident, it is necessary first of all for the coarser levels of ordinary mind, caught up with thoughts and concepts, to be harnessed by yogas, such as the yoga of vital energies, *prāṇayoga*, or the yoga of inner heat, *tummo*. On the basis of these yogic practices, and in the wake of those adventitious thought patterns of ordinary mind being harnessed and purified, the fundamental innate mind of clear light—'mind' in that sense— becomes fully evident.

From the point of view of Dzogchen, the understanding is that the adventitious level of mind, which is caught up with concepts and thoughts, is by its very nature permeated by pure awareness. In an experiential manner, the student can be directly introduced by an authentic master to the very nature of his or her mind as pure awareness. If the master is able to effect this direct introduction, the student then experiences all of these adventitious layers of conceptual thought as permeated by the pure awareness which is their nature, so that these layers of ordinary thoughts and concepts need not continue. Rather, the student experiences the nature that permeates them as the fundamental innate mind of clear light, expressing itself in all its nakedness. That is the principle by which practice proceeds on the path of Dzogchen.

THE ROLE OF AN AUTHENTIC GURU

So in Dzogchen, the direct introduction to rigpa requires that we rely upon an authentic guru, who already has this experience. It is when the blessings of the guru infuse our mindstream that this direct introduction is effected. But it is not an easy process. In the early translation school of the Nyingma, which is to say the Dzogchen teachings, the role of the master is therefore crucial.

In the Vajrayāna approach, and especially in the context of Dzogchen, it is necessary for the instructions to be given by a qualified master. That is why, in such approaches, we take refuge in the guru as well as in the Buddha, Dharma, and Saṅgha. In some sense, it is not sufficient simply to take refuge in the three sources of refuge; a fourth element is added, that of taking refuge in the guru. And so we say, "I take refuge in the guru; I take refuge in the Buddha; I take refuge in the Dharma; I take refuge in the Saṅgha." It is not so much that the guru is in any way separate or different from the Three Jewels, but rather that there is a particular value in counting the guru separately. I have a German friend who said to me, "You Tibetans seem to hold the guru higher than the Buddha". He was astonished. But this is not quite the way to understand it. It is not as though the guru is in any way separate from the Three Jewels, but because of the crucial nature of our relationship with the guru in such practice and teachings, the guru is considered of great importance.

Now this requires that the master be qualified and authentic. If a master is authentic, he or she will be either a member of the saṅgha that requires no more training, or at least the saṅgha that still requires training but is at an advanced level of realization. An authentic guru, and I stress the word 'authentic', must fall into one of these two categories. So it is because of the crucial importance of a qualified and authentic guru, one who has such realization, that such emphasis is placed, in this tradition, on the role of the guru. This may have given rise to a misconception, in that people have sometimes referred to Tibetan Buddhism as a distinct school of practice called 'Lamaism', on account of this emphasis on the role of the guru. All that is really being said is that it is important to have a master, and that it is important for that master to be authentic and qualified.

Even in the case of an authentic guru, it is crucial for the student to examine the guru's behaviour and teachings. You will recall that earlier I referred to the 'Four Reliances.' These can be stated as follows:

> Do not rely upon the individual, but rely upon the teaching.
> As far as the teachings go, do not rely upon the words alone, but rely upon the meaning that underlies them.
> Regarding the meaning, do not rely upon the provisional meaning alone, but rely upon the definitive meaning.
> And regarding the definitive meaning, do not rely upon ordinary consciousness, but rely upon wisdom awareness.

This is how a student should examine a teacher, using these four reliances. Our teacher, Lord Buddha, said,

> O bhikṣus and wise men,
> Just as a goldsmith would test his gold
> By burning, cutting, and rubbing it,
> So you must examine my words and accept them,
> But not merely out of reverence for me.[16]

All of the foregoing comments have been my way of introducing you to the background to this empowerment. What is most important during an empowerment of this nature is that: as Buddhists, we place great emphasis on taking refuge; as Mahāyāna Buddhists, we place great emphasis on the bodhisattva vow and arousing bodhicitta; and, as Vajrayāna practitioners, we lessen our fixation on perceiving things in an ordinary way, and rely upon pure perception. This is how you should receive an empowerment.

PART TWO

HITTING THE ESSENCE IN THREE WORDS

London, 1984

HITTING THE ESSENCE IN THREE WORDS

THE BACKGROUND

There was something glorious about the Dalai Lama's arrival in Scotland. In a sudden burst of afternoon sunlight, his car drew up in front of the seventeenth century hotel outside Edinburgh. Images and sounds followed in rapid profusion: the solitary pipe major pacing slowly down the path, the meadow behind with its primeval looking Highland cattle, the plangent cry of two peacocks mingling with the skirl of the pipes, and in the far distance, the ancient volcanic rock of King Arthur's Seat. Taking it all in within a few seconds, His Holiness beamed in gratitude and stepped inside the grey stone archway. His first visit to Scotland had begun.

The Dalai Lama's name is synonymous with non-violence, peace and forgiveness, and peace stood out as the dominant theme during his two week tour of Britain in 1984, a theme that aroused an electric response everywhere he went. There could have been few more evocative sights than His Holiness pausing silently to pray in the ruins of Coventry Cathedral, on what became known as his 'pilgrimage of peace'. Much of Coventry, the cathedral included, was destroyed in an air raid on 14 November 1940. The next day the decision was taken to rebuild the cathedral, not out of defiance, but as a sign of faith, trust and hope for the future of the world, so turning the people of the city away from bitterness and hatred. The ruins of the old were left alongside the new, to form one living cathedral, as much a reminder as a startling symbol of what would be Coventry's world-wide ministry of peace and reconciliation. Two thousand people filled the cathedral to hear His Holiness speak on 'The Contribution of the Individual to World Peace'. The title 'Peace Through Human Understanding' was given to his public talk in Edinburgh, where he was fêted with unbridled enthusiasm, many unable to squeeze into the music hall at the Assembly Rooms. Finally, five thousand crammed into the Royal Albert Hall in London, where His Holiness spoke on 'Peace of Mind; Peace in Action'.

One of the great motifs of the Dalai Lama's life is his quest to build respect and understanding among the world's religions. His first stop in Britain was at the Benedictine monastery and college of Ampleforth in Yorkshire, where he met and spoke to the monks and students. He also made a visit to the bedside of one of the community, Dom Aelred Graham, who at the age of seventy-seven was in his final illness. With his books *Conversations: Christian and Buddhist* and *Zen Catholicism*, Aelred Graham had been one of the first to bring an awareness of Buddhism to the Christian world, and it was through him that Thomas Merton came to meet the Dalai Lama on his Asian journey in 1968. His Holiness came out of Dom Aelred's room, visibly moved. In him, he said later, he had seen how, even weakened by illness and in the face of death, a person could find peace and confidence through his faith and spiritual practice.

In London, the Dalai Lama stayed with his dear friend, Edward Carpenter, the Dean of Westminster, with whom he shared some of the most intimate moments, whether it was at a birthday party for his fifty-ninth birthday, or speaking at his side in Westminster Abbey. There the Dean called His Holiness's life and work "a gospel for today", and, seeking words to depict the constancy and depth of his compassion, borrowed them from Shakespeare:

> Love is not love
> Which alters when it alteration finds,
> Or bends with the remover to remove.
> O no, it is an ever-fixed mark

That looks on tempests and is never shaken;
It is the star to every wand'ring bark,
Whose worth's unknown although his height be taken.

All through his days in Westminster, His Holiness continued to explore the common ground of religion in three separate meetings, with: western Tibetan Buddhist monks and nuns, Theravādin monks, and Benedictine abbots and monks, a number of whom were deeply engaged in the inter-monastic dialogue and exchange with Tibetan monasteries.

The Dalai Lama's abiding fascination with science is well-known, and in London he met his friend, the great physicist, David Bohm. On 3 July, he visited the Old Royal Observatory on its hilltop overlooking the Thames at Greenwich. Founded by Charles II in 1675, during the lifetime of the fifth Dalai Lama, the first 'Royal Observator' John Flamsteed had been instructed by the king "to find the longitude of places", a problem that had haunted astronomers and navigators for centuries. What fascinated His Holiness was how this village on the outskirts of London could have become the centre of the world—at zero degrees of longitude, the place where time and space converge. This very year, in fact, was Greenwich's centenary celebration. At a conference in Washington in 1884, by a vote of twenty-two to one, the Greenwich meridian had been adopted as 'the initial meridian for longitude'. The observatory is now under the control of the National Maritime Museum, and His Holiness questioned its Head of Astronomy and Navigation, and its Director, closely before examining the Airy Transit Circle, the instrument which had defined the meridian, and the 28 inch refracting telescope. He completed his visit by stepping across the prime meridian, the bronze strip laid into the courtyard, that seems to divide east from west.

HITTING THE ESSENCE IN THREE WORDS

In the sober, functional hall of the Camden Centre in London, opposite the Victorian triumph of St. Pancras station, His Holiness delivered a two and a half day seminar on Buddhist philosophy, structured around an explanation of the twelve links of dependent origination. He delved into the different levels of practice in Mahāyāna and Vajrayāna, concluding with a comparison of the view according to the four schools of Tibetan Buddhism, which foreshadowed certain points he would address again in his teachings in San Jose in 1989. The lectures were translated by Professor Jeffrey Hopkins and published in 1992 as *The Meaning of Life from a Buddhist Perspective.*

On the following day, 7 July, His Holiness gave a teaching on Dzogchen, at the request of Rigpa and Sogyal Rinpoche. As a preliminary, he conferred on the nine hundred people present a blessing of *Takdrol*—'Liberation through contact or touch',[17] explaining that such a teaching as Dzogchen really requires an empowerment of some kind. His Holiness drew out some of the special features of Dzogchen, and wove further explanations and instructions into the words of the brief ritual.

His Holiness had chosen to teach on Dzogchen by giving a commentary on Patrul Rinpoche's famous teaching on *Tsik Sum Né Dek—Hitting the Essence in Three Words.*[18] This instruction is the final testament of the first human Dzogchen master Garab Dorje, or Prahevajra. Histories of the Dzogchen lineage tell how, as Garab Dorje attained nirvāṇa, his body dissolved into space in the midst of a great cloud of rainbow light; the earth shuddered and miraculous sounds were heard.[19] His disciple Mañjuśrīmitra, who had studied the Nyingtik teachings with him for seventy-five years, saw him in the sky, surrounded by light, and cried out "Alas, alas! O vast expanse! If the light that is our teacher is extinguished, who will there be to dispel the darkness of the world?" It is said that, at this, Garab Dorje's right hand and forearm appeared holding a golden casket, the size of a thumbnail, which circled round Mañjuśrīmitra three times, and descended into the palm of his hand. Inside it he found the *Hitting the Essence in Three Words,* Garab Dorje's final testament, written in ink of liquid lapis lazuli on a leaf of five precious substances. Simply seeing it, Mañjuśrīmitra attained the same realization as his master. In fact, all four of the first vidyādharas of the Dzogchen lineage—Garab Dorje, Mañjuśrīmitra, Śrī Siṅgha and Jñānasūtra—bequeathed a testament in a similar way to their disciples, whereupon the minds of the disciples and wisdom minds of the masters became inseparable. *Hitting the Essence in Three Words* has been revered by masters and practitioners throughout the centuries as embodying in its key points the very essence of the path of Dzogchen.

Patrul Rinpoche's *Special Teaching of the Wise and Glorious King*, an elaboration, with its own commentary, on *Hitting the Essence in Three Words*, is treasured as the most crucial instruction for the practice of Dzogchen. Brief yet exceedingly profound, it captures the understanding of the trekchö practice, and is "the infallible key point of the path of primordial purity in the natural Dzogpachenpo". Patrul Rinpoche (1808-1887) was a great figure in the transmission of the Longchen Nyingtik, the cycle of teachings revealed as a mind treasure by Jikmé Lingpa (1730-98), who attained boundless realization after three visions of the great Dzogchen master Longchen Rabjam (1308-63). Patrul Rinpoche invokes these two masters, along with his root guru Jikmé Gyalwé Nyugu (1765-1843), in his *Special Teaching of the Wise and Glorious King*.

One of the best loved masters in Tibetan Buddhist history, Patrul Rinpoche was known for his amazing erudition, wisdom, simplicity and sanctity. He played a vital part in the renaissance of Buddhism in Tibet in the nineteenth century, and left an indelible mark on his times.[20] He was regarded as the speech emanation of Jikmé Lingpa, and studied under a wealth of great masters, such as Jikmé Gyalwé Nyugu, Do Khyentse, Gyalsé Shyenpen Thayé, and the fourth Dzogchen Rinpoche, Mingyur Namkhé Dorje. He received the preliminary practices of the Longchen Nyingtik teachings twenty-five times from Jikmé Gyalwé Nyugu, and compiled them in his famous *Kunzang Lamé Shyalung*, 'The Words of My Perfect Teacher', to which His Holiness refers at the close of his teaching in 1989. He wrote this in a cave high up above the Dzogchen monastery, an area where he spent many years, studying, practising and, later, teaching. Zenkar Rinpoche writes: "Dwelling for long periods near Dzogchen monastery in the isolated hermitages of Rudam, such as the Yamāntaka Cave, and the Long Life Cave, he put all his energy into the practice of meditation, and attained a realization that was as vast as space."[21]

Patrul Rinpoche's spirit continues to inspire generations of practitioners. His Holiness the Dalai Lama has frequently spoken of him with deep admiration, particularly when commenting on that teaching so close to his own heart, the *Bodhicaryāvatāra*. In 1991, when commenting on the first eight chapters in the Dordogne in France, His Holiness referred to Patrul Rinpoche's particular way of relating the ten chapters of the *Bodhicaryāvatāra* to the lines of the famous prayer:

> O precious, sublime bodhicitta:
> May it arise in those in whom it has not arisen;
> May it never decline where it has arisen;
> May it go on increasing, further and further!

and commented: "This is how Patrul Rinpoche explained it, and I find it very profound".[22] In 1993, when teaching on the ninth chapter in France at the Vajrayoginī Institute, he recalled the master from whom he had received the *Bodhicaryāvatāra*, Khunu Lama Tenzin Gyaltsen (1894/5-1977), who held Patrul Rinpoche's lineage, having received it from one of the great khenpos at Dzogchen monastery. He reminisced:

> Dza Patrul Rinpoche was a master in whom three qualities were united: learning, ethics and kindness. He was an outstanding figure, a scholar who attained the very highest spiritual realization. After having made a special study of the Bodhicaryāvatāra, he made bodhicitta the heart of his practice and was soon recognized far and wide as a superlative and fully

accomplished master. Later, his lineage came to Khunu
Lama Rinpoche…who was someone quite exceptional, to an extent that we can not even imagine. He
too had made bodhicitta the heart of his practice, and
it was from him that I received the transmission.[23]

As a preliminary teaching to the empowerments of the *Sangwa
Gyachen* cycle at Dzogchen monastery in 1992, His Holiness taught
on Patrul Rinpoche's *Good in the Beginning, Good in the Middle and
Good at the End*,[24] when he remarked:

> Dza Patrul Rinpoche was a great master and a great
> scholar, one who practised bodhicitta as his heart
> practice, and principally the Bodhicaryāvatāra. When
> he would teach the Bodhicaryāvatāra, special flowers
> would blossom, which became known as
> 'bodhicaryāvatāra flowers'. This I was told by Khunu
> Rinpoche. It is a story which underlines the unique-
> ness of his practice of bodhicitta.[25]

The *Special Teaching of the Wise and Glorious King* bears the stamp of
Patrul Rinpoche's greatness as a teacher. Reviewing his writings,
Zenkar Rinpoche comments: "He did not make them elaborate so
as to show off his knowledge, but explained things in order to fit
the capacity of students. The extraordinary and special character of
his teachings was described by Dodrupchen Jikmé Tenpé Nyima in
his biography of Patrul:

> If analyzed by the wise, they are found to be very
> meaningful. If heard by the dim-witted, they are easy
> to understand. As they condense the vital points, they
> are easy to remember. Just the right length, everything
> is coherent and connected from beginning to end.
> They are delightful to the ear, and whatever words he
> uses, hard or gentle, they become 'of one taste' with

the instructions, and so captivate the minds of all,
whether wise, confused, or somewhere in between".[26]

There is, it seems, no way to overstate the importance of this
teaching on *Hitting the Essence in Three Words*. Dilgo Khyentse
Rinpoche said, "Imagine you heard all eighty-four thousand
teachings of Buddha and then contemplated on them. You would
find that ultimately there was nothing that needed to be introduced
beyond 'Hitting the Essence in Three Words'. Compare these 'three
words' to the teachings of a hundred paṇḍitas or a thousand siddhas,
and there is nothing they can teach you beyond this. The omniscient
Longchen Rabjam had realized completely the meaning of the
three categories and nine spaces of Dzogpachenpo, and became
inseparable from the Primordial Buddha Samantabhadra. Yet
suppose you actually met him face to face: there would be nothing
he could teach you beyond 'Hitting the Essence in Three Words'.
Rigdzin Jikmé Lingpa, Jikmé Gyalwé Nyugu and all the
vidyādharas and masters of the three lineages—they could not
possibly teach us anything beyond this one instruction."

HIS HOLINESS THE DALAI LAMA

INTRODUCTION

Today I am giving the blessing for what is known as a *takdrol*—that
which 'brings liberation on contact'. It is based on a text, *The Tantra
that Brings Liberation Upon Contact*, which contains mantras and other
items to be worn on the body. There are many such takdrol, each
with its own specific contents, and the one I am going to transmit
today comes from the *Changter* or Northern Treasure tradition.[27]
The blessing is conferred by being touched with the text in which
these *dhāraṇī* mantras[28] are written, or through wearing them.
Someone receiving this blessing should really have already had an
empowerment into the highest level of tantra. Those of you who

received my transmission, two years ago, of the mind sādhana 'The Union of All the Innermost Essences' from the Sangwa Gyachen cycle, have received just such an empowerment. Others definitely need to have had some empowerment into the highest level of tantra.

The guru who grants such an empowerment—that is, who confers the blessing—should, of course, be someone whose realization is quite advanced. It is then that the blessing can be transmitted, by being transferred from the mindstream of an experienced guru and implanted, or aroused, in the mind of the student. But such a thing is rare, isn't it? From my own point of view, although I practise and have confidence in this path, it is difficult for me to claim any realization.

THE SPECIAL FEATURES OF DZOGCHEN

In the early translation school of the Nyingma, a system of nine yānas is taught. Three of these—the paths of the śrāvaka, pratyekabuddha, and bodhisattva—constitute the sūtra tradition, while the tantric tradition consists of six levels—the three outer tantras and the three inner tantras. The tradition of Dzogchen, or Atiyoga, is considered to be the pinnacle of these nine yānas. The other, lower, yānas are said to be philosophical systems that depend on ordinary consciousness, and so the path is based on that ordinary consciousness. Here the distinction being made is between ordinary mind—*sem*—and pure awareness—*rigpa*. The ninth yāna, the most majestic, is beyond ordinary consciousness, for its path is based on rigpa, not on the ordinary mind.

Throughout beginningless time, there has always been present, within us all, a pure awareness—that in-dwelling rigpa which in Atiyoga is evoked in all its nakedness, and which constitutes the practice. In other words, in Dzogchen the whole path is based on this rigpa: first you are introduced to it directly, and then you put it into practice. So this is known as the 'effortless yāna'. Now, such terminology carries its own special significance, and must be understood in a particular way. 'Effortless' here does not mean 'with absolutely no effort at all'; it would be quite inappropriate to take this to mean that all you needed to do was lie around and sleep.[29] In this tradition, there is indeed a practice, and it consists of focusing uniquely on rigpa—that is, practising on the basis of rigpa alone.

As I mentioned the other day, all the sources of Highest Yoga Tantra agree on this point as their ultimate intention.[30] The *ground* for all the phenomena of saṃsāra and nirvāṇa is the fundamental innate mind of clear light, and these phenomena are its radiance or display. While we are following the *path*, in order for all the impure aspects of our experience to be purified on the basis of that rigpa— or, you can say, that fundamental innate mind of clear light—there is no other means apart from that fundamental and innate state itself, which is therefore the very essence of the path. Finally, when the *fruition* is made fully evident, it is just this fundamental innate mind of clear light itself, free from obscuration, that constitutes the attainment of fruition. All the tantras of Highest Yoga Tantra agree on this explanation.

So phenomena based on conceptual elaboration, in all their variety, must be allowed to subside into the space of the fundamental innate mind of clear light. In fact, when the state of clear light reveals itself to us at the time of death, all our perceptions of appearances based on conceptual elaboration dissolve into the space of the pure state of clear light. This takes place through what are called the 'three visions', known as 'appearance', 'increase', and 'attainment'. Because of the power of our karma, this dissolution process takes place automatically. We do not have the capacity to remain in that pure state, and so out of it once more all the phenomena based on conceptual elaboration will arise. The *Guhyasamāja Tantra* explains these two processes—the dissolution process in the usual step-by-step progression and the process of reappearance with the steps in the reverse order.

Referring back to what I said earlier, how are we to base the path on rigpa, right now? Any given state of consciousness is permeated by the clear light of rigpa's pure awareness. However solid ice may be, it never loses its true nature, which is water. In the same way, even very obvious concepts are such that their 'place', as it were, their final resting place, does not fall outside the expanse of rigpa. They arise within the expanse of rigpa and that is where they dissolve. On this point, Dodrupchen Jikmé Tenpé Nyima says that all objects of knowledge are permeated by clear light, just as a sesame seed is permeated by its oil.[31] Therefore, even while the coarser states of the six consciousnesses[32] are functioning, their subtle aspect—that of clear light—can be directly introduced by means of those states themselves, through blessings and through pith instructions.

Here lies the extraordinary and profound implication of the Dzogchen teachings. When you are basing your path on the fundamental innate mind of clear light, you will employ skilful means to block the coarse and subtle states of energy and mind, as a result of which the state of clear light becomes evident, and on this you base your path. But in Dzogchen, even while the six consciousnesses are fully functioning, by means of those very states you can be directly introduced to their subtle aspect of clear light in your immediate experience, and you then meditate by focusing one-pointedly on that aspect. As you meditate in this way, resting in this non-conceptual state, gradually your experience of clear light becomes increasingly profound, while coarser thoughts and concepts dwindle away.

The most difficult task is to differentiate between ordinary mind and rigpa. It is easy enough to talk about it. You can say, for example, that rigpa has never been confused, while ordinary mind has fallen under the influence of concepts and is mired in confusion. But to be introduced to the direct experience of the essence of rigpa is far from being easy. And so Dodrupchen says[33] that although your arrogance might be such that you assume you are meditating on the ultimate meaning of rigpa, there is a danger that "you could end up meditating on the clear, empty qualities of your ordinary mind, which even non-Buddhist practitioners are capable of doing." He is warning us to be careful.

However, as regards view, meditation, and action, once you have gained experience of the view, there is no need for some additional technique of meditation or action. Rather, you maintain your practice by experiencing the expanse, or basic space, of the view. In the Dzogchen teachings four *chokshyak*—'states of imperturbable rest' or 'ways of leaving things in their natural simplicity'[34]—are discussed. Among them:

— *The View* is a state of imperturbable rest like a mountain, for a mountain is unmoving.
— *Meditation* is a state of imperturbable rest like an ocean, for no matter how many waves there are on the surface, the depths of the ocean remain calm and still. In this meditation there is what is known as a 'natural and genuine mindfulness'. Once you have been directly introduced to the experience of rigpa, this genuine mindfulness arises like the rays shining from the sun. At this point, you have no need for a mindfulness that requires effort on the part of ordinary consciousness.
— *Action* is a state of imperturbable rest in the face of perceptions. You have been introduced to the view and to rigpa, and you have that experience. As long as you do not follow and get caught up in sense objects, or the concepts that arise in their wake, but you remain in the vivid immediacy of rigpa, your actions will not be based on accepting some things and rejecting others. So action is a state of imperturbable rest in the face of sensory appearances, beyond suppression or indulgence, hope or fear.

These are special features of the Dzogchen approach.

In the sources of the Nyingma school, three lineages are distinguished—the extensive lineage, called *kama*; the shorter lineage, called *terma*; and the profound transmissions that are called *dak nang* or 'pure visions'. The extensive kama lineage consists of the teachings brought from India to Tibet. The terma lineage primarily stems from the Great Master, Padmasambhava. For the sake of those in future generations who would have the fortunate karma to be guided by him, he concealed these profound treasure teachings. No matter how many hundreds, or even thousands, of years have elapsed, when the time is right these teachings are revealed. This is due to a number of factors: the Great Master's innate compassion, our own merit as his followers, and the karma and aspirations of the *tertön*, the master who reveals the terma. Although the intervening period may be quite long, the transmission from the Great Master is extremely direct, so this is called the short lineage of terma. As for the profound transmissions through pure visions, there are three kinds of such visions—those that arise as meditative experiences, those that arise from the imaginative faculty of the mind, and those that arise directly to one's sensory consciousness. It is this third kind of vision, those that arise directly to the senses, that constitutes the lineage of profound pure visions.

Liberation Upon Contact

Now, as for the articles used during the empowerment, first there is the volume of *The Tantra that Brings Liberation Upon Contact*. If there is time, the master reads the text aloud, but we do not have time for that today. Then there is a crystal; in the Dzogchen cycles, this is a metaphor that illustrates, and so brings about your understanding of, the unity of rigpa and emptiness. In some traditions, a peacock feather is placed above the crystal, and in such cases, the crystal primarily symbolizes the practice of trekchö, the peacock feather that of tögal.

The ritual implements used by the master are simply the vajra and bell, nothing more. But they have a very important significance. The vajra symbolizes skilful means or upāya, and the bell wisdom or prajñā. It is said that together they signify the primordial unity of upāya and prajñā, which is the essence of ultimate bodhicitta. This unity can be understood according to the sūtra tradition, the tantric tradition, and the very highest teachings. So there are progressive levels of understanding, and the union of skilful means and wisdom can be interpreted from the point of view of appearances, or from the point of view of emptiness, and so on. A master should use these implements with an awareness of their significance; otherwise, the only use of ringing a bell would be to wake people who were dozing off. Perhaps I should use the bell to wake you up, and the vajra to wake myself up!

> *At this point, His Holiness explained how, in order to effect the empowerment, those who are taking part forge a connection with the vajra master, visualizing him as Lama Rigdzin, the embodiment of all the buddhas.*[35] *They consider that, as he recites the verses that follow, they are introduced directly to rigpa:*

THE VERSES

> Ema! Phenomena are, without exception,
> Perfect within the continuum of self-arising rigpa.

Now, the verses begin with "Ema!", an expression of wonder. For none of the phenomena of saṃsāra and nirvāṇa are, in their ultimate nature, things that are suddenly and newly created through causes and conditions. Their natural state is one of primordial and natural perfection within the continuum of self-arising pure awareness—that is, they are all embraced within its expanse. In the lower sense, the phenomena of saṃsāra depend on ordinary mind, while in the higher sense, the phenomena of nirvāṇa depend on rigpa.

According to the newer schools of Vajrayāna in Tibet, the fundamental innate mind of clear light is termed *sugatagarbha*, or buddha nature. In the textual sources of the Dzogchen and Mahāmudrā traditions, it is referred to as 'uncompounded clear light'. This term 'uncompounded' or 'non-composite' can be understood in various ways. More generally, it means something that does not depend on causes and conditions. But it can also signify 'that which is not contrived as something temporary and new', and so something that is primordially present—a 'continuous and permanent state'. Take, for example, the enlightened activity of buddhahood: *The Ornament for Clear Realization* refers to it as 'permanent', that is, some continuous permanent state; but it is in the sense that this activity is without interruption that it is labelled 'permanent':[36]

> Thus, since its enlightened deeds are so vast,
> Buddhahood can definitely be described as pervasive;
> And since those deeds are not subject to degeneration,
> They can in fact be described as 'permanent'.

Similarly, clear light is primordially as it is; it is beginningless, and not contrived as something new. It is something that abides continuously, or 'permanently'. That is one way of interpreting the term 'uncompounded'. Such terms need to be understood in context. For example, some scholars state, "All that exists is necessarily compounded". This is to be understood in the sense that things are of necessity 'put together' on the basis of concepts, and from that point of view are 'compounded'.[37]

Yet self-arising rigpa is beyond ordinary consciousness altogether. Concepts such as 'compounded' or 'uncompounded,' 'originating' or 'ceasing' are all still part of the concepts of the ordinary mind. Since the nature of self-arising rigpa is beyond the ordinary mind, the conventions created by our ordinary consciousness will be at odds with it. For rigpa is beyond all imagining or expression.

Personally I find this topic of considerable interest, and the reason I am explaining it is because of the statement made by many scholars, that the four schools of Tibetan Buddhism—Sakya, Geluk, Kagyü, and Nyingma—all meet at a certain point, with the same intention. This statement has aroused controversies as well, and is the subject of some debate. But it would seem that those scholars who say that there is this point of identical intention where all the schools meet, are saying so because there *is*, in fact, such a point, and not just for the sake of hearing the sound of their own voices. I give a lot of thought to this question, and I mention it because of my personal interest in what is a fundamental issue. True, different vocabularies are used to discuss this, and each school has its own unique interpretations, but these are individual ways of drawing out this truth and each has its own internal consistency and meaning that can bring you to an extraordinary level of understanding.

In the Guhyasamāja cycle, the self-arising wisdom of rigpa is termed the 'fundamental innate mind of clear light'; the Kālacakra cycle speaks of it as the 'all-pervading vajra space'; and in the *Hevajra Tantra*, its explanatory tantra, the *Vajra Tent*,[38] and related texts, it is referred to as the 'precious mind', as in the following verse:

> Other than the precious mind, there is no buddha, no
> ordinary being.

In the Dzogchen tradition the term *thamal gyi shépa*, 'ordinary awareness' is used, and often *rigpa*, 'pure awareness'. To elaborate on this further, use is made of terms such as *rang drol*, *cher drol* and *zangthal*—'self-liberating', 'nakedly free' and 'unobstructed'.

So the verses in the text point out that this self-arising rigpa is the ground of the phenomena of saṃsāra and nirvāṇa. They continue:

> This is the path of the heart essence, where knowing one
> liberates all.

If this one crucial point is explained on the basis of your personal experience, it can bring you freedom concerning many other key points, and so it is 'the path of the heart essence, in which knowing one thing liberates all.'

> Tantras, commentaries and pith instructions are all
> contained within this.

These terms—tantra, commentary, and pith instruction[39]—can have different connotations and interpretations, but here they correspond to Mahāyoga, Anuyoga, and Atiyoga.

Threefold wisdom is the experience of purity,

Since this is a Dzogchen teaching, 'threefold wisdom' is explained as constituting essence, nature, and energy or responsiveness. It would seem that this can be explained as: 'primordial wisdom of rigpa that is the essence', 'primordial wisdom of rigpa that is the nature', and 'primordial wisdom of rigpa that is the energy'. This line "Threefold wisdom is the experience of purity" denotes trekchö. Then:

The four visions are the supreme path.

This line denotes the practice of tögal, and refers to its four visions.

Buddhahood is attained, in simultaneous realization and liberation,

If an individual with extremely sharp faculties, and who has merit as a support, comes to understand this key point, realization and liberation can be simultaneous, as in the case of King Indrabhūti. For example, during empowerments some individuals can experience the awakening in their mindstreams of the wisdom that is the true meaning and point of the empowerment. Simultaneous realization and liberation such as this brings about a very swift awakening to buddhahood, and so this is an extremely special path. Since it consists of maintaining the state of rigpa, the next line of the text advises that you look directly at it, without any distraction:

So look, without distraction, directly at the essence of rigpa.

And then:

A A A

The verses conclude with three 'A' syllables. This is the single syllable of the perfection of wisdom, the Prajñāpāramitā.[40]

So as I read through this slowly, sit so that your body is straight, and do not let your minds be distracted. One method spoken of in the Dzogchen tradition is "to direct your mind into your eyes and direct your eyes toward space".[41] This is useful because our visual consciousness is so powerful. This doesn't mean you are looking *at* something in the outside world, but rather that you direct your gaze toward the space between you and external phenomena.

Now despite my explanation, you may still have doubts, but at this point you should not be thinking concepts of all kinds with your ordinary consciousness, such as "This is this, that is that". Rather, your mind should be uncorrupted by any sense of grasping: simply clear, simply aware. See if you can remain steadfast in the state of rigpa itself—essentially empty by nature, simply clear, simply aware, primordially pure in its very essence.

> Ema! Phenomena are, without exception,
> Perfect within the continuum of self-arising rigpa.
> This is the path of the heart essence, where knowing one
>   liberates all.
> Tantras, commentaries and pith instructions are all
>   contained within this.
> Threefold wisdom is the experience of purity,
> The four visions are the supreme path.
> Buddhahood is attained, in simultaneous realization and
>   liberation,
> So look, without distraction, directly at the essence of
>   rigpa.
> A A A

"THE SPECIAL TEACHING OF THE WISE AND GLORIOUS KING"

To begin with, there is something that I think we all need to know. Fundamentally, from the Buddhist point of view, there is no division in the teachings between theory and practice. There are not some teachings to be explained on a theoretical level, as distinct from some other teachings which are to be practised. Yet there can, of course, be different emphases. There *are* teachings that emphasize the stages of practice, and there are those that emphasize arriving at a more theoretical conclusion in your mind. Take the writings of the great and learned masters of India, for example. In Nāgārjuna's *Six Collections of Reasoning*, we find that the emphasis is on reaching this decisive kind of conclusion. On the other hand, in works like Śāntideva's *Bodhicaryāvatāra*, the emphasis is on the stages of practice. Nevertheless, even in this text, the ninth chapter on wisdom is intended for those individuals who cannot gain certainty concerning the view without arriving at such a decisive conclusion. In his *Collection of Praises*, however, Nāgārjuna explains things in a somewhat different way. It is said that these praises, such as *In Praise of the Dharmadhātu*, concern the Buddha's final series of teachings, the third turning of the wheel of Dharma, which is also the main concern of the *Sublime Continuum*, one of the five treatises of Maitreya. These works are commentaries on the tathāgatagarbha sutras found in this final series of teachings.

Then, of particular note here are the *dohās*, or experiential songs, of the mahāsiddhas which are, in a sense, commentaries on the path of Anuttarayoga, the highest level of Vajrayāna. These were spoken spontaneously, expressing direct personal experience without much emphasis on complex wording. In the writings of the great masters of all the Buddhist schools in Tibet—Sakya, Geluk, Kagyü and Nyingma—some of their works emphasize the reaching of a theoretical decision, and others emphasize personal experience. This text by Dza Patrul Rinpoche, *Hitting the Essence in Three Words*, belongs to this spontaneous, experiential genre of teachings.

Extremely learned and an incredible bodhisattva, Dza Patrul Rinpoche always maintained a very humble profile. On one occasion, a large number of students began to gather in the place where he was living. Longing for somewhere quieter, he gave them the slip and made off to another valley altogether, where he took up residence with a family. In fact, he became the personal servant of the old lady who was the mother of the household, doing all kinds of chores for her, even emptying her chamber pot. His students searched for him far and wide, asking everyone they met, "Where is Patrul Rinpoche?" At last they arrived at the house where this family lived and asked the mother, who replied, "No, there's no lama here. All we have is an old man who is always dressed in ancient, ragged clothes. He's working as my servant." It took the students no time to guess the truth, and they told the old lady who her servant really was. When she realized that such a great master had been serving her, she was so ashamed and embarrassed that she simply took to her heels and fled. This story was related to me by Khunu Lama Tenzin Gyaltsen, the teacher with whom I studied the *Bodhicaryāvatāra*.

Now let me read you the root text:

> Herein is contained *The Special Teaching of the Wise and
> Glorious King*, together with its commentary.[42]
> Homage to the master!
> The view is Longchen Rabjam: infinite, vast expanse.
> Meditation is Khyentse Özer: rays of wisdom and love.
> Action is Gyalwé Nyugu, that of the bodhisattvas.
> One who practises in such a way,
> May well attain enlightenment in this very life.
> And even if not, what happiness! What joy!
> As for the view, Longchen Rabjam,
> Three words hit the vital point.
> First, relax and release your mind,
> Neither scattered, nor concentrated, without thoughts.
> While resting in this even state, at ease,
> Suddenly let out a mind-shattering 'phaṭ!',
> Fierce, forceful and abrupt. Amazing!
> There is nothing there: transfixed in wonder,
> Struck by wonder, and yet all is transparent and clear.
> Fresh, pure and sudden, so beyond description:
> Recognize this as the pure awareness of dharmakāya.
> The first vital point is: introducing directly the face of
> rigpa in itself.

So, this text discusses view, meditation, and action. In fact, the view itself is presented in three 'words' or statements, and the first of these is "introducing directly the face of rigpa in itself". In this context, as I mentioned earlier, the view is a matter of reaching a sense of decisiveness.

> Then, whether in a state of movement or stillness,
> Of anger or attachment, happiness or sorrow,
> All the time, in any situation,
> Recognize that dharmakāya you recognized before,
> And mother and child clear light, already acquainted, will
>   reunite.
> Rest in the aspect of awareness, beyond all description.
> Stillness and bliss, clarity and thinking: disrupt them, again
>   and again,
> Suddenly striking with the syllable of skilful means and
>   wisdom.
> With no difference between meditation and post-
>   meditation,
> No division between sessions and breaks,
> Always remain in this indivisible state.
> But, until stability is attained,
> It is vital to meditate, away from all distractions and
>   busyness,
> Dividing the practice into proper meditation sessions.
> All the time, in any situation,
> Abide by the flow of what is just dharmakāya.
> Decide with absolute conviction that there is nothing other
>   than this—
> The second vital point is: decide upon one thing, and one
>   thing only.
>
> At that point, whether attachment or aversion, happiness or
>   sorrow—
> All momentary thoughts, each and every one,
> Upon recognition, leave not a trace behind.

For recognize the dharmakāya in which they are freed,
And just as writing vanishes on water,
Arising and liberation become natural and continuous.
And whatever arises is food for the bare rigpa emptiness,
Whatever stirs in the mind is the inner power of the
     dharmakāya king,
Leaving no trace, and innately pure. What joy!
The way things arise may be the same as before,
But the difference lies in the way they are liberated: that's
     the key.
Without this, meditation is but the path of delusion,
With it, even without meditating, there's the state of
     dharmakāya—
The third vital point is: confidence directly in the liberation
     of rising thoughts.

Then there follows the colophon:

For the View which has the three vital points,
Meditation, the union of wisdom and love,
Is accompanied by the Action common to all the
     bodhisattvas.
Were all the buddhas to confer,
No instruction would they find greater than this,

And now the historical context is given:

Brought out as a treasure from the depth of transcendental
     insight,
By the tertön of dharmakāya, the inner power of rigpa,
Nothing like ordinary treasures of earth and stone,
For it is the final testament of Garab Dorje,
The essence of the wisdom mind of the three
     transmissions.
It is entrusted to my heart disciples, sealed to be secret.

It is profound in meaning, my heart's words.
It is the words of my heart, the crucial key point.
This crucial point: never hold it cheap.
Never let this instruction slip away from you.
This is the special teaching of the wise and glorious king.

Now I shall return to the beginning of the text, and explain the commentary.

> Homage to the incomparable lord of compassion, my root master, in all his kindness!
> Here will be explained, in a few crucial points, how to take to heart and practise view, meditation, and action. First of all, as the master embodies completely the Buddha, Dharma and Saṅgha, simply to pay homage to him alone is to pay homage to all sources of refuge everywhere. And so: **"Homage to the master!"**

As I have said before, in the general context of Vajrayāna practice the connection with the master is of crucial importance. This is especially so in Dzogchen, for devotion to the master plays a vital role if you are to be introduced directly to self-arising rigpa, and then to put that into practice. This is why the text pays homage to the master as embodying all sources of refuge.

> Now for the main subject: If you take the practice to heart, while recognizing that the root and lineage masters are all inseparable from the true nature of your mind, this embodies the actual practice of view, meditation, and action. So view, meditation, and action are explained here by relating them to the meaning of the root and lineage masters' names.

Because of the importance of the master, Patrul Rinpoche uses the names of his lamas to explain the three points of view, meditation, and action. First he refers to Longchen Rabjam, who is one of the lamas in the lineage. Next he refers to Jikmé Lingpa, another lineage master, by one of his other names, Khyentse Özer. Finally he evokes the name of his own root guru, Gyalwé Nyugu, that is to say, Dza Trama Lama Jikmé Gyalwé Nyugu. Patrul Rinpoche employs the names of these three masters to explain the three essences of view, meditation, and action.

> First, the View is the realization that all the infinite appearances (*rabjam*) of saṃsāra and nirvāṇa, in their entirety, are perfectly contained and by nature equal within the all-encompassing space of the vast expanse (*longchen*) of buddha nature, which is the true nature of reality, free from any elaboration. And so: **"The view is Longchen Rabjam: infinite, vast expanse"**.

The dharmadhātu, which is free from all elaboration, is also called 'tathāgatagarbha'. All schools of Vajrayāna, both the older and the more recent, speak about this buddha nature, the wisdom of clear light. Because it cannot be established to have true existence or to be autonomous, it is termed 'free from elaboration.' In essence it is primordially pure, by nature it is spontaneously present. It is this buddha nature that serves as the ground for all saṃsāra and nirvāṇa, a vast expanse, within which all elaborations—the phenomena of saṃsāra and nirvāṇa—arise and subside. Pure by its very nature, this is what we term 'view', an expanse that permeates everything and within which everything is contained and complete.

> Meditation is the union of emptiness and compassion: with the wisdom (*khyen*) of the insight practice of vipaśyana, to realize conclusively the nature of the view of freedom from elaboration, and to rest one-pointedly in that emptiness united with the skilful means of the śamatha of loving compassion (*tse*). So, **"Meditation is Khyentse Özer: rays of wisdom and love"**.

Once you have the view, then automatically there arises in you a compassion for beings who are unaware of the essence of this view. That is what I feel is meant by saying that meditation is "Khyentse Özer: the rays of wisdom and love."

> Action is to be imbued with such a view and meditation and then to practise the six perfections so as to benefit others, in keeping with the ways of the bodhisattvas, "the new shoots of the buddhas". So, **"Action is Gyalwé Nyugu, that of the bodhisattvas".**

When you are imbued with this union of skilful means and wisdom, that forms the basis whereby the action of a bodhisattva, which ensures benefit for others, can ensue. So the text says that "Action is Gyalwé Nyugu, that of the bodhisattvas."

> To show how fortunate is the person who practises such view, meditation, and action, **"One who practises in such a way,"**
>
> Those who are able to seclude themselves in an isolated retreat, put aside the worldly cares and activities of this life and practise single-mindedly, will gain liberation—in their very lifetime—in the ground of primordial purity. So, **"May well attain enlightenment in this very life".**

If your practice is authentic, and imbued with these key points of view, meditation and action, it allows you to attain buddhahood in this lifetime.

> However, even if not, simply by turning your mind towards such view, meditation, and action, you will know how to transform all life's difficulties into the path, you will have less hope and fear about the preoccupations of this life, and in the next life you will

go from happiness to happiness. So, **"And even if not, what happiness! What joy!"**

Even though you may not attain buddhahood in this life, if your practice, combining skilful means and wisdom, brings you a stable realization, one in which you have confidence, then you will not fall under the sway of negative circumstances, but you will be able to incorporate them into the path. Also, in future lifetimes, the strength of this practice will carry you to steadily greater states of happiness. So this is something about which you can truly rejoice. To sum up: in this lifetime, you do not fall prey to hope, fear and other negative circumstances, but transform them into the path, and in future lives, you will experience greater and greater states of happiness.

> In order to explain, step by step, such a beneficial view, meditation, and action, first I wish to set out at greater length how to take to heart and practise the view. And **"As for the view, Longchen Rabjam,"**
>
> The entire meaning is in this instruction on the three words, for when they hit the essence of the practice, delusion is put to death. So: **"Three words hit the vital point"**.

The view is covered in three words that touch on, or 'hit', the essential meaning.

I. INTRODUCING DIRECTLY THE FACE OF RIGPA IN ITSELF

> First is the method of introducing the view that has not yet been revealed. Generally speaking, there are many ways of bringing the view to realization. In the sūtrayāna path of dialectics the method of *lung rig*[43] is employed; that is, using the scriptural authority of the teaching of Buddha and the great masters, and through logic and reasoning, arriving at the realization

of the view. According to the common approach of
Secret Mantrayāna, by means of the wisdom of
example in the third empowerment, one is introduced
to the real, ultimate wisdom in the fourth empowerment. Here, according to the special approach of the
great masters of the practice lineage, the nature of
mind, the face of rigpa, is introduced in and upon the
very dissolution of conceptual mind.

Amidst the churning waves of delusory thinking, the
gross arising thoughts which run after the objects of
perception obscure the actual face of mind's true
nature. So even if it were introduced, you would not
recognize it. Therefore, in order to allow these gross
discursive thoughts to settle and clear, **"First, relax
and release your mind,"**

This view, the self-arising rigpa to which you are directly introduced, is being pointed out right here. What makes it difficult at the
beginning for us to be introduced to this rigpa is that there are so
many positive and negative thoughts arising, one after another, in
our minds. In just the same way, it is difficult to have someone
pointed out to you and recognize them in a crowd, but once you
have been introduced to that person, you can identify him or her
readily, even in the midst of a huge gathering.

Now, it is true that all thoughts are permeated by the quality of
pure awareness, but as long as these thoughts bind the mind, rigpa
cannot be laid bare in all its nakedness. That is why the root text
says, "First, relax and release your mind", so that you do not allow
thoughts to create that kind of disturbance, and instead you relax.

However, to leave your own mind relaxed and uncontrived is itself the wisdom of clear light. So paths
that are contrived will never bring you to the
realization of your true nature, and to signify that this
uncontrived innate wisdom is there within you:

> "Neither scattered, nor concentrated, without thoughts".

This self-arising rigpa is already present within us. It is what we might call our 'genuine nature'. But the temporary influence of thoughts prevents it from becoming evident. In order for this genuine and continuous state of utterly natural rigpa to become clear, you must dispense with adventitious thoughts. This is why the root text says, "Neither scattered, nor concentrated, without thoughts".

> A beginner may be able to let the mind rest naturally in itself, and try to maintain it. However, it is impossible for them to be free from fixation on the many experiences such as 'bliss', 'clarity' and 'non-conceptuality' that come in the state of calm and stillness: **"While resting in this even state, at ease".**

It is not enough for the mind simply to rest without stirring, for even while it does, you will experience the taste of bliss, clarity, and states of non-conceptuality, and these can create obstacles to your recognition of rigpa.

> To free yourself from the cocoon of attachment to experience, lay bare the all-penetrating rigpa and reveal explicitly its true state, **"Suddenly let out a mind-shattering 'phaṭ!',"**
>
> Since it is vital to cut through the flow of arising thoughts, and destroy meditation made by the mind, the sound 'phaṭ!' should be fierce, forceful and abrupt: **"Fierce, forceful, and abrupt. Amazing!"**

So as to dispel, suddenly, all the thoughts that cause such busyness in the mind, you use the sound of 'phaṭ!'—fierce, forceful, and abrupt. Used in this way, it has the effect of suddenly startling your mind.

When a boat moves through the water, for just an instant there is an empty space behind the stern. In the same way, there is a gap between a previous thought that has been suddenly dispelled, and a new thought that has yet to arise.

> At this moment, you are free from all fixed notions of
> what mind might be, and liberation itself is actualized:
> **"There is nothing there: transfixed in wonder,"**

As a means to dispel thoughts, by preventing a previous thought continuing and a fresh one arising, you use the forceful sound of 'phaṭ!' All the fragmentation of thought vanishes without trace, and the mind is left simply clear and aware. At that point, it is as though your mind were somewhat startled or astonished. It is a little difficult to explain what is being indicated here, but think of it in this way: the continuous experience of mind as 'ālaya', the basis of all ordinary experience, is cut through with the sharp edge of rigpa. The usual experience of the ordinary mind fades, and in the gap before the onset of grasping—for just an instant—naked rigpa can be perceived.

Mangtö Ludrup Gyatso[44] cites many scriptural sources on this point. In one of his texts he says, "In the gap between the previous thought and the next, luminous rigpa is uninterrupted". In another context, it is said, "In the gap between the previous thought and the next, wisdom continues uninterruptedly".[45] This awareness of the present instant, which is experienced in the gap between a previous thought and the next one, is easily evoked by this approach, it would seem, with the result that you are able both to identify it and to understand the significance of what it is you are identifying.

> In that state of dharmakāya, devoid of any reference
> or reliance whatsoever, all-penetrating, naked aware-
> ness dwells, just as it is, as the wisdom that transcends
> the mind, and so it is: **"Struck by wonder, and yet all
> is transparently clear"**.

So in the gap between a previous thought and the subsequent one, it is easier to introduce the self-arising rigpa directly, and easier for it to become clear.

> This all-penetrating, unimpeded awareness is the key point of inexpressible and naturally inherent wisdom, being beyond all extremes such as rising and ceasing, existing and non-existing, so beyond words and out of reach of mental enquiry. So: **"Fresh, pure and sudden, so beyond description:"**

Since this is beyond ordinary concepts such as existence and nonexistence, origination and cessation, and beyond any kind of verbalization, the root text says, "Fresh, pure and sudden, so beyond description."

> That key here is that rigpa, which abides in the ground of dharmakāya, is the primordial purity of the path of the yogins, the absolute view of freedom from all elaboration. Until you recognize this one point, then whatever meditation or practice you do, you can never get beyond a fabricated mind-made view and meditation. The difference between this and the approach of the natural Dzogpachenpo is greater than that between earth and sky, as it does not possess the essential point—the unceasing flow of clear light, which is non-meditation. So it is most important, first of all, to recognize this and this alone, and: **"Recognize this as the pure awareness of dharmakāya"**.

It is said that rigpa in this sense, which is dharmakāya, must be identified on the basis of personal experience. If you have not been directly introduced, and so cannot recognize it as such, you do not have the Dzogchen view. Remember that in the context of

Dzogchen, the view is a matter of focusing uniquely on rigpa and making that experience into meditation.

In this respect, Dodrupchen Jikmé Tenpé Nyima says that once you understand all phenomena to be the energy, or the display, of this self-arising rigpa, then it is very straightforward to realize that all phenomena only seem to exist as a result of concepts, of them being labelled to be so.[46] So, in this present case the view is where you are introduced directly to rigpa, and you practise by maintaining that recognition. If you have already gained direct introduction to rigpa, you do not necessarily have to go through the preliminary of examining the arising, remaining, and ceasing of thoughts to reveal 'the mind's hidden flaw', and so arrive at a decisive conclusion about it.[47] In the Madhyamaka approach of the sūtra tradition, however, all of these steps are necessary.

> This then is the first of the three words which hit the essence. If the view has not been introduced and re-cognized, there is nothing to maintain in meditation. This is why it is so important, first and foremost, to be introduced to the view. Then since the natural, in-herent wisdom is introduced as something natural and inherent in you, it is neither to be sought elsewhere, nor is it something that you did not have before and that now arises newly in your mind. So: **"The first vital point is: introducing directly the face of rigpa in itself"**.

Such a view is the direct introduction to the face of rigpa in itself, introduced on the basis of your personal experience. You must then meditate on it, or rather abide in it one-pointedly. What is happening is that you are being directly introduced, on the basis of your own experience, to the rigpa that is present within you already. Other than this, there is nothing that mind needs to create as something new, or about which it has to reach some conclusion. It is simply the true nature that each one of us already has, just as it is.

Since this is introduced directly, and it is in this that you abide, the first essence is, "Introducing directly the face of rigpa in itself".

As regards this direct introduction to the view, as I have said before, it is only when a master who has the authentic experience meets a student with faith and devotion that it can take place. It is not at all easy under any other circumstances.

II. DECIDE UPON ONE THING, AND ONE THING ONLY

Once you have been directly introduced to such a view, there is a means of maintaining this experience, which is the process of meditation.

> Now to give a more detailed explanation of how to take the practice of meditation to heart:
> In a natural state of rest, all the time and in any situation, your meditation is like the continuous flow of a river. Without cultivating stillness or suppressing the movement of thought, simply maintain the recognition that when stillness occurs, it is the dharmakāya's own face, and when movement arises, it is the inherent power of wisdom. And: **"Then, whether in a state of movement or stillness,"**

Once the face of rigpa itself has been introduced, regardless of what thoughts arise in your mind there is no need to react to them, by encouraging some and blocking others. As it is said, if thoughts arise, they arise within the space of rigpa, while they also cease within that space. So as long as you can maintain that natural state of rigpa, none of these thoughts, whatever they may be, can pose any threat.

When rigpa has been directly introduced, whatever thoughts arise within that state, be they positive or negative, there is no need to use some specific and deliberate means to block these thoughts from arising or to avoid indulging in them. Simply hold to the natural state of rigpa—the face of rigpa in itself—that has been introduced, without ever losing that context. Then even if thoughts do arise they can only do so within the space of rigpa. And where else would they go when they dissolve?

> From the energy of mind's thinking come negative emotions like anger and attachment that represent the truth of the origin of suffering, as well as feelings like happiness and sorrow, which constitute the truth of suffering itself. Yet whatever experiences arise, if you can realize that the true nature of these thoughts and emotions is the very nature of reality, they will be just the flow of dharmakāya. And so: **"Of anger or attachment, happiness or sorrow,"**

> But that is not all. Generally speaking, even though you may have recognized the view, if you do not sustain it in meditation, and you slip into the ordinary proliferation of delusion, the same old patterns of thought will bind you to saṃsāra. As a result, the Dharma and you become divorced, and you end up no different from an ordinary person. That is why you must never be apart from this supreme state of naturally resting in non-meditation, and why: **"All the time, in any situation,"**

> So, whether the mind is still, active or whatever, it is not a question of overcoming each individual negative emotion and thought with its own separate remedy. Instead, the sole remedy for whatever thought or emotion may occur, the one remedy for all, is the recognition of that view which was introduced previously, and that alone. So: **"Recognize that dharmakāya you recognized before,"**

So, at any time and whatever the situation, regardless of the variety of thoughts that arise, you do not need to rely on individual antidotes for each individual thought and emotion. Rather, you

simply recognize the dharmakāya wisdom which was directly
introduced before. This brings to mind one of the songs of Jetsün
Milarepa, in which he sings of how the clouds arise within the space
of the sky, and dissolve back into its expanse again.[48] There are other
examples: the ice that melts to become water again, or the water
that turns turbid the more it is stirred, but becomes clear once left
alone. Just so, rigpa is the true nature of all the thoughts that stir
within the mind; rest in rigpa and within that state thoughts will
simply vanish.

Here there is an important distinction to be made. In the
mainstream tradition of Madhyamaka philosophy, what is refuted is
the mind's grasping at things as though they had true existence. This
is the ignorance that is the first of the twelve links of interdependence, that initial ignorance which causes us to grasp at things as true.
Here, however, the focus is on that which has never been subject to
that grasping, which makes this quite a different approach.

> So, whatever thought or emotion arises, in itself it is
> no other than the wisdom of dharmakāya, and the
> true nature of these thoughts and emotions is the
> actual clear light of the ground of dharmakāya. When
> you recognize this, that is what is known as 'the
> mother clear light present as the ground'. To recognize
> your own nature in that view of the clear light of self-
> knowing rigpa introduced earlier by the master is
> what is known as 'the path clear light of practice'. To
> remain in the state where these two, the clear light of
> ground and path, are inseparable is known as 'the
> meeting of mother and child clear light'. So: **"And
> mother and child clear light, already acquainted,
> will reunite"**.

Fundamentally, no matter who we are, whether we meditate or not,
the self-arising wisdom of rigpa is already primordially present, and
we have never strayed from it. Then there is rigpa as it is directly

introduced to us by a master, on the basis of our personal practice. The nature of rigpa in both cases is identical—it is uncontrived rigpa—but in the one case it is simply so, without having been directly introduced, while in the other case we are recognizing our true nature for what it is. So one can talk about rigpa in two ways. But actually, there are not two things, one reuniting and another being reunited. The direct introduction to what is naturally present as the ground of being is metaphorically called 'reuniting mother and child'.

In other traditions, this expression 'reuniting' or sometimes 'merging' mother and child clear light is connected to the dawning of the ground clear light at death, experienced even by ordinary people when they die. Specifically the expression describes the ability of a practitioner, through the power of yoga, to transform this experience, as it arises, into the essence of the path. And this is what is meant by reuniting mother and child clear light, the 'mother' clear light being that which arises for even ordinary people at death and which is transformed into the path.

Also the mother clear light can be a reference to the state of emptiness, with the child clear light as the mind—not really considered as rigpa in these particular traditions—that maintains a continuous awareness of that emptiness. So in these traditions 'reuniting mother and child' refers to the way in which the mind, the child, experiences emptiness, the mother.

> In this way, always remind yourself of the view, which
> is the clear light recognized in you as your true nature,
> and rest in that state. Apart from that, the crucial point
> is neither to suppress nor indulge, neither accept nor
> reject, in any way, the thoughts or emotions which are
> the energy of rigpa: **"Rest in the aspect of awareness,
> beyond all description"**.

Patrul Rinpoche describes how to maintain the recognition of rigpa, on the basis of your experience of the direct introduction to the face of rigpa in itself. This is what is meant by "Rest in the aspect of awareness, beyond all description".

In other texts, those of the Highest Yoga Tantra tradition, the term 'clear light' is used to refer to a subtle state of mind that is coemergent with being itself. This corresponds to what in the Dzogchen tradition is referred to as 'ground rigpa'—for a distinction is made between the 'ground' and the 'manifestation of the ground'. When you are directly introduced to rigpa through the six consciousnesses, this is termed 'rigpa as energy' or 'effulgent rigpa'. On the basis of being introduced to rigpa as energy, you meet the ground rigpa, face to face.[49]

> When you maintain that state for a long time, as a beginner you will have experiences of bliss, clarity or non-conceptuality, which will mask the face of your true nature. So if you free it from this shell of attachment-to-experience, and lay bare the actual face of rigpa, then wisdom will shine out from within. There is a saying:

> > The more it is disrupted,
> > The better the meditation of a yogin.
> > The further it has to drop,
> > The greater the force of a waterfall.

> So: **"Stillness and bliss, clarity and thinking: disrupt them, again and again,"**

Meditative experiences of stillness, bliss, or clarity will obscure the rigpa when they arise, and so they must be disrupted.

> "How to disrupt them?" you might ask. Whenever experiences of stillness, bliss or clarity arise and intensify, or feelings of joy, glee or delight, you must pulverize your shell of attachment to experience,

shattering it as if by a bolt of lightning, with the forceful sound of 'phaṭ!' which is the combination of 'pha', the syllable of skilful means that concentrates and gathers, and 'ṭ', the syllable of prajñā, which cuts through. So: **"Suddenly striking with the syllable of skilful means and wisdom"**.

At such times, says Patrul Rinpoche, you must dispel thoughts with a forceful exclamation of this syllable 'phaṭ!'

> When you do not lose this vital point of personal experience, and you maintain, at all times and in all situations, that indescribable, all-penetrating rigpa, formal meditation and post-meditation will no longer be distinct: **"With no difference between meditation and post-meditation,"**

In the phrase "that indescribable all-penetrating rigpa", the word *zangthal*—all-penetrating—carries the sense of a lack of obstruction. Although the manifest objects of rigpa continue to arise unimpeded, outwardly your mind does not fixate on these objects, and inwardly you simply rest in the state of rigpa itself. So whether you are in meditation or in post-meditation, that is to say, in the formal sessions or the periods in between them, there is no real difference between the two.

> That is why the meditation just in sessions and the meditation when you are active during breaks are not separate: **"No division between sessions and breaks,"**
>
> In this 'great meditation with nothing to meditate on', the continuous river-like yoga of inherent, even and all-pervasive wisdom,[50] there is not even a hair's breadth of anything to meditate on, nor an instant of distraction. This is what is meant by the saying:

> Neither do I ever meditate, nor am I ever separate
> from it;
> So I have never been separate from the true
> meaning of 'non-meditation'.[51]

And that is why: **"Always remain in this indivisible
state"**.

Without making any division between formal practice sessions and
the periods between them, you should rest in a continuous and
vivid state of rigpa.

> If someone is a suitable and receptive vessel for the
> unique path of Dzogpachenpo, just as the teachings
> themselves intend, and they belong to the 'instant-
> aneous' type of person who is liberated upon hearing
> the teaching, then, for such a person, perception and
> thoughts are the supreme ground for liberation, and
> anything that happens becomes the flow of
> dharmakāya. There is nothing to meditate on, and no
> one to meditate. However others who are less
> fortunate and who still fall prey to delusory thinking
> must find stability in 'gradual stages'. Until they do so,
> they must engage in the practice of meditation.
> Therefore: **"But until stability is attained,"**

Those for whom the arising and liberation of a thought are
simultaneous are of the very highest capacity. For beginners
however, it is not enough that the rigpa has been directly introduced; they must meditate in order to extend this experience over
time, and this they must do, "away from all distractions and
busyness".

> That meditation must be done when all the condi-
> tions favourable for meditative stability are complete;

only then will real experience occur. No matter how long you spend meditating in the midst of busyness and distraction, true meditation experience will not arise, and so: **"It is vital to meditate, away from all distractions and busyness"**.

While meditating too, though there is no difference between practice in formal sessions and post-meditation, if you are not truly grounded in your meditation first, you will be unable to blend the wisdom you experience with your post-meditation. However hard you try to turn your daily life into the path, your vague and generalized understanding makes you prone to slip into your old negative patterns and habits. Therefore: **"Dividing the practice into proper meditation sessions"**.

You might have the sort of practice which makes you confident that you can keep up this state of meditation by dividing the practice into proper sessions. Even so, if you do not understand how to integrate that practice with the activities of post-meditation and how to maintain it continuously, then this practice will not serve as a remedy when difficulties arise. When some discursive thought leads you off, you will sink back into very ordinary things. This is why it is so very important to abide in that all-penetrating state of awareness after meditation: **"All the time, in any situation,"**

More especially, when we are not practising formally, but doing other kinds of things like meeting people, we run the risk, because of our strong past habits, of falling under the influence of powerful attachment and aversion. This is why the experience that was directly introduced must be stabilized without interruption, "all the time, in any situation," while we continue to develop certainty about it, again and again.

At that point, there is no need to seek for anything
else on which to meditate. Instead, in a state of
meditative equipoise that never parts from this very
view of dharmakāya, maintain an unconcerned,
carefree nonchalance towards all actions and all
thoughts, without suppressing or indulging them, but
letting things come and go, one after another, and
leaving them be: **"Abide by the flow of what is just
dharmakāya"**.

"Abide by the flow of what is just dharmakāya" means that though
all manner of thoughts can arise and usher in all kinds of
experiences, pleasant or unpleasant, none of these thoughts falls
outside the expanse of the self-arising rigpa, the wisdom of
dharmakāya. That is what they initially arise from, and what they
dissolve back into in the end—the expanse of dharmakāya. In the
meantime, these perceptions and appearances, in all their variety,
arise like the images we see in our dreams. So the text is saying, in
effect, understand them to be the flow of dharmakāya, which is also
termed 'Samantabhadra'—'all-good' and 'mind without beginning
or end'.

A practice such as this, which is the indivisible union
of śamatha and vipaśyana, the yoga of the natural state
free from elaboration, uncontrived and innate, the
abiding by the face of the intrinsic nature of reality, is
the heart of the practice of all the tantras of the Secret
Mantra Vajrayāna. It is the ultimate wisdom of the
fourth empowerment. It is the speciality, the wish-
fulfilling gem, of the practice lineage. It is the flawless
wisdom mind of all the accomplished masters and
their lineages, of India and Tibet, of both old and new
traditions. So decide on this, with absolute conviction, and do not hanker after other pith instructions,
your mouth watering with an insatiable appetite and

greed. Otherwise it is like keeping your elephant at home and looking for its footprints in the forest. You walk into the trap of unending mental research, and then liberation will never have a chance. Therefore you must decide on your practice, and: **"Decide with absolute conviction that there is nothing other than this—"**

While you are seeking this certainty within yourself, if your mind goes everywhere, thinking, "Perhaps this will be better, or maybe that..." grabbing at one thing after another, you will end up getting nowhere. So it is important that you start by coming to a decision, and then proceed on the basis of that decision. You need to "Decide with absolute conviction that there is nothing other than this".

Make a decision then that this naked wisdom of dharmakāya, naturally present, is the awakened state, which has never known delusion, and abide by its flow: this is the second secret and vital word. Since it is so crucially important: **"The second vital point is: decide upon one thing, and one thing only".**

This phrase, "the awakened state, which has never known delusion," calls to mind two lines from the *Sublime Continuum*:[52]

It has flaws that are only superficial,
While it has enlightened qualities by its very nature.

The significance of the first line "It has flaws that are only superficial" is that all the flaws of distortion are capable of being overcome by antidotes. However, the qualities of buddhahood that come from realization—all the qualities unique to self-arising rigpa, or the fundamental innate mind of clear light—are primordially established. Hence the second line: "While it has enlightened qualities by its very nature".

III. CONFIDENCE DIRECTLY IN THE LIBERATION OF RISING
THOUGHTS

> Now, at such times as these, if there is not the
> confidence of the method of liberation, and your
> meditation is merely relaxing in the stillness of mind,
> you will not get beyond being side-tracked into the
> samādhi of the gods. Such a meditation will not be
> able to overcome your attachment or anger. It will not
> be able to put a stop to the flow of karmic formations.
> Nor will it be able to bring you the deep confidence
> of direct certainty. Therefore, this method of libera-
> tion is of vital importance.
>
> What is more, when a burning attachment is aroused
> towards some object of desire, or violent anger towards
> an object of aversion, when you feel joy about favour-
> able circumstances, material possessions and the like,
> or you are afflicted by sorrow on account of unfavour-
> able circumstances and things like illness—no matter
> what happens—at that moment it is a test of the
> power of your rigpa, and so it is vital to recognize the
> wisdom that is the ground for liberation. So: **"At that
> point, whether attachment or aversion, happiness
> or sorrow—"**

Whenever you experience some strong attachment or aversion, or
some intense feeling of joy or sadness, and you are able to maintain
your practice well, it will be because you have been directly introduced to rigpa. For as the text says, "it is a test of the power of your
rigpa, and so it is vital to recognize the wisdom that is the ground
of liberation". It is a question here of not losing the context of the
wisdom that is the ground for liberation, and of that self-arising
rigpa to which you have been directly introduced.

> Besides, if your practice lacks the key point of "libera-
> tion upon arising", whatever subtle thoughts creep

unnoticed into your mind will all accumulate more saṃsāric karma. So, the crucial point is to maintain this simultaneous arising and liberation with every thought that rises, whether gross or subtle, so that they leave no trace behind them. **"All momentary thoughts, each and every one,"**

Therefore, whatever thoughts arise, you do not allow them to proliferate into a welter of subtle delusion, while at the same time you do not apply some narrow mind-made mindfulness. Instead what you must do is never separate from a natural genuine mindfulness, but recognize the true nature of whatever thoughts arise and sustain this "liberation upon arising" which leaves no trace behind, as if writing on the surface of water. So: **"Upon recognition, leave not a trace behind"**.

At this point, if the arising thoughts are not purified, dissolving as they liberate themselves, the mere recognition of thoughts on its own will not be able to cut the chain of the karma that perpetuates delusion. So at the very same instant as you recognize, by seeing the true nature of the thought nakedly, you will simultaneously identify the wisdom with which you are familiar from before, and when you rest in that state, thoughts are purified, dissolving so that they leave no trace. That dissolution is a crucial point. So: **"For recognize the dharmakāya in which they are freed,"**

To take an example: writing or drawing on water. The very instant it is written, it dissolves—the writing and its disappearance are simultaneous. Likewise, as soon as thoughts arise, liberation is simultaneous, and so it becomes an unbroken flow of "self-arising and self-liberating": **"And just as writing vanishes on water,"**

Experiencing thoughts "like writing on water", you do not stray from the state of rigpa, which is the very nature of the thoughts. If you can remain in that state, none of the thoughts that arise will last, no more than does writing on water.

> And so, without suppressing the risings, you allow
> whatever arises to arise, and any thoughts that do arise
> actually become the path for purifying into their true
> nature. This is what you must hold to as the essence
> of the practice: **"Arising and liberation become
> natural and continuous"**.

Since you remain within the experience of rigpa, thoughts—which are "self-arising"—are liberated within that space of rigpa. If your practice goes well, any thoughts that arise are simply upheavals and tests of the energy of rigpa, and so they serve as food, only nourishing and increasing your experience of the naked union of rigpa and emptiness. This is the meaning of "And whatever arises is food for the bare rigpa emptiness":

> So by training in thoughts like this as being the sport
> of dharmakāya, then whatever thoughts occur arise as
> a training in the power of rigpa. And however gross
> the thoughts of the five poisons are, that much more
> will they invest the rigpa in which they are liberated
> with clarity and sharpness. **"And whatever arises is
> food for the bare rigpa emptiness,"**
>
> When any thoughts that stir all arise from the all-
> penetrating true face of rigpa itself as its own inner
> power, simply abide in this, without accepting or
> rejecting. Then at the very instant they arise, they are
> liberated, and they are never outside the flow of the
> dharmakāya: **"Whatever stirs in the mind is the
> inner power of the dharmakāya king"**.

So if you do not fall under the influence of thoughts, but you are able to maintain your recognition of the true nature of rigpa, no matter how many thoughts occur, they will all arise as the energy of rigpa— the "dharmakāya king". Self-arising rigpa is called the "dharmakāya king", and thoughts arise as its energy or display like the retinue of this king. And since thoughts are not prolonged, the root text goes on to say, "Leaving no trace, and innately pure. What joy!"

> Thoughts in the mind, the delusory perceptions of ignorance, are pure within the expanse of dharmakāya that is the wisdom of rigpa, so within that expanse of uninterrupted clear light whatever thoughts stir and arise are by their very nature empty. So: **"Leaving no trace, and innately pure. What joy!"**

> When you have become used to integrating thoughts into your path like this over a long period of time, thoughts arise as meditation, the boundary between stillness and movement falls away, and as a result, nothing that arises ever harms or disturbs your dwelling in awareness: **"The way things arise may be the same as before,"**

Patrul Rinpoche is saying that when you have mastered such experience, thoughts will still arise in all their variety, as they did before, but there is a vital difference—the way they are liberated.

> At that juncture, the way that thoughts, the energy of rigpa, arise as joy and sorrow, hope and fear, may be similar as in an ordinary person. Yet with ordinary people, their experience is a very solid one of suppressing or indulging, with the result that they accumulate karmic formations and fall prey to attachment and aggression. On the other hand, for a Dzogchen yogin, thoughts are liberated the moment they arise:

—at the beginning, arising thoughts are liberated
upon being recognized, like meeting an old friend;
—in the middle, thoughts are liberated by themselves,
like a snake uncoiling its own knots;
—at the end, arising thoughts are liberated without
being of either benefit or harm, like a thief breaking
into an empty house.

Here Patrul Rinpoche is talking about the three modes of liberation, of which the third is considered the best. The self-liberating
quality of thoughts here is compared to a thief entering an empty
house. The house has nothing to lose and the thief has nothing to
gain. This seems to me to mean that when you maintain "the face
of rigpa in itself" and you do not lose its natural state, thoughts can
do no harm. They will arise, but they liberate themselves. And of
the many ways in which liberation occurs, the final one that Patrul
Rinpoche discusses here is the most profound. He concludes:

So, the Dzogchen yogin possesses the vital point of the
methods of liberation such as these. And so: **"But the
difference lies in the way they are liberated: that's
the key"**.

That is why it is said:
    To know how to meditate,
    But not how to liberate—
    How does that differ from the meditation of the
    gods?

What this means is that those who put their trust in a
meditation which lacks this vital point of the method
of liberation, and is merely some state of mental
quiescence, will only stray into the meditation states of
the higher realms. People who claim that it is sufficient
simply to recognize stillness and movement are no

different from ordinary people with their deluded thinking. And as for those who give it all kinds of labels like 'emptiness' and 'dharmakāya', the basic flaw in their remedy is exposed when it fails to hold up under the first misfortune or difficulty they meet. So: **"Without this, meditation is but the path of delusion"**.

'Liberation on arising', 'self-liberation', 'naked liberation', whatever name you give it, this manner of liberation where thoughts liberate themselves and are purified without a trace is the same crucial point, which is actually to show this self-liberation explicitly. It is the extraordinary speciality of the natural Dzogpachenpo, and so if you possess this key point, then whatever negative emotions or thoughts arise simply turn into dharmakāya. All delusory thoughts are purified as wisdom. All harmful circumstances arise as friends. All negative emotions become the path. Saṃsāra is purified in its own natural state, without your having to renounce it, and you are freed from the chains of either conditioned existence or the state of peace. You have arrived at such a complete and final state, there is no effort, nothing to achieve, and nothing left to do. And **"With it, even without meditating, there's the state of dharmakāya"**.

If you can meditate on the basis of pith instructions like these on personal experience, you do not need to make some mental effort to construct something when you meditate. You reach a decisive experience in the state of dharmakāya.

If you do not have the confidence of such a way of liberation, you can claim your view is high and your meditation is deep, but it will not really help your mind, and nor will it prove a remedy for your negative emotions. Therefore, this is not the true path. On the other hand, if you do have the key point of 'self-arising and self-liberating', then without even the minutest attitude of a 'high view' or notion of a 'deep meditation', it is quite impossible for your mind not to be liberated from the bonds of dualistic grasping. When you go to the fabled Island of Gold, you can never find ordinary earth or stones, however hard you look. In just the same way, stillness, movement and thoughts all arise now as meditation, and even if you search for real, solid delusions, you will not find any. And this alone is the measure to determine whether your practice has hit the mark or not; so: **"The third vital point is: confidence directly in the liberation of rising thoughts"**.

Here it seems that Patrul Rinpoche is emphasizing that on the basis of this experience, you have to establish confidence in the essence of that self-liberating quality of thoughts.

IV. THE COLOPHON

These three key points are the unerring essence which brings the view, meditation, action and fruition of natural Dzogpachenpo all together within the state of the all-penetrating awareness of rigpa. So in fact it constitutes the pith instructions for meditation and action, as well as for the view.

However this is not some abstract concept about which, to use the Dharma terminology of the mainstream textual tradition, a definitive conclusion is reached after evaluating it with scripture, logic and reasoning. Rather, whenever you actually realize wisdom itself, directly and in all its nakedness, that is the view of the wisdom of rigpa. Since all the many views and meditations have but 'one taste', there is no contradiction in explaining the three vital points as the practice of the view. So: **"For the View which has the three vital points,"**

A practice such as this is the infallible key point of the path of primordial purity in the natural Dzogpachenpo, the very pinnacle of the nine graduated vehicles. Just as it is impossible for a king to travel without his courtiers, in the same way the key points of all yānas serve as steps and supports for the Dzogchen path.

Not only this, but when you see the face of the lamp of naturally arising wisdom—the primordial purity of rigpa—its power will blaze as the insight which comes from meditation, and then the expanse of your wisdom swells like a rising summer river, while the nature of emptiness dawns as great compassion, and so infuses you with a loving compassion which is without limits or bias. This is how it is, and so: **"Meditation, the union of wisdom and love,"**

Patrul Rinpoche is saying that, with regard to the view that is imbued with these three points of view, meditation, and action, the practice of meditation will be one that combines wisdom and love.

What is said about meditation here also relates to the practice of tögal. In the Dzogchen tradition, the ground is explained from the point of view of its essence, nature, and energy or responsiveness, but the emphasis is on the first two: its primordial purity and spontaneous presence. When we consider the terminology used in other traditions, 'primordial purity' corresponds to the aspect of emptiness, and 'spontaneous presence' to the aspect of form. So the union of emptiness and form could be thought of as analogous to that of primordial purity and spontaneous presence. It is all very well to explain it in that way, but in that case your point of view would be that what is ultimate is the fundamental innate mind of clear light. The *shyentong* or 'empty of other' school of Madhyamaka describes this innate mind as being 'empty of other, adventitious conditions'. You would be considering that to be the ultimate, with primordial purity and spontaneous presence as its aspects. As well as the union of emptiness and form, this could also be compared to that of wisdom and skilful means. But here, in this uniquely Dzogchen explanation of the two truths, their primordial unity is what is ultimate.

The term 'primordial purity' relates to the middle series of the Buddha's teachings, and in general it refers to this middle series, although there are situations where it applies to rigpa. The term 'spontaneous presence' relates to the final series of teachings and the ultimate enlightened intent of the Buddha. In the Dzogchen tradition, this profound subject of spontaneous presence is only dealt with in the highest teachings. I should point out that learned masters have held different opinions on these topics.

Given the primordial purity and spontaneous presence of the ground, when it comes to the practice of the path, you practise trekchö on the basis of the primordially pure ground, and tögal on the basis of the spontaneously present ground. By means of these two paths, the result that comes about is conventionally termed 'primordial purity as the inner lucidity of dharmakāya' or 'spontaneous presence as the outer lucidity of sambhogakāya'.

> Once this key point on the path, the unity of empti-
> ness and compassion, is directly realized, the ocean-like
> actions of the bodhisattvas, all included within the path
> of the six pāramitās, arise as its own natural energy, like
> rays which shine from the sun. Since action is related to
> the accumulation of merit, anything you do will be for
> the benefit of others, helping you to avoid seeking
> peace and happiness for yourself alone, and so deviating
> from the correct view. So it: **"Is accompanied by the
> Action common to all the bodhisattvas"**.
>
> This kind of view, meditation and action is the very
> core of the enlightened vision of all the buddhas who
> ever came, who are here now or who will ever come,
> and so: **"Were all the buddhas to confer,"**

The supreme peak of all the yānas, the key point on the path of the Vajra Heart Essence of the Nyingtik, the quintessence of all fruition—nothing surpasses this. And so: **"No instruction would they find greater than this"**.

Since this is the most excellent of spiritual advice, "Were all the buddhas to confer, no instruction would they find greater than this". Until you have based your path on this clear light, there can be no awakening to buddhahood. And in the main texts of Dzogchen, it is said that the profound and rapid method is to approach rigpa as the ground through rigpa as the energy of that ground.[53]

The real meaning of what is expressed in this instruction is the heart-essence of the pith instructions of the lineage, it is certain; yet even the lines that express it, these few words, should arise, too, out of the creative power of rigpa. So: **"By the tertön of dharmakāya, the inner power of rigpa,"**

When the root text says, "Brought out as a treasure from the depth of transcendental insight by the tertön of the dharmakāya", it implies Dza Patrul Rinpoche himself.[54]

I have not the slightest experience of the actual meaning behind these words as a result of 'the wisdom that comes from meditation'. Yet by hearing the unerring oral transmission of my holy master I cleared away all doubts completely with 'the wisdom that comes from listening', and then came to a conclusive understanding through 'the wisdom born of contemplation', whereupon I composed this. And so it was: **"Brought out as a treasure from the depth of transcendental insight,"**

It is unlike any ordinary kind of worldly treasure, which might simply bring temporary relief from poverty. **"Nothing like ordinary treasures of earth and stone,"**

These three vital points of the view, known as 'Hitting the Essence in Three Words', were given by the nirmāṇakāya Garab Dorje, from within a cloud of light in the sky as he passed into nirvāṇa, to the great master Mañjuśrīmitra. These are the very pith-instructions through which their realization became inseparable. **"For it is the final testament of Garab Dorje,"**

It was through penetrating to the essential meaning of this instruction that the omniscient king of Dharma, Longchen Rabjam, in his very life-time directly realized the 'wisdom mind' of primordial purity, where all phenomena are exhausted, and so awakened to complete and perfect buddhahood. Actually appearing in his wisdom body to the vidyādhara Jikmé Lingpa, he blessed him in the manner of the 'sign transmission of the vidyādharas'. From him in turn, by means of 'the transmission from mouth to ear', our own kind root master, Jikmé Gyalwé Nyugu, received the introduction through this instruction, and encountered the true nature of reality face to face. And this is the instruction I heard from Jikmé Gyalwé Nyugu, while he was present among us as the glorious protector of all beings. That is why it is: **"The essence of the wisdom mind of the three transmissions"**.

Patrul Rinpoche here is referring to the victorious Longchenpa, the omniscient Jikmé Lingpa, and Jikmé Gyalwé Nyugu as embodying the three lineages of transmission.

Pith instructions such as these are like the finest of gold, like the very core of the heart. It would be a pity to teach them to people who would not put them into practice. But then again it would be a pity, too, not to teach them to a person who would cherish these instructions like his or her own life, put their essential meaning into practice, and attain buddhahood in a single lifetime. So:

> "It is entrusted to my heart-disciples, sealed to be secret.
> It is profound in meaning, my heart's words.
> It is the words of my heart, the crucial key point.
> This crucial point, never hold it cheap!
> Never let this instruction slip away from you!"

With this brief commentary, 'The Special Teaching of the Wise and Glorious King' is completed at this point. Virtue! Virtue! Virtue!

For more than a year now, Sogyal Rinpoche has been requesting me to give a teaching, and since we did not have much time, I thought it would be good to teach on this text, which is quite short but of great substance. We have spent the last few days together in this same hall, and I have enjoyed myself very much. I think, at least I hope, that you all have as well.

Now, the most important thing for spiritual practitioners is for us to practise in our everyday lives. For that, we need great courage, determination and hope. Also we need to follow our own religion sincerely; that's crucial too. Religion must be inside us, not simply on our lips. There is no sense in it just remaining in our mouths, and nor is it much use if religion just stays in a temple or a church. Religion or spirituality must live within us.

Then again, what is religious, or spiritual, must work for us, for it is when we are faced with problems or tragedy that we need spiritual help. All will depend then on what we are familiar with. Dodrupchen Jikmé Tenpé Nyima tells us:

Whether realization awakens depends on your practice
   being well planted;
Whether your practice takes root depends on your courage
   and determination.[55]

In fact whatever we do, we need to make an effort. It will not do to
expect it all to be very easy, and for something great to happen, just
like that. So that is all. Thank you very much.

PART THREE

DZOGCHEN AND THE BUDDHADHARMA

Helsinki, 1988

DZOGCHEN AND THE
BUDDHADHARMA

THE BACKGROUND

Turning to a reporter at Helsinki airport at the beginning of his first visit to Finland in 1988, His Holiness the Dalai Lama told her that he was looking forward to hearing how a nation of only five million had managed to maintain its autonomy and stay on good terms with such a powerful neighbour. "Maybe we can learn something", he mused. A few days later, in a casual discussion over breakfast, it emerged that His Holiness had paid special attention to broadcasts about Finland while listening to the BBC news in the 1940s on his radio in the Potala. The conversation then turned to the remarkable figure of Baron C.G. Mannerheim (1867-1951), a larger than life character who had played an intimate role in the autonomy of Finland. His rounceval career spanned more than fifty years, during which he saw action in five wars, served twice as commander in chief of the Finnish Army, shot tigers in India, became Marshal of Finland, maintained his country's independence and finally, at the age of seventy-seven, was elected President.

As a cavalry colonel aged forty in the Russian army, at a time when Finland was a grand duchy of Russia, Mannerheim was sent secretly on an expedition into Central Asia and China to gather military intelligence.[56] Posing as an explorer, he nevertheless did undertake ethnological, anthropological and even archaeological work, compiling maps and bringing back to Finland thousands of objects and photographs. His ultimate aim was to assess whether a strike by Russian armies could successfully sever China in half, but it seems Mannerheim's subterfuge was penetrated by the Chinese at an early stage. For two years and fourteen thousand miles, most of them in the saddle, he followed the northern tracks of the silk road on the edge of the Taklamakan desert, through Russian Turkestan, Xinjiang and western China and on to Beijing.

One of his tasks was to gauge the role played by the Dalai Lama in the advancement of local peoples towards autonomy. So it was that on 26 June 1908, Mannerheim came to meet the thirteenth Dalai Lama at Wutai Shan. The Dalai Lama had left Lhasa in 1904 and travelled to Mongolia, and then Amdo and Kumbum, the birthplace of Tsongkhapa, before arriving at the holy mountain of Mañjuśrī, where he stayed for five months, and had many visionary experiences. His residence was the temple built for the fifth Dalai Lama over two centuries before. The meeting with Mannerheim was a ponderous exercise in diplomacy, until its final moments. After two years in the saddle, the Baron was at a loss what gift to offer the greatest spiritual eminence in Asia. The only possession he had of any value was his Browning revolver. The Dalai Lama watched spellbound, his face alight with mirth, as Mannerheim demonstrated the speed with which it could be reloaded, and solemnly presented his gift, explaining: "The times are such that a revolver may be of greater use, even to a holy man like yourself, than a prayer wheel".

Exactly eighty years later, back in Helsinki, and intrigued by the Baron's travels, His Holiness insisted on an impromptu visit to the Mannerheim Museum. Meanwhile, in his scheduled programme, at the cathedral, the university and the Rosicrucian Temple, a familiar pattern unfolded, as huge crowds began to gather, of a size that took everyone by surprise.

The teaching on Dzogchen, requested by one of the members of the organizing committee, took place at 10am on 30 September in the Rosicrucian Temple. The Finnish Rosicrucians are an offshoot of H.P. Blavatsky's Theosophical Society, but emphasize the universal message of love taught in the Gospels, along with the heritage of the Kalevala, Finland's epic myth of the origin of humanity and the world, and the struggle between light and darkness. The striking temple, with its Egyptian columns, paintings of Christ, and motifs from the Kalevala was packed to overflowing, with many left outside. What moved all those present, more than any words, was when His Holiness made three prostrations towards the seat from which he would teach, behind which stood a life-size statue of Christ. In this teaching, His Holiness, concerned that there might be many there who were fresh to Buddhism, set the practice of Dzogchen within a wider Buddhist framework: the Four Noble Truths and the Four Seals.

HIS HOLINESS THE DALAI LAMA

THE FOUR TRUTHS, FOUR SEALS AND DZOGCHEN

Brothers, sisters, today I am going to give a talk on Buddhism, and, as a Buddhist, I shall naturally be explaining my thoughts from the Buddhist point of view.

Unlike other living things, we human beings are endowed with a special gift, the ability to apply methods to overcome our suffering and achieve the happiness we all desire. Over the ages, as a result of the deep examination and analysis of human feelings of suffering and happiness, a variety of religious systems has emerged, each of them inspired by this common aim of overcoming suffering. These faiths and systems of practice are methods through which human beings, acknowledging that individually they cannot cope with the challenges they face, seek to solve their problems and achieve what they desire. Time, place, and cultural background account for the variety of religious traditions that have sprung up in different parts of the world. And because of the different needs even within one single community, sub-divisions and branches of religions have also appeared. Yet all of these religions and all of these systems of faith have one thing in common, and that is a message for all humanity: to be a good human being, and to develop a good heart.

In this modern age, with the advances in systems of communication, we see much closer contact between the world's major religions, and as a result greater mutual respect and understanding between the faiths. I think this is a very positive sign. Today I am very happy to have this opportunity, here in this temple, to give a brief explanation of Buddhist thought and practice, and I would like to thank all those who have been involved in organizing this teaching.

In Buddhism, generally speaking, there are two major traditions: one which flourished and is practised in countries like Sri Lanka, Thailand, Burma, Cambodia and so on, and which we could call the Fundamental Vehicle, and another which flourished in countries like Tibet, China, Mongolia, Japan and Korea, which is known as the vehicle of the bodhisattvas, or Mahāyāna.

The system of Buddhism practised in Tibet incorporates all the essential practices of these different traditions of Buddhism. Tibetan Buddhism includes, for example, the main practices of the Fundamental Vehicle, such as the vinaya vows, the practices of śamatha or single-pointed concentration and vipaśyana or special insight, and the thirty-seven aspects of the path to enlightenment. It also comprises the main elements of the Mahāyāna sūtra tradition, which are the cultivation of compassion and altruism, coupled with wisdom— which means the realization of the ultimate nature of phenomena— and the practice of the six perfections. The Buddhist tradition of Tibet also includes the practices of the tantric vehicle of Vajrayāna, such as deity yoga. In fact, what has become more apparent, the closer the contact we have had with other traditions of Buddhism, is that the Tibetan tradition represents a very complete form of Buddhism.

THE FOUR NOBLE TRUTHS

The general structure of Buddhist practice is based on what are called the Four Noble Truths, which the Buddha taught in his very first public teaching. They constitute the foundation for the entire Buddhist path. They are:

1) the truth of suffering
2) the truth of its origin
3) the truth of its cessation
4) the truth of the path which leads to that cessation

Perhaps my giving an explanation of the general structure of Buddhist practice might seem a little repetitive if you already know about basic Buddhism, and especially as I am supposed to be speaking today about Dzogchen. However, whenever I give teachings, I normally make a point of explaining the general structure of the Buddhist path, so that listeners can get a complete picture and then fit their understanding of specific practices into the overall context.

Buddha's teaching on the Four Noble Truths is based on the natural needs and desires of living beings. All of us have a natural instinct to desire happiness and avoid suffering. Therefore the practice of Dharma should be a technique whereby we can fulfil that need. Since what we desire is happiness and what we do not desire is suffering, Buddha first taught the truth of *suffering*, so that we would be able to recognize suffering for what it is.

Then, although we may enjoy certain degrees of happiness even while we are subject to suffering, true happiness will always elude us as long as we carry the causes of suffering inside us. This is why in the second noble truth Buddha taught the importance of eliminating the *origin* of suffering, by first of all identifying it. With the third noble truth, he explained that as a result of recognizing that origin of suffering there is *cessation*, a state that is free from all suffering. Buddha then taught the fourth noble truth, the path that will ultimately lead us to that cessation.

The conclusion, then, which we can derive from the teaching on the Four Noble Truths, is that this suffering that we do not want, and the happiness we long for, are both dependent, in the sense that they only arise in dependence upon their causes and conditions. The teaching on the Four Noble Truths in fact teaches us the principle of interdependent origination. Happiness, it shows us, comes about only as a result of the interaction of causes and conditions. At the same time, suffering can be avoided, but only if we are able to put an end to the causes and conditions that give rise to it. The teaching on the Four Noble Truths points out that this is our responsibility and we should take the initiative, on our own, to pursue a path that will lead to this end.

So how to go about it? The Four Noble Truths teach us, first of all, that suffering has to be identified and recognized as suffering. Next, we need to seek out the origin of suffering, the cause that gives rise to such experiences. Then we should strive to put an end to that suffering, and that can only be achieved through the realization of the path that leads to that cessation. So, in short, suffering is to be recognized as suffering, the causes for this suffering should be searched for, an end must be put to the suffering, and the path that leads to such a cessation must be actualized.[57]

How to recognize suffering as suffering? There are three levels or types of suffering. The first is suffering which is obvious, technically called 'the suffering of suffering'. The second is 'the suffering of change', and the third, 'the pervasive suffering of conditioning'.

1) 'The suffering of suffering' refers to all those self-evident experiences of suffering, like pain for example, which we would normally identify as suffering.

2) 'The suffering of change' refers to experiences that we usually regard as pleasure or happiness but which, when we are engaged in them for too long, end up leading to frustration, dissatisfaction and suffering. Say we buy a new television set, the latest camera or car. At the beginning, when we first get it, we feel satisfied and it gives us great pleasure and happiness. But then as time goes by, gradually we begin to get bored with it and want something else. Eventually it only causes us frustration. The experience that we initially thought of as pleasure or happiness is revealed as something which does not last, since it changes into feelings of dissatisfaction. This kind of experience is 'the suffering of change'.

3) The third type of suffering, 'the pervasive suffering of conditioning', embodies a recognition which is unique to Buddhism.

To explain this third level of suffering in greater detail, the fundamental tenets of Buddhist philosophy known as the four 'seals' or axioms of Buddhism need to be understood. They are:
1) all conditioned phenomena are impermanent and transitory
2) all contaminated phenomena are, by nature, suffering
3) all phenomena are empty of self-existence
4) nirvāṇa is true peace.

CONDITIONED PHENOMENA ARE IMPERMANENT

What is the true meaning of impermanence? It is that any phenomenon that depends for its origination on causes and conditions must be impermanent, for the reason that the very causes and conditions that give rise to its existence are also the causes for its disintegration and cessation. All these phenomena are momentary, in the sense that they all go through a process of change moment by moment, and they do not require secondary conditions for their disintegration. The very fact that the causes and conditions which produce them are adequate causes and conditions for their disintegration shows that these phenomena must be, by nature, momentary and impermanent.[58]

Look at external matter, for instance. Take an object like this plant by my side. In terms of its continuity, it appears to us to be something which is enduring, in the sense that we saw this plant yesterday and we see it again today. We assume that it is the same plant today as it was yesterday, but if we analyze it more deeply, and get down to the level of elementary particles, we find that the plant has been going through a constant process of change. The plant that we look at today is not the same plant that was here yesterday. In fact it is only because this plant is by nature momentary that it is possible for it to have gone through the whole cycle of sprouting from the seed, growing, flowering, and finally dying.

The same is true of our own inner experiences, that is, for our mind and mental processes. It is difficult for us to recognize and identify what mind or consciousness is, yet from our own experience we know that our mind goes through a process of change, and we all experience different levels of consciousness. This shows that the mind is momentary. It also shows that there is a possibility for us to change and transform our own minds.

So not only external matter, but also our own internal phenomena, are subject to change. Anything that is dependent on causes and conditions for its production and existence is transitory and impermanent. Phenomena which are subject to change and are dependent on causes and conditions for their existence are called 'otherpowered', in the sense that they are under the power and control of their causes.

So, as we saw, there are the first two kinds of suffering: obvious suffering and the suffering of change. Now we are talking about what serves as a basis for these two to come about, and a foundation for them to develop. This third level of suffering embraces the aggregates of our own body and mind, as well as external phenomena, all of which serve as the basis for the other kinds of suffering. It is pervasive in that all our painful experiences of suffering come about because of the very fact of our unenlightened existence. This very basic nature of our existence is called 'the suffering of conditioning'.[59]

CONTAMINATED PHENOMENA ARE, BY NATURE, SUFFERING

Now, if these experiences of suffering are entirely other-powered and so depend on their causes and conditions, what are the causes? In the Buddhist teachings, when we search for the causes of suffering, we find what is called 'the truth of the origin of suffering', namely that negative actions—karma—and the negative emotions that induce such actions are the causes of suffering.

Talking about causes, if we take a step further and investigate more deeply, we find that the cause alone is not sufficient for bringing about the results. Causes themselves have to come in contact with co-operative circumstances or conditions. For instance, say we search for a material or substantial cause for this plant, we will find that it has a continuity stretching back into beginningless time. There are certain Buddhist texts that speak of space particles, existing before the evolution of this present universe. According to these texts, the space particles serve as the material and substantial cause for matter, such as this plant. Now if the essential and substantial cause for matter is traced to these space particles, which are all the same, how do we account for the diversity that we see in the material world? It is here that the question of conditions and circumstances comes into play. When these substantial causes come in contact with different circumstances and conditions, they give rise to different effects, that is, different kinds of matter. So we find that the cause alone is not sufficient for bringing about a result. What is required is an aggregation of many different conditions and circumstances.

Although you can find certain differences among the Buddhist philosophical schools about how the universe came into being, the basic common question addressed is how the two fundamental principles—external matter and internal mind or consciousness— although distinct, affect one another. External causes and conditions are responsible for certain of our experiences of happiness and suffering. Yet we find that it is principally our own feelings, our thoughts and our emotions, that really determine whether we are going to suffer or be happy.

In the realm of matter, for example, one and the same object can serve as a cause of happiness for some living beings, and a cause of suffering for others. Certain plants, for example, function as medicine for some creatures, but for other species they can be poisonous. From the point of view of the object itself there is no difference, but because of the physical constitution and the material state of the particular living being, that single self-same object can affect them in different ways. Then, in the sphere of our own experiences, the same holds true. A certain individual may appear to some as very friendly, kind and gentle, and so gives them feelings of happiness and pleasure. Yet to others that same person can appear harmful and wicked, and so cause them discomfort and unhappiness.

What this kind of example points to is that, although external matter may act as a cause for our experience of pain and pleasure, the principal cause that determines whether we experience happiness or suffering lies within. This is the reason why, when Buddha identified the origin of suffering, he pointed within and not outside, because he knew that the principal causes of our suffering are our own negative emotions and the actions they drive us to do.

So this is where the second axiom comes in. Any phenomena which are under the control and domination of negative emotions and actions are 'contaminated' and therefore, by nature, suffering. Now the question is: What is the purpose, all along, of recognizing suffering as suffering? What is the next step? Is it really possible to put an end to this suffering?

All Phenomena are Empty of Self-Existence

Then the third axiom was taught, that all phenomena are empty of self-existence. How exactly does this third axiom answer the question of whether or not there is a possibility to put an end to suffering? Here, in this respect, our understanding of the 'emptiness' of phenomena should be a correct one. When we say that phenomena are empty, it does not mean that they are non-existent. When we hit the table we feel pain, and this experience of pain is proof enough to show us that the table exists; this very experience will refute and negate any misconception of the table being non-existent. So what is the meaning of phenomena being empty? Phenomena are empty in the sense that they do not have any *independent* or *inherent* existence.

When we talk about the cause of suffering, we talk about negative emotions, and if we examine them, we find that all these emotions are rooted in ignorance. This is very clear, for example, when we have obvious experiences of strong emotion, like hatred, or passion, or desire for someone. At that moment we perceive the object of our emotion as being inherently existent. If it is an object of desire, it appears to us as independently and inherently desirable. This shows that these negative emotions arise because of the ignorance that underlies them, and which apprehends phenomena as having an inherent existence of their own.

So there is a discrepancy, a gap, between how things appear to us and how things really are. We ordinary beings grasp at phenomena as they appear. Something appears to us as inherently existent, and we do not question that superficial appearance. Immediately we run after it and grasp at it, just as it appears. If we examine this analytically, we will find that there is a discrepancy: things do not in fact exist as they appear to. To realize this, and to understand that things are dependent, only coming into being through the aggregation of causes and conditions, is what is meant by realizing the ultimate nature, or the emptiness, of phenomena.

Now when that ignorance which grasps and apprehends things as inherently existent is realized to be erroneous, it opens up a possibility for us to see through the deception, and so put an end to the negative emotions that ignorance causes. Therefore there is a possibility of putting an end to suffering.

NIRVĀṆA IS TRUE PEACE

Just as with external phenomena, so mind, too, lacks any inherent existence, and is therefore, by nature, emptiness. That emptiness or lack of inherent existence of mind is its ultimate nature, or mode of being. To realize that is to realize the nature of the mind itself, and so to pierce and see through the deception of ignorance. Thereafter we will be able to free the mind from the influence of ignorance. And, when freedom from ignorance is achieved, that state is called 'cessation', or nirvāṇa, a state of true peace. And here we come to the fourth axiom: "Nirvāṇa is true peace".

As a consequence of recognizing the third category of suffering, that is 'the pervasive suffering of conditioning', you will begin to develop a deep sense of disenchantment with worldly experience and everything that is by nature suffering. This will engender in you a genuine desire and aspiration to achieve a state of liberation that is totally free from such dissatisfaction and suffering. That type of aspiration is called 'renunciation'. When you are inspired by such a deep and genuine sense of renunciation, and engage in the practices of 'śamatha' and 'vipaśyana'—single pointedness of mind and special insight into the nature of phenomena—you will have embraced what is the essence of the practice of the Fundamental Vehicle.

With this as your basis, when your aspiration to attain liberation is not confined to seeking your own liberation from suffering, but is extended to encompass the welfare and benefit of all sentient beings, every one of them equal to you in desiring happiness and wishing to avoid suffering, then you will have created a proper foundation for the practice of Mahāyāna. When you are imbued with this altruistic attitude and then engage in the practice of the six perfections, that comprises the essence of the practice of the Mahāyāna path.

The practice of the six perfections can be summed up as the practice of method and wisdom. In fact the general procedure in the Mahāyāna is to follow a path characterized by the union of method and wisdom. That is to say, method must not be isolated from wisdom, nor wisdom isolated from method. But although the sūtra system of the Mahāyāna does speak of the union of method and wisdom, it is only on the path of tantra that we find an indivisible union, where both aspects of the path, method and wisdom, are complete within a single entity of consciousness.[60] In Highest Yoga Tantra, this union of method and wisdom takes place not on the gross level of mind, but at an extremely subtle level of consciousness.

How can we exemplify different levels of consciousness in our experience? When the sensory perceptions such as seeing, hearing and so on are active, we are at a level where our state of mind is quite coarse. Compared to this, the consciousness of the dream state is regarded as much subtler. Even subtler still is the state of consciousness associated with particular experiences like fainting, or falling unconscious. The subtlest level of consciousness is experienced at the time of death. The unique approach found in the practices of Highest Yoga Tantra is to utilize the subtlest level of consciousness as a state of wisdom that realizes emptiness. This is a very swift and profound approach.

THE TRUE ENEMY

The fundamental philosophical principle of Buddhism is that all our suffering comes about as a result of an undisciplined mind, and this untamed mind itself comes about because of ignorance and negative emotions. For the Buddhist practitioner then, regardless of whether he or she follows the approach of the Fundamental Vehicle, Mahāyāna or Vajrayāna, negative emotions are always the true enemy, a factor that has to be overcome and eliminated. And it is only by applying methods for training the mind that these negative emotions can be dispelled and eliminated. This is why in Buddhist writings and teachings we find such an extensive explanation of the mind and its different processes and functions. Since these negative emotions are states of mind, the method or technique for overcoming them must be developed from within. There is no alternative. They can not be removed by some external technique, like a surgical operation.

It is because Buddhism places such emphasis on eliminating the root of suffering through a process of mental training, rather than relying on principles based on a belief in a divine being or theory of creation, that a number of people have observed that Buddhism is not a religion in the true sense of the word, but, more properly speaking, is a science of mind. There seem to be some genuine grounds for such a conclusion.

The various traditions of Buddhist practice explain different methods for overcoming our negative emotions. In the Fundamental Vehicle, the method for dealing with negative emotions is based on abandoning and uprooting them altogether. In this kind of practice, you eliminate the negative emotions completely, without ever generating them within yourself in order to use them as your path. For bodhisattvas, however, there are certain situations where some types of negative emotion, for example desire, can be utilized, under particular circumstances, in order to benefit other sentient beings. In Highest Yoga Tantra, sophisticated and unique techniques are explained for transforming these negative emotions into the path itself.

These negative emotions we all have within us are innate, spontaneous and natural, and also possess great energy and force. In Vajrayāna practice, there are techniques in which you can utilize that energy, but without letting yourself be influenced or dominated by the negative emotions. This is how negative emotions like desire,

anger, and so on, can be transformed into the path. It is because of
these unique methods that we find different imagery and symbol-
ism, such as the wrathful and passionate deities, in the visualizations
and meditation of Vajrayāna practice.

Four major traditions—Nyingma, Kagyü, Sakya and Geluk—
emerged as a result of the earlier and later dissemination of the
Buddhist teachings in Tibet, and also because of the emphasis placed
by great masters of the past on different scriptures, techniques of
meditation and, in some cases, terms used to express particular
experiences. Often people call these different traditions the 'black
hats', 'red hats', 'yellow hats', and the like. But if the only criterion
we had to distinguish traditions was the colour of the hat they wore,
since Lord Buddha was not given to wearing any headgear, we
would be obliged to call his the 'hatless' tradition!

What is common to all the four major traditions of Tibetan
Buddhism is their emphasis on the practice of the entire structure of
the Buddhist path, which comprises, as explained earlier, the essence
of not only the Vajrayāna teachings, but also the Mahāyāna practices
of the bodhisattvas, and the basic practices of the Fundamental
Vehicle. In India, based on differences in philosophical standpoint,
four major Buddhist schools of thought emerged: Vaibhāṣika,
Sautrāntika, Yogacāra and Madhyamaka. All four major traditions
of Tibetan Buddhism, however, uphold the philosophical standpoint
of the Madhyamaka school, and to that extent, there are no fundamental philosophical differences between them.

THE GROUND AND PRACTICE OF DZOGCHEN

The profound and unique feature of the Nyingma tradition is the
teaching and practice of Dzogchen. Of the two aspects of Dzogchen,
trekchö and tögal, the practice of trekchö is the more basic approach,
and anyone intending to take up the practice of trekchö must first of
all train in the preliminary practices. The practice of Dzogchen,
moreover, depends on the extraordinary blessings of an experienced
master—a man or woman who has realization—infusing your
mindstream.

When Dzogchen is explained, first there is the *ground*; on the basis of how the ground abides there is the *path*; and on the basis of that, the *fruition*.

The ground in Dzogchen is fundamentally the buddha nature, the tathāgatagarbha. In the sources of the Madhyamaka philosophical school, this buddha nature is primarily described as being the very nature of the mind itself. Its nature is emptiness, and it is such that there is a continuum of consciousness, clear and aware, that has always been there and that will finally attain buddhahood. For this buddha nature is the fundamental factor that allows us to attain the level of buddhahood, and the kāyas of buddhahood. This is what is actually meant by the ground in Dzogchen.

In the context of the ground, we can speak of an impure state, in that there is a failure to recognize the true nature of this clear and pure awareness, rigpa. Instead, we fall under the influence of rigpa's own energy and inner power, and when that energy cannot stay in its own place, we slip under the control of—or rather follow after—arising thoughts. Since rigpa cannot stand on its own, what results is saṃsāra. On the other hand, if rigpa can hold its own ground, without falling under the influence of thoughts, that is the basis for nirvāṇa. Given that the basis of all saṃsāra and nirvāṇa is to be found in this fundamental innate mind of clear light—uncompounded rigpa—this is the ground for Dzogchen.

When we come to meditation, it is practised with the "three immovables".

The first, the immovable body, is the physical posture, in which the body is kept straight, with the hands either folded in the lap in the pose of meditation, or lightly resting on the knees. Your body is held upright, yet not too rigid, but natural and relaxed.

The second immovable concerns the senses, primarily the eyes. Keep them neither closed nor too widely open, but simply gazing naturally in front of you.

The third immovable refers to the mind itself. Here the mind is not active. You do not entertain any thoughts at all, whether recalling the past or thinking about the future. Simply rest in the present moment of awareness, fresh and uncontrived. Without any kind of examining or analyzing whatsoever, the mind dwells, tranquil and at peace, in a non-conceptual state.

This is the basis from which you start.

This kind of consciousness that rests steadfastly without indulging any thoughts is, to use Dzogchen terminology, a calm, placid and undisturbed experience of ālaya. It is a state of mind that possesses a quality of slight stupidity and dullness, because while it is not entertaining thoughts, it lacks the quality of clarity. So this is what is termed 'the calm ālaya, endowed with a stupid dullness'.

As you maintain this state and continue your practice over a period of time, this stupidity and dullness can, when certain factors come into play, be gradually removed. Rigpa—because there is a distinction to be made between the ordinary mind and rigpa here—becomes fully evident, extremely clear and lucid, undistorted by the thoughts and concepts of the ordinary mind, and divested of the stupid quality of the stable ālaya. Rigpa is capable of being aware of anything, but is not sullied by ordinary thought processes or by grasping at and following after objects. This extraordinary essence of rigpa is what is to be recognized and experienced, and trekchö practice consists of maintaining the presence of that natural state of rigpa.

There is a distinction to be made here, however. The term 'quality of stupid dullness' refers to ignorance, but in this context it is in the sense of coemergent ignorance.[61] In the Madhyamaka philosophical texts, ignorance—*marigpa*—refers to a mistaken mode of apprehending the ultimate nature of things. That is not what is meant by this term here, where it simply implies a slightly stupid quality that is sullying and obscuring the mind. Here the term 'ignorance' then is to be understood as that which obscures the experience of rigpa bursting forth in all its nakedness. These comments apply here solely to the context of the practice of Dzogchen.

Our fundamental nature, this essence of rigpa which is utterly natural, is already present and not something that needs to be newly developed. It is simply the nature of the consciousness we already have, and so as long as there is consciousness, its nature will be that of unimpeded all-penetrating rigpa. Therefore in Dzogchen you are being directly introduced to what is already, and has always been, present. Once you have been directly introduced to this, if you experience this fundamental state of rigpa as a stable presence, then the power of conceptual thinking gradually weakens, while the power of love, compassion and the like automatically increase. So an extraordinary kind of experience can result.

I feel very happy that we have been able to discuss an extremely profound subject like this in three languages and at some length, and so I would like to thank you all for your patience. You have gathered here, motivated by a genuine interest in the spiritual path. Now, the essence of spirituality is constantly to look within, to examine and check our own minds, our attitudes and actions, and to become better human beings. This means to nurture positive thoughts, and to try to restrain and discipline our negative thoughts. The ultimate aim is that we should all become good human beings—human beings with smiles on their faces.

PART FOUR

THE PINNACLE OF ALL YĀNAS

San Jose, 1989

THE PINNACLE OF ALL YĀNAS

THE BACKGROUND

In September 1989, His Holiness the Dalai Lama began a three-week visit to the United States, taking in the East Coast, California, and Wisconsin. In Newport Beach, California, on October 5 and 6, he took part in the second of the 'Mind and Life' conferences. This remarkable series of encounters was pioneered by Francisco Varela, a neurobiologist at the National Centre for Scientific Research in Paris, and Adam Engle, an American attorney and businessman. Between 1987 and 2000 seven Mind and Life dialogues took place, between His Holiness and groups of scientists and specialists that have included neurologists, biologists, physicists, and philosophers. They focused on a range of topics: emotions and health; sleep, dreams, and dying; altruism, ethics, and compassion; physics and cosmology; and destructive emotions.[62] The conference that took place in Newport Beach in 1989 lasted two days, and focused on neuroscience, treating issues such as the mind and the brain, the nature and types of consciousness, and memory. Immediately before it, His Holiness had taken part in a three-day dialogue on suffering and compassion with a panel of psychotherapists, psychologists and individuals serving the dying.[63] These meetings threw into vivid relief His Holiness's engagement with modern thinking and his deep concern for humanity, and at the time seemed uncannily appropriate as a setting for what happened next.

Early in the morning of October 5, news came from Oslo that His Holiness had been awarded the Nobel Peace Prize. The Nobel Committee explained their choice: "The Committee wants to emphasize the fact that the Dalai Lama, in his struggle for the liberation of Tibet, consistently has opposed the use of violence. He has instead advocated peaceful solutions based upon tolerance and mutual respect in order to preserve the historical and cultural heritage of his people. The Dalai Lama has developed his philosophy of peace from a great reverence for all things living, and upon the concept of universal responsibility, embracing all mankind as well as nature. In the opinion of the Committee, the Dalai Lama has come forward with constructive and forward-looking proposals for the solution of international conflicts, human rights issues, and global environmental problems."

In his response His Holiness remarked: "As this dramatic century draws to a close, it is clear that the renewed yearning for freedom and democracy sweeping the globe provides an unprecedented opportunity for building a better world. Freedom is the real source of human happiness and creativity. Only when it is allowed to flourish can a genuinely stable international climate exist." When the award was presented in December that year, the Nobel Committee specified that it was in part in memory of Mahatma Gandhi, and His Holiness accepted it in that spirit, as a tribute to "the man who founded the modern tradition of non-violent action for change—Mahatma Gandhi, whose life taught and inspired me". In October 1989, nothing could have come as a greater encouragement and impetus to the Tibetans and their friends and sympathizers, and it sparked off an atmosphere of euphoria everywhere there was an interest in Tibet, Buddhism or non-violence. It could not have come either in a more poignant and momentous year, one that witnessed the tragedy of Tiananmen Square, the withdrawal of Vietnamese troops from Cambodia and Russian soldiers from Afghanistan, the collapse of six of the prevailing régimes in Eastern Europe and the fall of the Berlin Wall.

THE DZOGCHEN TEACHINGS IN SAN JOSE

On 7 October, His Holiness arrived in Santa Cruz to begin the series of teachings he had been invited to give by Rigpa and Sogyal Rinpoche. In the Santa Cruz Civic Auditorium, he was introduced by local leader and environmentalist Gary Patton, and gave a public talk carried by a number of radio stations, entitled: 'Compassion, the Heart of Enlightenment', which appears as the appendix to this book. Such was the demand for tickets that the box office had distributed them all within forty minutes of opening, to people who had queued from 5.30am.

The Dalai Lama's Dzogchen teachings were originally scheduled to be given in Santa Cruz, but when thousands had registered within two weeks they were relocated to the nearest venue large enough, the newly constructed Student Union Recreation and Event Centre at San Jose State University, in California's Silicon Valley. Above the stage hung two rows of thangkas, including the complete set of visionary paintings commissioned by Jamyang Khyentse Chökyi Lodrö, as well as the eight manifestations of Guru Padmasambhava. The centrepiece, directly above His Holiness's throne, was a huge thangka of Guru Rinpoche appearing as 'The Fulfilment of All Aspirations'—*Sampa Lhundrupma*, from the terma of Chokgyur Dechen Lingpa. To His Holiness's right stood the exquisite maṇḍala house constructed by Ven. Tenzin Dakpa, His Holiness's ritual master from the Namgyal Monastery. Tibetan carpets covered the stage, and banners hung right and left along the sides of the hall, which was packed to its 5,500 capacity. From all over the United States, and from other countries, followers of all Buddhist traditions had been drawn by the opportunity of receiving these teachings from an authority like His Holiness. Lamas, geshes and ordained saṅgha filled the stage during the teachings, headed by H.E. Sakya Dagchen Rinpoche, Dzogchen Rinpoche, Nyoshul Khen Rinpoche, Lama Zöpa Rinpoche, Geshe Tsultim Gyeltsen, Geshe Tsephel, Gyatrul Rinpoche and Sogyal Rinpoche. At the time, it was one of the largest gatherings seen in the west of lamas and practitioners of the Buddhadharma. Nyoshul Khen Rinpoche gave a number of teachings during this period, one of them on the evening of 8 October, a teaching that appears as the afterword to this book, entitled 'A Gift to the World'.

This was the first time His Holiness had taught on Dzogchen in such depth in the west, and the first time in the United States. On the opening day, he emphasized the importance of having a strong grounding in the different vehicles of Buddhadharma. He gave the bodhisattva vow, and responded to a wide range of issues in two question and answer sessions. On the second day, 9 October, he showed how the ultimate intention of all four schools of Tibetan Buddhism comes down to the fundamental innate mind of clear light. He had explored this in London in 1984, and also in a remarkable address given in Virginia in the United States in 1979 entitled 'The Union of the Old and New Schools'.[64] There, he had demonstrated with great clarity how the final goal of all the different Tibetan Buddhist traditions comes down to the same point, since "the various systems present what are merely different techniques for manifesting the fundamental innate mind of clear light".[65] As he points out: "This innate fundamental mind of clear light is emphasized equally in the Highest Yoga Tantra systems of the new translation schools and in the Nyingma system of the Great Perfection, and is the proper place for comparison of the old and new schools."

His Holiness then high-lighted the special features of Dzogchen, drawing from Longchen Rabjam's *Chöying Rinpoche Dzö*, 'The Precious Treasury of the Dharmadhātu', and its commentary the *Lung gi Ter Dzö*, 'The Treasury of Scriptural Transmission'. In choosing one of the *Seven Treasuries* of Longchen Rabjam (1308-1363), His Holiness reached right into the very heart of Dzogchen, by invoking one of the greatest scholars and realized masters of Tibet, in whom all the streams of Dzogchen had converged, and whose overarching genius set out an entire foundation for the study and practice of Dzogchen in his writings such as *The Seven Treasuries, The Trilogy of Comfort and Ease, The Trilogy of Natural Freedom* and *The Three Inner Essences*. Nyoshul Khenpo explains:

The omniscient Longchenpa's *Seven Treasuries* were written to elucidate the extraordinarily profound meaning of the seventeen tantras of Dzogpachenpo as well as the teachings of all the nine yānas. For the purpose of the actual practice of Dzogchen according to these tantras, Longchenpa gathered his own termas as well as those of Chetsün Senge Wangchuk (who was later reborn as Jamyang Khyentse Wangpo) and Pema Lédrel Tsal (Longchenpa's previous incarnation) in the form of the thirteen volume collection known as *Nyingtik Yabshyi.* This *Yabshyi* is the practice aspect of Longchenpa's writings, and the basis of the Old Nyingtik. In it he synthesized the Vima Nyingtik of Vimalamitra and the Khandro Nyingtik of Guru Rinpoche and explained all the practical details in the light of his own realization.[66]

The Treasury of the Dharmadhātu is regarded as expressing the essence of Longchenpa's teachings on Dzogchen, and distils the three categories of Dzogchen: mind, space, and pith instructions. Patrul Rinpoche calls this work, which is used as a practice, a prayer and meditation instruction, "a living buddha...the vivid array of pure dharmakāya as teaching". His Holiness made reference to it during a teaching in London in 1988, when he emphasized the need to study the key texts in order to arrive at a thorough understanding of Dzogchen.

One can begin to appreciate the profundity and difficulty of attaining this view by reading Longchen Rabjam's own text on the practices of the Great Perfection, *The Treasury of the Supreme Vehicle.* The root text is very difficult and the auto-commentary is rather copious and itself difficult to comprehend. Another text by Longchenpa is *The Treasury of the Expanse of Reality* (The Treasury of the Dharmadhātu),

in which he also outlines the practices of the Great
Perfection. In fact this second text is like the key to
Dzogchen. Only by comprehending the practices of
Great Perfection based on these two texts can you
hope to have a good, reliable understanding of the
Great Perfection.[67]

At a number of points in his teaching at San Jose, His Holiness also
quotes the writings of Dodrupchen Jikmé Tenpé Nyima (1865-
1926). The third incarnation of Jikmé Lingpa's great Dharma-heir
Jikmé Trinlé Özer (1745-1821), Dodrupchen Jikmé Tenpé Nyima
was a student of Patrul Rinpoche, Jamyang Khyentse Wangpo,
Dzogchen Khenpo Pema Dorje, the fourth Dzogchen Rinpoche,
Mipham, Jamgön Kongtrul and Lerab Lingpa. The thirteenth Dalai
Lama, when he saw one of his compositions, remarked: "Today a
writer of this quality is very rare in this land". His Holiness calls
him "a great scholar and remarkable yogi", and says of him:

> This very special being was the student of Jamyang
> Khyentse Wangpo, who was himself an incarnation
> of the King Trisongdetsen, as well as an amazing
> lama free from bias concerning the views of Nyingma,
> Sakya, Kagyü and Geluk. In his late teens, Dodrupchen
> was already skilled in many texts of the Middle Way,
> the Perfection of Wisdom, Valid Cognition, and the
> new translation schools' interpretation of the Kālacakra
> Tantra and the Guhyasamāja Tantra, as well as the Great
> Perfection, his own unique specialty.[68]

In developing his own understanding of the correspondences
between Highest Yoga Tantra and Dzogchen, the Dalai Lama adds,
"Reading Dodrupchen was as if he were stroking my head in confirmation, giving me confidence that my insight was not un-
founded". His Holiness referred to Dodrupchen in his 1984
teachings in London, and quoted extensively from his writings

during his teachings at Dzogchen monastery in 1992. Among the
third Dodrupchen's many great disciples was Jamyang Khyentse
Chökyi Lodrö, whose explanation of the quotation from the
Prajñāpāramitā His Holiness used as the structure for his entire
teaching in San Jose.

When the Dalai Lama came on stage at San Jose, it was to
rapturous applause. Sogyal Rinpoche welcomed him and congratu-
lated him on the Nobel Peace Prize, paying tribute to his courage,
vision and determination:

> This is a triumph for the Tibetan people and all their
> hopes, a signal that the world acknowledges the justice
> of their struggle and supports their aspirations for
> freedom, borne through so much suffering. It is a
> message of victory for all those throughout the world
> who cherish peace and human values, and a signal of
> hope to encourage all those other people who are
> struggling for their rights and their happiness. It is a
> tribute to your unwavering stand on non-violence,
> and to your message of compassion and love, which
> has moved so many millions around the globe. And it
> is the long-awaited confirmation of your place as the
> most important spokesman for world peace in this
> troubled world of ours. For no one else has cham-
> pioned the cause of universal brotherhood and sister-
> hood, of reconciliation and forgiveness as you have
> done. At long last the world has recognized what so
> many have known for so long.

His Holiness replied:

> First, I would like to extend my greetings to you all,
> my Dharma brothers and sisters, gathered here. Also I
> wish to thank Sogyal Rinpoche and all of you for your
> congratulations upon my receiving the Nobel Peace

Prize. I consider this prize to be some kind of recognition of my motivation and its sincerity. So essentially the credit goes not to this monk Tenzin Gyatso, but rather to the sincere motivation of altruism.

Every human being has the same potential for compassion; the only question is whether we really take any care of that potential, and develop and implement it in our daily life. My hope is that more and more people will realize the value of compassion, and so follow the path of altruism. As for myself, ever since I became a Buddhist monk, that has been my real destiny—for usually I think of myself as just one simple Buddhist monk, no more and no less.

HIS HOLINESS THE DALAI LAMA

THE PURE MOTIVATION

We have gathered here today for a teaching on Dzogchen. When we embark on a teaching, it is important for both the teacher and the students to begin by arousing pure motivation. On the part of the teacher, if he is motivated to give the teaching merely by self-importance, arrogance, or desire for fame and the admiration of his students, then his motivation is wrong. On the contrary, the teaching should be motivated solely by an altruistic attitude—to be of the greatest possible benefit to the students. In fact the attitude of a teacher when conducting a teaching should be the same as that explained in *The Eight Verses on Training the Mind*:

> Whenever I associate with others, I will learn
> To think of myself as the lowest among all,
> And respectfully hold others to be supreme
> From the very depths of my heart.[69]

Whenever we associate with others, that is the kind of outlook we should always have towards them. And when giving a teaching, it is the attitude a teacher should have towards his students.

On the part of the listeners, if your motivation and your attitude in attending these teachings is to be a spiritual one—to search for ways to improve and advance your spiritual practice—then your motivation must not be influenced by negative emotions like hatred, anger, jealousy or attachment. This is especially the case because the teaching I will be explaining today belongs to the Mahāyāna. So your motivation should also be governed by the altruistic aspiration of benefiting and helping others.

This is why, before receiving the teachings, we take refuge in the Three Jewels and generate the altruistic aspiration to attain enlightenment for the benefit of all other beings. Among those here in the audience today, it is possible that there are a few who do not consider themselves Buddhist practitioners, but who have some interest in Tibetan culture, or Buddhist meditation, or certain aspects of Buddhism. You do not need to cultivate this initial motivation, and you can listen to the teachings in the same way as you might listen to a lecture.

When we take refuge in the Three Jewels, it is important to be aware of the ultimate significance of refuge. Its ultimate meaning comes from understanding the potential or seed that we all possess within us, which is known as 'the buddha nature'. This is a potential that allows us, through the process of spiritual training, to attain the state of complete enlightenment. Once we are able to activate this potential seed within, and explore it to its fullest, then ultimate refuge is achieved.

This potential is something that is inherent within our mind stream, and it is sometimes called the Primordial Buddha Samantabhadra, in Tibetan *Kuntuzangpo*, meaning 'all-good'. Every living being possesses this self-arising potential to attain, eventually, the state of the Primordial Buddha. So after taking refuge in the Three Jewels, we should cultivate the altruistic aspiration to be able to realize the highest enlightenment for the benefit of all sentient beings, and so that we can lead them to the same perfect state of Samantabhadra, every single one.

THE TRADITIONAL APPROACH

The actual format of this teaching will not follow any particular text, although I shall be primarily drawing upon *The Treasury of the Dharmadhātu*[70], composed by the omniscient Longchen Rabjam.

The traditional approach in Tibet when conducting this type of teaching is to emphasize the aspect of personal experience. So the teachings are not given altogether in one stretch, but each different stage of the practice is taught separately. After one particular element of the practice is given, then the student is advised to meditate on it for as long as possible, but at least for a prescribed number of days. One can find explicit mention of this, for instance, in the writings of Khenpo Ngakchung, who identifies different sections of the practice and specifies that, having received the teaching, you should meditate on that particular topic for at least three or four days, or whatever is required.[71]

That has been the traditional approach in Tibet for this type of teaching; it was never given all at once, along with all the different aspects of the visualization and meditation. But since we have no time in this modern age, we can always quote our 'lack of time' as a pretext for sweeping through the details of the meditation and covering it all in one go. In our case today, neither the students nor the teacher have time to follow the traditional pattern. However during our teaching sessions we will pause at various points, to allow ourselves a minute or two to concentrate on specific topics.

So although you may receive the transmission, and inspiration, from these sessions of teaching, you should not be satisfied with that alone. You should make a point of listening to further commentaries and teachings from your masters, and then meditate on them over a lengthy period of time. Otherwise, if you were to be satisfied with this one brief teaching, then your listening to this teaching would become like the fleeting experience of a dream. And if this were true of the way you listened to the teaching and absorbed it, you would find that the result of your meditation would be simply a fleeting experience as well. Therefore it is of vital importance to cultivate a continuous and enduring effort in applying yourself to the practice.

Within a short time-span, it is impossible to change all our concepts or the entire attitude of our mind. It needs constant application. Speaking from my own small experience, from the age of about sixteen or seventeen, I began to make some serious effort to change and improve my outlook. Now at fifty-five, some thirty-nine years have gone by, several decades have passed, yet still the result is not satisfactory! We do have to struggle, and to work hard— and that is the reality.

Besides, as Buddhist practitioners, we are not counting in hours or weeks or months. We count in aeons—billions and billions of years, billions and billions of lives. Sometimes you might find this quite daunting. But if we do take a very long-term view of the future, what it gives us is real determination; it gives us some kind of inner strength, because from that vantage point, time counts for nothing. What is important is that we must change, and we must improve, no matter how long it takes. So a firm determination is vital, isn't it?

Now, the special feature of Dzogchen is that the path is created through wisdom. In the Nyingma tradition, the teachings are divided into nine vehicles. Among them are the eight vehicles which are philosophical systems that depend on ordinary consciousness, meaning that they employ the ordinary mind. In Dzogchen, or Atiyoga, however, the path is created with wisdom, which transcends the ordinary mind or consciousness altogether. There is an enormous difference between a path created with the ordinary mind and a path created through wisdom.

To help us understand how the path is created through wisdom, first of all we need to be aware that there are different categories of trainees. There are some whose predispositions from previous lifetimes have awakened, and whose faculties are very sharp. When they meet a master with authentic experience, it is possible for him to give them instructions—it might only be a few words—on which they meditate one-pointedly, and realization and liberation occur simultaneously. This is the profound path for 'those who can progress in instantaneous leaps'. They are, however, extremely rare.

Individuals whose abilities are more ordinary can not follow such a path, and for them it is vital to proceed 'step by step'. When their mindstreams have become fully matured, they will be capable of meditating in this extraordinary way, and of using its profound key points, because then they will be ready and their minds will be able to fathom such an approach. Until then, however, they need to train and prepare in gradual stages.

Fundamentally, then, there is one path that is the pinnacle and peak of all the nine yānas, and all the other yānas are taught beforehand, in order to prepare practitioners for this supreme path. In this way, when all the circumstances needed are complete, they will not fall into error and their practice will bear fruit.

So that the special features of Dzogchen can be pointed out and you can recognize them, you must have a thorough, overall understanding of the principles of all the different vehicles of the Buddhadharma. This is the only basis on which you can truly appreciate the uniqueness and depth of Dzogchen. Without such an overview, it will be difficult for your mind to feel any certainty as to why these teachings are so special. That is why you need to understand the whole spectrum of the Buddhadharma, from the lower yānas to the higher yānas. Therefore this morning and this afternoon I will focus on the different vehicles in general, and especially on the Mahāyāna and the Secret Mantrayāna.

1. THE PRIMACY OF MIND

According to the approach of Jamyang Khyentse Chökyi Lodrö, handed down by Dilgo Khyentse Rinpoche, the entire spectrum of Buddhist philosophy and practice can be explained by means of this famous quotation by the Buddha:

> **The mind is devoid of mind,**
> **For the nature of mind is clear light.**[72]

The first words of this quotation "The mind..." encompass the entire meaning of the teachings on the Four Noble Truths, the first turning of the wheel of Dharma.

The remaining part of the first line "...is devoid of mind" encompasses the meaning of all the wisdom sūtras, the second turning of the wheel of Dharma.

The meaning of the second line of the quotation "For the nature of mind is clear light" embraces the entire subject matter of the third turning of the wheel of Dharma. This refers not to the sūtras which are taken as the scriptural sources of the Cittamātra teachings, that is the Yogacāra school, but rather to sūtras like the *Essence of Buddhahood Sūtra* which is the source sūtra for treatises like Maitreya's *Sublime Continuum of the Great Vehicle*, in which the meaning of the primordial clear light nature of mind is taught.

This line "For the nature of mind is clear light" embodies the ultimate intention of the teachings of Highest Yoga Tantra, where the whole emphasis of the practice is on accomplishing the fundamental innate mind of clear light. However in Dzogchen, it is the clear light, and that alone, which is practised and laid bare in all its nakedness. Dzogchen in fact is uniquely the practice of clear light or naked rigpa, alone.

The fact that both the fundamental innate mind of clear light in the new translation schools and Highest Yoga Tantra, and the pristine awareness of rigpa in the Dzogchen teachings ultimately come down to the same meaning can be found in the writings of Longchen Rabjam, and in Jikmé Lingpa's commentary to his own *Treasury of Enlightened Attributes*. You can also find the same point in the writings of the fifth Dalai Lama, and particularly in the later writings of Dodrupchen Jikmé Tenpé Nyima, the third Dodrupchen Rinpoche, who was not only a very great scholar but also a great meditator and adept. He had a vast knowledge of sūtra and tantra, and of both the new translation schools of tantra and the old translation school, in addition to which his understanding of Madhyamaka philosophy and Sautrāntika epistemology and logic was extremely profound. In his writings you can find explicit references to how the ultimate

meaning of what is spoken of in the new translation schools as 'the
fundamental innate mind of clear light' and in Dzogchen terminology as 'rigpa'" are one and the same thing.[73] You will also find
specific mention of this fact in the writings of Khenpo Ngakchung,
especially when he distinguishes between the ground and the
appearances from the ground, referring to the ground as rigpa.
These are my sources for the claim that ultimately the fundamental
innate mind of clear light of the new translation schools and the
pristine awareness of rigpa in Dzogchen come down to the same
point.

Although I cannot claim to have authentic, advanced realization
of rigpa or the fundamental innate mind of clear light, yet when I
read and compare the writings of various masters from different
traditions, and particularly when this point is analysed in relation to
the writings of the different schools of Buddhist philosophy, including both the sūtra system and all four classes of tantra, in both old
and new translation schools, I find myself inclined towards sharing
this opinion. I find this particular insight of real help in understanding the fundamental unity of all the different traditions of Tibetan
Buddhism. It not only draws out and clarifies the profound points
of the various systems, but also enables me to develop a genuine
respect towards all the diverse approaches within the Buddhist
tradition of Tibet.

VALID COGNITION

Now the first question to arise in any philosophical enquiry—and
it is a very basic one—is how to determine whether or not something exists. The Buddhist answer to this is that if something is
verifiable through experience or awareness at any level of cognition,
that is a criterion for its being existent. Conversely, any event or
thing that is not verifiable through our experience or awareness can
not be considered to exist.

However, it is vital to bear in mind that there are many different
types and levels of verifying awareness or cognition, which could
even extend to include the heightened states of awareness of a

meditative experience such as primordial wisdom. In addition, different philosophical systems have different viewpoints on exactly how to define something as 'a valid cognition'.

The reason why we find so much discussion of epistemology, or how to define something as a valid cognition, in Buddhist writings is because all our problems, suffering and confusion derive from a misconceived way of perceiving things. This explains why it is so important for a practitioner to determine whether a cognitive event is a misconception or true knowledge. For it is only by generating insight which sees through delusion that we can become liberated.

Even in our own experience we can see how our state of mind passes through different stages, eventually leading to a state of true knowledge. For instance, our initial attitude or standpoint on any given topic might be a very hardened misconception, thinking and grasping at a totally mistaken notion. But when that strong grasping at the wrong notion is countered with reasoning, it can then turn into a kind of lingering doubt, an uncertainty where we wonder: "Maybe it is the case, but then again maybe it is not". That would represent a second stage. When further exposed to reason or evidence, this doubt of ours can turn into an assumption, tending towards the right decision. However, it is still just a presumption, just a belief. When that belief is yet further exposed to reason and reflection, eventually we could arrive at what is called 'inference generated through a reasoning process'. Yet that inference remains conceptual, and it is not a direct knowledge of the object. Finally, when we have developed this inference and constantly familiarized ourselves with it, it could turn into an intuitive and direct realization—a direct experience of the event. So we can see through our own experience how our mind, as a result of being exposed to reason and reflection, goes through different stages, eventually leading to a direct experience of a phenomenon or event.

However, as to the question of whether or not a true knowledge or valid cognition might still be deceptive or deluded, the philosophical systems differ in their viewpoints. For example, the great Buddhist philosopher, Nāgārjuna, as interpreted by Candrakīrti, maintains that a state of mind could be a true knowledge and a valid cognition, and yet at the same time contain a certain degree of delusion. Yet other schools of thought maintain the contrary standpoint. For them a true knowledge or a valid cognition cannot be deceptive.[74]

Because some philosophical systems maintain that a true knowledge can incorporate a certain element of delusion, they distinguish different aspects of the object of the mind. One state of mind, for example, could have 'an appearing object', and 'an object of apprehension'. This means that a true knowledge can be deceived in relation to its appearing object, while being unmistaken in relation to the object of apprehension. According to this view, consciousness or awareness can only be posited in relation to an object, be it a distorted or a veridical state of mind. Without an object, there would not be a consciousness, and without a consciousness there would not be an object. Therefore consciousness and the object are posited in a mutual relationship with one another, because of the fundamental belief held by the proponents of these systems in the principle of relativity.

However, other philosophical systems maintain that although the object exists in relation to an awareness, in order to establish the existence of an awareness, what is called an 'apperceptive nature of the mind' is required, meaning that mind should be aware of itself. It is important here not to confuse the term that is used in such philosophical systems—'apperception' or 'reflexive awareness', *rang rig* in Tibetan[75]—with the same term employed in other contexts, for example in the tantras.

DIFFERENT CLASSES OF PHENOMENA

Having established that phenomena do exist, within the category of existent phenomena two classes are identified. The first embraces things that do not exist permanently, but only occasionally, which indicates that they depend on certain causes, conditions and circumstances in order to arise. The other type of phenomena are those which are permanent and do not depend upon any such causes, conditions or circumstances.

Phenomena that depend for their existence on causes, conditions and circumstances are called 'other-powered', meaning that they are subject to the power of these causes and conditions. The very fact that they depend upon their causes and conditions in order to arise is sufficient to illustrate that equally they have the potential to disintegrate. Therefore anything that is produced has the potential eventually to disintegrate, as if through an in-built mechanism.

Within the category of phenomena that arise as a result of causes and conditions, which are known as the 'produced' phenomena, there are again three different types: *First*, there are those that are physical, material and tangible, which we can perceive through our sense faculties. *Second*, there are certain types of phenomena that figure only within the domain of our experience, such as our sensations, our experiences, awareness and so on. *Third*, there is still another type of phenomena, which are purely mental constructions, abstract and of a kind which can only be conceived within the mind, for example: time, mathematical entities and also concepts like production, disintegration, process and pattern. Included among these are even ourselves, what we call human beings, the self, or 'I'. They form a category of phenomena of an entirely different level, quite unlike the first two categories.

The first two types of phenomena have a certain basis through which you can identify them. So, for example, we can perceive and come into contact with form and physical matter through our sense faculties. And experiences, awareness and so on, although not within the realm of physical contact, can at least be experienced subject-ively, and we can have an awareness of them. Phenomena of the third type, however, are to be understood solely in terms of concept. For instance, when we talk about a human being, we might ask: what is a human being? If we investigate and search for its essence, none can be found. The human being is neither our body nor our mind, but a label imputed upon the combination of body and mind. It is a metaphysical entity.

Similarly, take what we call 'awareness' or 'consciousness'. We are quite certain of its existence, and we claim that we can feel it,

experience it, and be conscious of it. But when we discuss the existence and nature of consciousness with specialists like neuroscientists,
it often poses quite a problem even to attempt to identify what
exactly it is. This is an area, I feel, which needs a lot of research.

THE MIND

Now, the reason we take such interest in all these metaphysical or
philosophical questions is because of the natural tendency that all
human beings possess, that is, to desire happiness and to avoid
suffering. It is that natural desire which inspires and induces us to
think about such questions. When we embark on philosophical
enquiry, the subject that we deal with directly is the area of body
and mind, and the relationship between them.

From our experience we know that there are certain sensations
of pain or pleasure which are primarily related to the body, and at
the same time there is another domain in our experience of pain
and pleasure, namely happiness and sorrow, which is mental. We also
know that if we are intent on a higher purpose, and so prepared
consciously to face the possibility of hardship, we can endure
physical difficulties or even pain, if necessary, to such an extent that
we can even rejoice in it. On the other hand, if our mind is not
calm and we lack stability and joy, we may be surrounded by the
greatest comfort and every kind of material facility and yet we feel
discontent, and time drags by with agonizing slowness.

Because of the primary role that our state of mind plays in our
experience of pain and pleasure, happiness and sorrow, it is crucial
for us to reflect upon the nature of mind, and discover how, if at all
possible, we can train our mind in such a way that we can transform
it for the better. On account of the mind's central position in our
experience of happiness and sorrow, it is the mind then that is
chosen, out of all these different categories of phenomena, and the
whole expanse of reality, as the subject here in the quotation from
the sūtra. Mind is identified as the basis on which the whole
enquiry is undertaken. And so, in the sūtra it says, "the *mind* is devoid
of mind".

Although all the Buddhist traditions and schools of thought concur on the question of mind being of primary importance among all types of phenomena, there are different philosophical explanations and understandings of how that is so. For instance, according to the Cittamātra 'Mind Only' school, the explanation of how the mind enjoys such a status is that external phenomena are not objectively existent, but are mere projections or extensions of the mind. In their view, when you have an awareness of an external, material object, it is not objectively existent. What that means is that it is not composed of atoms, but is only a projection of your mind. So mind is primary from the point of view of the Cittamātra philosophers, who maintain that external reality has no objective existence.

However, many Buddhist philosophical schools of thought maintain that mind and matter are distinct entities, but even so will uphold the supremacy or primacy of mind. A number of Buddhist traditions, for example, divide phenomena into two different types: those which are contaminated and fall into the category of the cycle of existence or saṃsāra; and those which are unstained and un-polluted, which belong to the category of liberation or nirvāṇa. By developing an insight into the ultimate nature of things and events, you are liberated, but when the ultimate nature of things is mis-understood and apprehended incorrectly, then you fall into the cycle of existence. This shows that the undisciplined and untrained mind leads into the saṃsāric cycle of life and death, while a trained and disciplined state of mind liberates that mind from the bondage of saṃsāra.

Then, some philosophical schools explain the primacy of mind from the point of view of how mind is instrumental in creating labels, providing concepts and giving designations for all phenom-ena. According to the highest philosophical tenets of Buddhism, of the Madhyamaka Prāsaṅgika, all phenomena are ultimately mere labels designated upon the collection of their bases of designation. There is no substantiality that could suggest the possibility of finding a true inference behind those labels. In other words, they do not exist, in-and-of themselves. Other philosophical schools of thought may speak of a category of 'imputed phenomena', but their understanding of the imputed nature differs from Madhyamaka Prāsaṅgika.

Although they reject the Cittamātra thesis that there is no external reality, so to speak, and the phenomena we perceive as externally real are projections of the mind, such schools as the Madhyamaka Prāsaṅgika maintain that external phenomena do depend upon the mind in that they are dependent upon the labelling of thought and concepts.

So the primacy or supremacy of mind is explained differently according to these various points of view and schools of thought.

SUFFERING AND ITS END

Now in our day-to-day lives we know that the more stable, calm and contented our mind is, the more feelings and experiences of happiness we will derive from it. The more undisciplined, untrained, and negative our mind is, the more we suffer mentally, and physically as well. So we can see only too well that a disciplined and contented mind is the source of our happiness. Now if such peace of mind, this disciplined state, is the route to happiness, a question arises: "Can we develop it even further, to its fullest extent? Or is it simply a state of mind which we may possess now, but can never be increased?"

When this disciplined and peaceful state of mind is explored and advanced to a high level, it is technically known as 'the true path', or 'the truth of the path which leads to cessation'. The reason why we can realize this true path is because it is possible for us to put an end to mental and physical suffering, along with the delusions that cause it. In other words, the possibility of 'cessation' does exist.

The reason, then, why delusions can be removed and separated from the mind is that at their root lies a misapprehension, one which grasps at things and events as existing in a way that does not accord with reality. We apprehend things as existing inherently and objectively in their own right. Yet if we examine this kind of outlook, using our wisdom and intelligence, we will find that it is simply not the case.

As soon as we realize the disparity between how we perceive things and how things and events actually exist, it prompts us to see through the deception, illusions, and misconceptions of this fundamental ignorance. This allows us, eventually, to release our minds from the influence of ignorance, and from the grip of conceptual thought processes. And this in turn makes it possible for the nature of mind to be released from the influence of negative emotions and delusions, and so attain true cessation of suffering.

Now the factors that make our mind undisciplined, and maintain it in such a state, are called delusions. The principal delusion is that fundamental ignorance which underlies all our deluded states of mind—the grasping at things as inherently existent. Among the delusions also figure the afflictive emotions like desire, hatred, jealousy, and anger. Together with the negative actions of our body, speech and mind to which they give rise, these delusions are the causes of suffering, and they are therefore known as 'the origin of suffering'.

The reason why we identify deluded states of mind, such as desire, hatred and anger, as 'afflictive' is because they lead to undesirable consequences—suffering and pain, both physical and mental. Suffering, in fact, is explained at three different levels. The first is technically known as 'the suffering of suffering', which refers to the obvious kinds of suffering like physical pain, which we can readily identify as suffering. The second type of suffering is called 'the suffering of change'. This involves the experiences and sensations which we usually identify as pleasurable, but are in fact suffering, because if we pursue them, eventually they will only lead to boredom and dissatisfaction. Their essential nature is suffering. The third level of suffering is what is called 'the pervasive suffering of conditioning', and this refers to the aggregates which all of us living in the cycle of existence possess, and which act as the basis for us to undergo all these different types of suffering. For as long as we are not free from these aggregates of body and mind produced by contaminated actions, we will always have the potential to suffer.

So, when you identify suffering correctly, you will be able to search for its causes and identify its true origins. Having examined and identified the true origins of suffering, you will be able to develop a genuine wish to be rid of this suffering—its origins as well—and have the power to break free from bondage. That in turn will enable you to arouse a genuine desire to seek liberation, and it is this that will inspire you to seek the path.

In short then, undesirable consequences, such as suffering and pain, derive from undisciplined and negative states of mind, and desirable experiences, like happiness and pleasure, arise from positive, disciplined states of mind. All depend entirely on our state of mind, disciplined or undisciplined, and this is why Buddha says in the sūtras that we are our own masters, and no other, external, master exists.

Dependent Origination

In order to illustrate the process through which the truth of suffering and its origin bind sentient beings within saṃsāra, Buddha taught the principle of the 'twelve links of dependent origination'.[76] In the sūtra called *The Rice Seedling Sūtra*,[77] Buddha spoke about how sentient beings are bound in this cycle of life and death by the twelve links of dependent origination. In this sūtra, he explained three kinds of conditions. The *first* is that because the causes are there, the effects or fruits will follow. Now this implies that, in order for there to be an effect, there must be a cause. Nothing can exist without any cause and conditions. Then he makes his *second* statement, that because the cause is produced, the effect ensues. What this implies is that in order for something to be a cause for a particular event or effect, it is not sufficient for it simply to exist, but the cause should be an impermanent phenomenon, something that is functional and has the capacity to produce something. Then he makes the *third* statement, saying that actions arise from ignorance. This implies that in order for a cause to produce its effect, it is not enough for it to be existent and at the same time functional and impermanent, but it should also be concordant with the effect or events that it produces. A specific cause can not produce entirely unrelated effects. Therefore the implication is that in order for a cause to produce the effect: *first* of all, it should be existent; the *second* qualification is that it should be impermanent and functional; and the *third* characteristic is that it should have the potential to produce a corresponding effect, meaning that it should be commensurate with the effect that it produces.

All Buddhist philosophical systems and tenets maintain that happiness is produced by positive states of mind, and unhappiness and suffering are the consequences of negative states of mind and negative actions. All Buddhist schools embrace the philosophical principle of dependent origination. Therefore, it is on the premise of interdependence that they will explain all the changes, minor or major, that take place in the evolutionary process of the universe. The reason that all these changes take place is because of their causes and conditions. No other external cause is posited. And when events take place, or effects ensue, they come about as a result of the interaction between an initial cause and circumstantial conditions. Therefore, it is important for us, when we talk about causes and conditions, to understand the distinction between the substantial cause, which is the primary cause of an event or phenomenon, and the co-operative causes, which are factors that interact with the substantial cause and so allow the event or phenomenon in question to evolve.

Now here when we speak of causes and conditions, we are talking mainly in relation to mind and matter. Matter comprises the physical entities and material things that we can perceive, see, touch, and feel. Then there is an entirely different class of phenomena, of which we spoke earlier, that belongs solely to the domain of experience, for example memory, awareness and perception. So, when we trace the substantial causes of these two different classes of phenomena we find that, according to Buddhist explanations, particularly the Kālacakra Tantra, the initial cause of matter in this universe is traced to what are called 'space particles', which pervaded space prior to the formation of this present universe. From these space particles evolved the entire range of material substances that we now see in the universe. It is only when the consciousness of a being interacts with the external matter of the universe that the evolution of life comes into being, as, for example, in the evolutionary theories of Darwin.

Now, as we have seen, it is the impact of circumstantial conditions which makes it possible for anything to go through a process of change. What is the reason that these circumstantial conditions should be there in the first place, to effect that change at a particular time, and in a particular place? It is here that the question of karma comes in. For a Buddhist to maintain that an event or phenomenon can exist without any cause at all is, logically speaking, totally incoherent. Also the position that there is an original cause like a creator, which gave rise to the whole of evolution, is uncomfortable and plagued with logical inconsistencies as well. Therefore Buddhists maintain that these interactions between mind and matter take place as a result of karmic actions. However, when discussing karma, it is very important to understand karma in terms of a dynamic process. We all know, for example, how our sensations of happiness, pleasure and pain come about as a result of the active process of ongoing events.

So, having reflected on these various fundamental philosophical questions, when we sum up, we find that the ultimate moral we can draw from them is that we should train our mind. This can not be achieved by some physical intervention like surgery or a course of injections, but only through a discipline, where the mind generates its own awareness and intelligence from within. To develop a powerful, effective wisdom and intelligence, we need a faculty of single-pointedness that will enable us to channel our energy and attention towards a chosen object. And for this, we need a proper foundation, provided by the discipline of pure morality. So, it is in this light that I am emphasizing the importance of the three higher trainings of wisdom, concentration, and ethical discipline.

This is how we can sum up the entire subject matter of the Buddha's first public discourse, the teachings on the Four Noble Truths, and so lay out a framework of basic Buddhist practice that is common to both the Fundamental Vehicle and the Mahāyāna.

2. "MIND IS DEVOID OF MIND"

Earlier we spoke of the mind as being the primary source and basis for the arising of the entire universe, including both the cycle of existence and the state of liberation beyond it. Now let us take the mind itself as our subject; let us examine it and search for its essence. What we discover, when we try to find the mind through some analytical process, is that it is unfindable. Yet mind is the basis and source of all events and all experience, in the sense that it creates our experiences of happiness and unhappiness, pain and pleasure. It is very evident that the mind exists. But if we search for it, if we investigate exactly what the mind is, it is nowhere to be found. That is why our quotation from the sūtra says: "The mind is devoid of mind".

Now, if we interpreted the meaning of "the mind is devoid of mind" to signify that mind does not exist at all, this would contradict our direct experience. For we have an experience of our own mind, we feel it, and we are aware of its presence. Therefore, we have to search for a deeper meaning to the statement that mind is devoid of mind. It is on this point that the understanding of the two truths becomes critical. Often, without a proper understanding of ultimate and conventional truths, seeming inconsistencies or contradictions will arise in our mind. For example we will think that, if mind is the source of happiness and it possesses the capacity to function as such, it must exist objectively. It cannot be the case that mind lacks inherent existence. How can mind possibly function like it does if it lacks any inherent or independent existence? If our understanding of the two truths is incomplete or incorrect, all kinds of contradictions will seem to appear.

Generally speaking, we find a presentation of the two truths in all the philosophical tenets of Buddhism, and also in the teachings of certain non-Buddhist philosophical schools. But the presentation of the two truths as dual aspects of a single entity can only be found in the teachings of the Mahāyāna schools of thought, such as the Mind Only or Cittamātra, and the Middle Way, or Madhyamaka.

Although this is the case, differences in the definition of conventional and ultimate truth can be found in the philosophical tenets of the various schools. The viewpoint given here is mainly from the standpoint of Madhyamaka, and particularly the Madhyamaka Prāsaṅgika.

ULTIMATE AND CONVENTIONAL TRUTHS

In the writings of Longchen Rabjam, and especially of Mipham, there is explicit mention of how the view of emptiness in the Dzogchen system should accord with the view of emptiness of Madhyamaka Prāsaṅgika.[78] In the writings on Dzogchen by these masters, you can find mention of two types of preliminary practices for Dzogchen: a common preliminary practice and an uncommon preliminary practice. The uncommon preliminary practices include what is technically called 'searching for the hidden flaw of mind', one of the preliminary trainings of body, speech and mind. This search is undertaken within a framework of three stages:

1) analysing where mind comes from—examining its origin;
2) analysing the state of mind itself—how it abides or remains;
3) analysing where a state of mind ceases, in other words, where it dissolves.

Examining the origin of the mind, the manner of its endurance, and how it ceases, is also explained from the point of view of the analytical approach of Madhyamaka Prāsaṅgika. Except for the difference in length, one being concise and the other elaborate, this practice is comparable to a certain type of analytical process called 'the diamond slivers', to be found in the Madhyamaka treatises. This analysis uses logical reasons to analyse an event from the point of view of its cause, and from the point of view of its effects, and to analyse the event on its own.[79]

The definition of ultimate truth and conventional truth according to the Madhyamaka Prāsaṅgika, taking into account the manner in which both non-conceptual and conceptual states of mind perceive them, is that any object or any phenomenon that is to be found in the wake of ultimate analysis is called ultimately true, and any phenomenon that is established only through a conventional analysis is called conventionally true.

But then, the terms 'ultimate truth' and 'conventional truth' are used again in a different way in Highest Yoga Tantra. There is also a distinctive presentation of the two truths in Longchen Rabjam's *Treasury of Wish-Fulfilment*. The eighteenth chapter contains a unique presentation of the two truths, which begins with a definition of the ultimate truth as the fundamental, innate nature, and the conventional truth as adventitious phenomena.[80] In other words, what is natural and innate is called ultimate truth, whereas what comes about newly because of adventitious conditions is held to be conventional truth.

Again, we find a presentation of the two truths in Highest Yoga Tantra according to the new translation schools, such as in the Guhyasamāja Tantra, where ultimate truth is spoken of in terms of clear light, and conventional truth in terms of the illusory body. Presented like this, the definition and meaning of the two truths differs totally from that expounded in the sūtra system.

As regards the clear light and illusory body—which are referred to as the two truths of the completion stage according to Highest Yoga Tantra—if these were to be categorized according to the two truths of the sūtra system, both of them would fall into the category of conventional truth. Conversely, as regards the ultimate truth referred to in the sūtra system—which is the ultimate nature of reality or emptiness—if it were compared to the two truths as explained in Highest Yoga Tantra, it would be an object of the clear light.

So when the fundamental innate mind of clear light is spoken of as ultimate truth in Highest Yoga Tantra, the use of the term "ultimate truth" has a certain parallel with the term ultimate truth in the Dzogchen tradition. Ultimate truth can be understood in the context of ground, path and fruition. Because it is primordially and spontaneously present as our true nature, this ultimate truth is fundamental and innate. However, something like the illusory body of Highest Yoga Tantra is an adventitious phenomenon, newly achieved through causes and conditions, and therefore constitutes a conventional truth. For when we explain things on the basis of how the two levels of truth are assigned, adventitious phenomena such as the experience of the illusory body, which are newly created through causes and conditions, cannot be assigned to the fundamental ground. They are the kind of phenomena that possess limits, and at some point they will cease. Ultimately, such conventional, adventitious phenomena are without origin or final cessation, but they are considered as things which occur adventitiously and newly, as a result of conditions and because of the make-up and interests of those to be guided.

A good example would be the 'supreme nirmāṇakāyas'.[81] Ultimately they have no final limits, and yet they occur newly, as a result of adventitious causes and conditions, because of the interdependence of cause and effect, and in response to the interests of those to be guided. So we can classify them as conventionally true.

However, the 'visions of the vajra kāya' that arise in the Dzogchen practice of tögal are *not* something that develops newly and adventitiously as a result of causes and conditions. These visions are there because of the primordial union of kāyas and wisdom, something that is primordially present, the natural self-radiance of our rigpa or fundamental innate mind of clear light. Whether these pure visions are evident or not, they are already present, and in place. This primordial ground, so to speak, is brought into evidence through the path, but other than this, there is nothing being newly achieved, or newly brought about.

Therefore, this fundamental, innate ultimate truth is empty, in the sense that it is empty of the adventitious phenomena of conventional truth. And the things of which it is empty are not non-existent.

Compare this with the sūtra system, where emptiness is understood in terms of the negation of an inherently existing mode of being, a mode of being which we have superimposed on things and events, and we find that the object of negation in this context is totally non-existent. Therefore, the meaning of emptiness differs here as well.

Also, in the Guhyasamāja Tantra different levels of emptiness, the so-called 'four empties' are explained, corresponding to the different levels in the process of dissolution of conceptual thoughts. And in the Kālacakra Tantra we find the term emptiness understood to signify emptiness of corporeality or material substance. So there are many different presentations of emptiness.

Even in the sūtra system itself, we find different uses of the term ultimate truth. For instance, Maitreya, in his *Discrimination of the Middle Way from the Extremes*, refers to the ultimate in three different contexts: ultimate meaning, ultimate practice, and ultimate attainment or result:[82]

> Meaning, attainment and practice;
> The ultimate is said to be threefold.

The terms ultimate and conventional are also found employed in the *Sublime Continuum*, in relation to taking refuge in the Three Jewels.[83] Here, they denote ultimate and conventional refuge, ultimate and conventional determined by whether or not the source of refuge has attained complete fulfilment and is ultimately liberated and released from the bondage of saṃsāra.

Let us return to the presentation of the two truths. Since the fundamental innate mind is empty of adventitious phenomena like conceptual processes and circumstantial conditions, and has always retained its continuity, so it is spoken of as emptiness or ultimate truth. This interpretation gave rise to a view of emptiness in Tibet where this fundamental innate mind, described as ultimate truth, was taken to mean something independently and ultimately existent. This type of view of emptiness is called 'emptiness of other' or *shyentong*. It has been refuted by many great Tibetan masters in the past, but Dilgo Khyentse Rinpoche stated that there are two different interpretations of shyentong, one of which is authentic and valid and one of which is erroneous and invalid.[84]

The reason why I am reviewing all these different references to ultimate and conventional truth in specific settings is so that you

will not allow yourselves to be confused by the uniformity of a term
that is being used in different contexts. For instance, if you are reading a text like the *Treasury of Knowledge*[85], a text on the Vaibhāṣika
philosophy, and you find mention of the terms ultimate and conventional truth, it is very dangerous to seek to understand those
terms from the point of view of the Madhyamaka Prāsaṅgika. In
fact, there is no way you can do that. As a rule, if you find terms
such as the two truths and so on in the text of a lower philosophical
school, the correct way to interpret them is in their own right. If
you find the very same term used in a source from a higher school
of thought, it is most important to examine whether the meaning
remains the same and is common to both schools, or whether it has
a different sense in that particular context. The same holds true
when you find the term ultimate truth in tantra. You should begin
by examining whether the meaning of that term in that particular
context is one that is common to both sūtra and tantra, or whether it
has acquired a different sense. And the same applies to ultimate truth
in the context of Dzogchen practice. So, all in all, it is very important
to examine what the reference of any particular term may be.

UNDERSTANDING EMPTINESS

Now we were speaking of the two truths seen from the point of
view of Madhyamaka Prāsaṅgika, which is the understanding of the
two truths common to both sūtra and tantra. Here, as I said earlier,
ultimate truth is defined as the mode of being of phenomena which
is established through an investigation into the ultimate nature of
things, and conventional truth is defined as the aspect which is
established by an analytical process that examines only the conventional nature of things. This definition of the two truths is
presented from the perspective of how both conceptual and non-
conceptual states of mind perceive things. However, if we were to
define ultimate and conventional truth purely from a direct experiential point of view—the manner in which a non-conceptual
awareness understands things—then we could say this: any phenomenon perceived by direct experience, in a manner in which all the

duality of subject and object is dissolved, is ultimate truth. Whereas any object that retains a subject-object duality when directly perceived is conventional truth.

Now, the understanding of these definitions of the two truths is important in understanding the opening line of the quotation from the sūtra, that is, "Mind is devoid of mind". If we were to take that quotation at face value, it would be totally illogical. We would have to maintain that mind does not exist as a mind, but this is not the case. The reason why Buddha spoke of mind being devoid of mind is that mind does not exist in its own right. Mind does not have an ultimate existence, but only exists in dependence upon other factors, causes and conditions. So that absence of independent existence of mind is the ultimate reality, or ultimate truth, of mind.

Here, when we use the term ultimate, it has two connotations. Firstly, from the point of view of how mind is perceived by direct experience, it should be noted that mind is *not* an object of a direct experience which realizes the ultimate nature of mind. This is because when you realize the ultimate nature of mind, that awareness only realizes the emptiness of mind and not the mind itself. Therefore mind is not ultimate. Secondly, mind is not ultimately existent for the reason that study, contemplation and meditation prove that it lacks an independent nature.

However, if we take ultimate reality—emptiness itself—what we will find is that emptiness is a phenomenon that is found as a result of an ultimate analysis upon a given object. Therefore, from that point of view, it is ultimate, and rightly called ultimate truth. Yet if we take the ultimate as an object in its own right and then examine it, search for its essence, and determine whether emptiness exists objectively, independently of other factors, and so on, we will find that this is not the case. This indicates that emptiness is also not ultimately existent. Understanding this will enable us to reconcile the seeming contradiction that arises when we say that emptiness is ultimate truth, but at the same time it is not ultimately existing.

All the phenomena that appear to our minds and exist in the universe, including the mind itself, depend for this very existence on causes and conditions. Since their nature is one of dependence, they are devoid of any independent existence. They cannot exist in their own right, and from their own side, and this absence or negation of independent existence is the ultimate reality or ultimate truth of all things.

Ultimate truth or emptiness, as presented in the writings of the Madhyamaka school of thought, such as Nāgārjuna's *Fundamental Treatise on the Middle Way*, the root text on wisdom, or Candrakīrti's *Entering the Middle Way*, is one of a type of phenomena called negative phenomena. Generally, phenomena are divided into two categories: affirmative phenomena and negative phenomena. Although there are references to fifteen types of negative phenomena in certain texts, these can all be subsumed under two broad categories: non-affirming negative phenomena and affirming negative phenomena. Emptiness is a non-affirming negative phenomenon.

This division of phenomena into two categories, affirmative and negative, is not made on the basis of things which are positive or negative, but rather from the viewpoint of a subjective awareness: how do we perceive things, how do we develop knowledge of things and events?

Let us take space as an example. Space could be understood merely in terms of negation, simply as an absence of obstruction, and an absence of form. Then that absence of an obstructive quality is called 'space', so whenever we perceive space we do so through negating an obstructive quality. But there are also phenomena that we can understand without having explicitly to negate something, and so it is on the basis of this different manner of perception that we make the division into categories of things which are negative and things which are affirmative.

For instance, there are two tables here, one by my side, and the other in front of me. On the table by my side, you can see there is a flower. In order to perceive that there is a flower, we do not need any other factor, such as having to negate something. Whereas the appearance of the flower presented to our perception enables us to perceive the presence of a flower on the table at my side, in order to perceive the absence of a flower on the table in front of me, first of all I have to identify 'flower', which is to be negated, and then by explicitly negating 'flower', I can understand the absence of any flower on the table before me. So we see that there are two different ways of understanding or perceiving things. And this emptiness that is simply the total absence of a flower on the table in front of me *is* a phenomenon which exists, because we can correctly perceive it.

To return to emptiness, if we were to question how the presence or absence of emptiness matters to us, the answer is: it doesn't! The fact that there is emptiness does not make any difference to us. What does make a difference, however, is our understanding and realization of the empty *nature* of things. This is of crucial importance, because understanding and realizing emptiness is directly related to our quest to purify our mind of afflictive emotions like hatred, anger, and desire.

Generally speaking, whenever we perceive things, our perception is deluded, in that we project onto things a status of existence and a mode of being which is simply not there. We exaggerate things, and the way they then appear falsely to our minds gives rise to afflictive emotions. When we see our friends or enemies, for instance, we superimpose on them a quality of desirability or undesirability that is beyond the actual facts of the situation, and this superimposition or exaggeration sparks off fluctuating states of emotion in our mind. Towards our friends we feel strong attachment and desire, and towards our enemies powerful anger and hatred. So if we are serious about trying to purify our minds of these afflictive emotions, an understanding of emptiness becomes crucial.

This understanding of emptiness, when furthered, advanced and directly experienced, is one of the principal factors of the true path. That direct realization of emptiness will have the power to serve as an antidote, to overcome and dispel ignorance and afflictive emotions from our minds. For such an insight cuts right through the illusion created by the misapprehension of grasping things and events as existing inherently, in and of themselves. When this function of the direct realization of emptiness as an antidote is taken further, it gradually eradicates delusions and ignorance from the mind altogether.

According to the philosophical school of Nāgārjuna and his followers, this direct realization of emptiness as an antidote that overcomes and removes delusions from the mind is a crucial and indispensable factor of wisdom not only for the practitioners of the Mahāyāna, but also for followers of both the 'listeners' vehicle' and the 'solitary realizers' vehicle'.[86] They maintain that for all three types of spiritual practitioners this realization of emptiness is a common requirement in order to attain liberation. Of course in the Mahāyāna sūtras, the teaching of emptiness is set out more elaborately and more explicitly. Yet this does not mean that emptiness is never spoken of in the teachings of the Fundamental Vehicle, for Nāgārjuna argues that there are explicit references to emptiness in the sūtras of the Fundamental Vehicle as well.

THE SKILFUL MEANS OF BODHICITTA

Since there is no difference between the three vehicles with respect to wisdom, the difference must lie in the domain of method or skilful means. Thus it is that the generation of bodhicitta, the altruistic aspiration to attain enlightenment for the benefit of all, is said to be the gateway to the Mahāyāna path, and it is this which distinguishes whether a practitioner is Mahāyāna or not. When a practitioner is initially motivated by this kind of altruistic principle to work for the benefit of all sentient beings, and when he or she puts this ideal into action, then the practice of the six perfections comes into play.

Bodhicitta can be defined as an expansive state of mind that is attained as a result of training in two kinds of aspiration. One is an altruistic aspiration to benefit all sentient beings, an attitude of deep compassion. The other is the conviction that comes from reflecting on the suffering of all sentient beings and realizing that for as long as we do not attain the highest enlightenment, we will be handicapped and limited in our ability to fulfil our aspiration to benefit others. The state of mind that is induced through these twin aspirations is called bodhicitta, or the mind of enlightenment.

However, our direct understanding of emptiness might be motivated by the wish to attain liberation for ourselves alone. By cultivating that understanding of emptiness, we can free ourselves from emotional obscurations and delusions, and so attain the state of arhat. Yet this will not have the power to free us from the cognitive obscurations, the 'obstructions to knowledge', left behind in our minds by these delusions.

If we follow what is said in *The Sublime Continuum*, these cognitive obscurations or obstructions to knowledge, can only be overcome by cultivating a direct realization of emptiness, accompanied by the factor of skilful means, such as bodhicitta, compassion, and so on. By understanding this emptiness, called the 'emptiness endowed with all the aspects of skilful means', we will be able not only to release our minds from delusion, but also to overcome the cognitive obscurations, the latent potencies left behind by the delusions.

HOW TO DEVELOP BODHICITTA

The question then is "How do we cultivate and develop this bodhicitta, the mind of enlightenment?" The key, and the root, is great compassion. Compassion here refers to a state of mind that makes it utterly unbearable for us to see the suffering of other sentient beings. The way to develop this is through understanding how we feel about our own suffering. When we become conscious of our own suffering, we have a spontaneous wish to be free from it. If we are able to extend that feeling to all other beings, through realizing the common instinctive desire we all have to avoid and overcome suffering, then that state of mind is called 'great compassion'.

All of us have the potential to develop that kind of compassion, because whenever we see people who are suffering, especially those close to us, we immediately feel empathy towards them, and witness a spontaneous response within our minds. So all we have to do is to bring that potential out, and then to develop it to become so impartial that it can include all sentient beings within its embrace, whether friend or foe.

To cultivate this great compassion within ourselves, first of all we need to develop what is called loving-kindness, a feeling of connectedness or closeness with all living creatures. This closeness and intimacy should not be confused with the kind of feeling we normally have toward our loved ones, which is tainted by attachment. This attachment, where we think: "These are *my* friends...they are *my* relatives..." is based on ego and on selfishness. When we develop loving kindness, we are not prompted by such selfish reasoning. On the contrary, we are seeking to develop a feeling of closeness towards other sentient beings, and affection for them, by reflecting: on the fact that suffering is inherent in their very nature, on the helplessness of their situation, and on the instinctive desire they all have to overcome suffering. The greater the force of our loving kindness towards other beings, the greater the force of our compassion. And the greater the force of our compassion, the easier it will be for us to develop a sense of responsibility for taking upon ourselves the task of working for others. The greater that sense of responsibility, the more successful we will be in generating bodhicitta, the genuine altruistic aspiration to attain buddhahood for the benefit of all.

Secondly, an important factor in cultivating compassion is to develop a deep insight into how, in this cycle of existence as a whole, the very nature of life is unsatisfactory, or *duḥkha*. This is in fact the first noble truth—the truth of suffering. If our insight into this truth is not sufficiently deep, rather than generating compassion for sentient beings, we may feel envy towards those who would, by worldly standards, be regarded as successful, wealthy, or powerful. If we have emotions like these, it indicates that our insight into suffering is too shallow to allow us really to appreciate the pervasiveness of suffering in the lives of people caught up in this vicious circle of saṃsāra. However, if our understanding of suffering is deep enough, then we will develop a spontaneous sense of how unbearable life is in the cycle of existence as a whole. To have that feeling of 'unbearableness' is what will enable us to appreciate the suffering of others more spontaneously. Otherwise, our cultivation of compassion will be somewhat hypocritical. As much as we may pretend to have compassion towards sentient beings, deep down we may remain envious and jealous of people who are seen as successful in the eyes of the world.

In short then, genuine compassion is cultivated when we have two factors within our mind. The *first* is a deep insight into how suffering is the nature of life in the cycle of existence in general, along with a feeling of its unbearableness. The *second* is to realize the sameness of ourselves and others: we all have the natural tendency to seek happiness and to try to avoid suffering, just as we all have a natural right as well to enjoy happiness and be free from suffering. This is the realization that will lead us to exchange ourselves for others, for although we all share this common natural inclination and right, the difference lies in numbers. When we are talking about our own welfare, no matter how important we might be, it remains a question of one, single individual, whereas others are infinite in number. From that point of view, they are much more important than we are, on our own.

These two factors of mind: a deep insight into suffering, coupled with a realization that others are more important than ourselves, will give rise to a sense of responsibility to work for the benefit of others. This will lead us to generate genuine compassion within ourselves.

Taking the Bodhisattva Pledge

In his *Entering the Middle Way*, Candrakīrti writes:

> Before all else I praise compassion:
> The seed of the abundant harvest of buddhahood,
> The water that makes it grow,
> And what ripens into the state of lasting enjoyment.[87]

Candrakīrti compares compassion, at the beginning of our practice, to a seed; during the path itself, it is like the moisture and the fertilizers that germinate and nourish the young plant as it grows;

and in the resultant state of buddhahood, it is like a ripened fruit, which can be enjoyed by all sentient beings. So the importance of compassion spans not only the beginning stage of spiritual practice, but also the path, and the result as well.

When we have cultivated a compassion such as this, it will become our inspiration for developing bodhicitta, the altruistic aspiration to attain full enlightenment. As for the method of generating bodhicitta, there emerged in India two techniques: the 'seven point cause and effect method' of Atiśa, and 'equalizing and exchanging oneself with others', a method developed by the master Śāntideva. It is very effective and beneficial to follow a method which combines both of these two approaches.

Training our mind through equalizing and exchanging ourselves with others is extremely powerful, and is in fact designed for bodhisattvas who have higher mental faculties. Training the mind through this approach is particularly effective in these modern times, in that it suits the mental outlook of our present age.

Now, once you have had a slight realization of bodhicitta through applying either of these two techniques, or combining the two, you can then reinforce your generation of this altruistic aspiration by going through the ceremony of generating what is called the 'aspirational aspect' of bodhicitta. This ceremony makes your generation of the altruistic mind all the more firm and powerful.

This we will do now, through your repeating after me the verse that I shall recite. As you are repeating it, say to yourself: "For the benefit of all sentient beings, I will aspire to attain complete enlightenment". If you generate this attitude with that kind of motivation, it will have great effect. And in the future, when you engage in the task of working for others, this ceremony will always be a reminder of the pledge you made today.

Those of you who have a keen interest in and respect for Buddhist practice, and who wish to pursue Buddhist meditation, especially according to the Mahāyāna, can reflect along these lines. Those who do not consider themselves Buddhist practitioners do not need to follow the visualization or contemplation explained at this point.

Visualize that in front of you and above you in space are all the buddhas and bodhisattvas. Imagine yourself surrounded by all sentient beings, reflect on the suffering inherent in their lives, and think: "Just like me, they too have a natural desire to be happy and to overcome all of their suffering".

Now build up an attitude of courage, saying to yourself: "May I be able to take upon myself the responsibility for helping all these sentient beings get rid of their suffering and the experiences they do not desire." Then, spurred on by such a sense of responsibility, you take the pledge that you will work to put this ideal into action.

> In the Buddha, Dharma and Saṅgha,
> I take refuge until enlightenment is reached.
> Through the merit of my practice of generosity
>   and the like,
> May I attain buddhahood, so as to benefit all beings!

Having generated this altruistic state of mind, make a pledge from the depth of your heart that from now on, you will always be a good human being; whenever the occasion arises, you will help other sentient beings and, if not, at least restrain yourself from harming them. What is most important is really to make this pledge and commitment with all your heart, so that now that you have generated this spirit of altruism, you will allow it to infuse your whole life.

But it is not enough to be content with this aspiration alone. Now that altruistic ideal should be put into action, through the practices of the six perfections. In brief, the bodhisattva's way of life or practice is the union of method or skilful means and wisdom. 'Method' here refers to practices like generating the altruistic mind of enlightenment, and allowing it to motivate you to engage in skilful means for helping others, such as: generosity, pure morality, patience, enthusiasm, and concentration. 'Wisdom' here means to develop and reinforce your understanding of, and insight into, emptiness.

THE UNION OF METHOD AND WISDOM

Now in the Perfection Vehicle, the union of method and wisdom is understood only in terms of two factors that complement one another: method is complemented and supported by the wisdom that realizes emptiness, or wisdom is supported and complemented by method.[88] So the unification of the two factors in the sūtra system is not ultimate and therefore not complete. However, in the tantric system there is a more refined and ultimate unification of method and wisdom. Here this union is brought to an extremely profound and subtle level, where both factors of method and wisdom are complete and present within the one entity of a single consciousness. Although there are many unique features that distinguish tantra from sūtra, this indivisible unification of method and wisdom is one of tantra's primary distinguishing characteristics.

The reason this union of method and wisdom can be achieved in such a subtle state and in such an indivisible manner is because in tantric meditation practice, especially in deity yoga meditation, one's ordinary aggregates of body and mind are dissolved into emptiness. Practitioners begin by reflecting on the empty nature of the aggregates of body and mind. Then they dissolve into emptiness not only their 'identity'—the mode of being superimposed on them by the ignorant mind—but also the very appearance of the ordinary aggregates of body and mind. Then, from within that emptiness, the practitioners arise as a pure, divine being. Taking that divine being as the focus of meditation, they then reflect again upon its empty nature. So here within one meditative state of mind you find meditation on the deity's body, combined with the apprehension of its empty nature. Both deity yoga and understanding of emptiness are complete and present within a single cognitive event of the mind.

This indivisible union, in which both of the factors of method and wisdom are present within a single moment of consciousness, is common to all the tantras including the three lower classes of tantra: Kriyā, Caryā, and Yoga tantra. There are, however, certain differences among these tantras, for example in subtle aspects of the yogas. In the case of Yoga tantra, for instance, one speaks of what are known as the 'four seals'.[89]

HIGHEST YOGA TANTRA

So far I have explained the approach to spiritual development from the point of view of the six yānas. In Dzogchen and Nyingma terminology, a sequence of nine vehicles is taught. The first three are the śrāvaka vehicle, pratyekabuddha vehicle, and bodhisattva vehicle, which are known collectively as 'the vehicles from the direction of the origin of suffering'. They comprise the vehicles of the sūtra tradition, and form what is called the outer vehicle. The tantras are divided into two: outer tantras and inner tantras. The first three classes of tantra—Kriyā, Caryā, and Yoga tantras—are called the outer tantras, and are also known as 'the vehicles of gaining awareness through austerities'.[90]

Apart from the presence or absence of deity yoga, the basic approach to meditation on emptiness is similar in all these first six vehicles. However, in Highest Yoga Tantra, although there is no difference in subtlety as far as the object, emptiness itself, is concerned, from the point of view of the subjective experience of emptiness, there certainly is a difference. So from the point of view of objective emptiness we can say that there is no difference between sūtra and tantra with regard to the view of emptiness. However, from the point of view of subjective experience there is a difference in the understanding or view of emptiness between sūtra and tantra. When we understand this, we can reconcile the two seemingly contradictory standpoints—that there is a difference in the view of emptiness between sūtra and tantra, and that there is no difference at all.

Now the difference in the subjective experience of emptiness between the sūtra practice and the practice of Highest Yoga Tantra emerges from the fact that in Highest Yoga Tantra much emphasis is

placed on dissolving conceptual thought processes—the coarse
levels of mind—so bringing the mind down to such a depth that
the fundamental innate mind of clear light becomes manifest and
active, and then can focus on emptiness and perceive it. Once that
is realized, then the subjective experience of emptiness becomes
very powerful, and quite different from the kind of mind that is
employed in understanding emptiness in the sūtra system.

Now although the basic aim of utilizing the innate mind of
clear light in realizing emptiness is the same in both the new
translation schools of tantra and the Dzogchen system, the
difference lies in the methodology. In the systems developed
within the new translation schools of tantra, the emphasis is more
on harnessing the coarse levels of mind and vital energy so that
gradually these coarser states cease, and the fundamental innate
mind of clear light becomes fully evident. However in Dzogchen,
from the very beginning, you are not concerned with harnessing
these coarse levels of mind and vital energy, but rather with
making the fundamental innate mind of clear light evident from
the very start.

It is from this point of view that the last three yānas or vehicles
are taught. They are: Mahāyoga, which refers to the generation
stage; Anuyoga, which is the completion stage; and Atiyoga which
is the great completion stage, Dzogpachenpo. These three are
known as 'the vehicles of overpowering means'.[91]

According to the systems that evolved within the new translation schools of tantra, the division of Highest Yoga Tantra is made
in terms of father tantra, mother tantra, and non-dual tantra. These
categories are determined on the basis of how particular tantras
emphasize a certain subject matter. For instance, out of the four
empowerments, the vase empowerment authorizes the practitioner
to practise the generation stage. The remaining three empowerments are specifically connected to the practice of the completion
stage. The secret empowerment authorizes the practitioner to
engage in the illusory body practice. From this point of view, tantras
that emphasize the practice of the illusory body as their subject

matter are known as father tantra. Tantras that emphasize the practice of clear light, which relates to the third empowerment, the wisdom-knowledge empowerment, are categorized as mother tantra. Any tantra that emphasizes equally these two aspects of the completion stage—the illusory body and clear light—and which is associated with the fourth empowerment, the word empowerment, is classified as non-dual tantra. Although all the tantras belonging to the Highest Yoga Tantra class deal with all four empowerments, there are different emphases on certain aspects of these empowerments, and the classification of father, mother and non-dual tantra is made on that basis.[92]

When we talk about Mahāmudrā, the Great Seal, it should be understood that there are different levels of Mahāmudrā. We can speak of Mahāmudrā that is common to both sūtra and tantra, and Mahāmudrā which specifically refers to the practice of clear light associated with the third empowerment, the wisdom-knowledge empowerment. And there is yet another level of Mahāmudrā that refers to the union of the illusory body and clear light.

Now, as I mentioned earlier, the significance of emphasizing the practice of clear light in Highest Yoga Tantra is to enable the practitioner to employ the fundamental innate mind of clear light for understanding and realizing emptiness, so that it can provide you with a unique wisdom—'the wisdom which realizes emptiness'.

Here I think it is crucial to understand that there are different types of meditation, because this will help us appreciate what we mean when we talk of meditating on clear light. For instance, there is meditation on emptiness or selflessness, where that emptiness or selflessness is taken as the object of the meditation. First you reflect on them, and then you apprehend them. Then there are other types of meditation, like meditation on love or compassion, which belong to a totally different category. When we speak of meditation on love, this does not mean taking love as an object, but rather seeking to transform our whole state of mind into that state of love or compassion. Meditation on clear light is similar to the meditation on love, because we are not taking clear light as an object, but generating our mind into that very state of clear light.

3. QUESTIONS AND ANSWERS

Question: *What is the difference between Mahāmudrā and Dzogchen?*

HHDL: Although ultimately the practice of Mahāmudrā and Dzogchen come down to the same point, at the initial stages there do seem to be certain differences in emphasis on particular aspects of the practice. The distinctiveness of the practices of Mahāmudrā and Dzogchen principally has its origins in the sources of the respective approaches. Mahāmudrā was transmitted mainly through the new translation schools of tantra. And yet it is also possible for Mahāmudrā teachers who have personal experience of Dzogchen in their own meditation to integrate Dzogchen techniques into their practice of Mahāmudrā. This is also true in the case of the practice of the Sakyapas called 'the union of emptiness and clarity'. A master who has a personal experience of Dzogchen meditation can integrate certain elements of Dzogchen techniques into their practice of the union of emptiness and clarity. This question will be addressed in greater depth later on.

Question: *Can a student objectively evaluate his own progress?*

HHDL: Yes, this is definitely possible. As you progress in your practice, you can always relate your new experiences to the teachings that you have received so far, and also relate them to the text that you are reading and studying. For instance, take the example of the great yogin Milarepa. In the latter part of his life when he spent most of his time in solitary retreat in the mountains, he did not have his teacher, Marpa, nearby where he could always refer to him. He had to evaluate his own experiences and progress for himself.

This question brings up the whole basic approach, which is to emphasize study and learning at the beginning, in order to develop a good understanding of the entire scope of Buddhist teaching and practice. It is like creating a proper blueprint, so to speak, or drawing a real plan for your future development. When you have learned enough, you can evaluate your progress, and advance in your practice. This is why study and learning are so important at the initial stages.

Question: *Can you please distinguish the terms rigpa, wisdom—yeshé, and clear light? They are often used in similar ways.*

HHDL: According to my own observation, I think that when these terms are employed in certain contexts, for example when referring to Dzogchen practice, they have specific definitions and meanings, whereas in another context or another text, the meaning will differ. So you might assume that certain terms have a common meaning, whereas in fact they have different levels of meaning, according to the particular context in which they are found.

The term 'rigpa' is employed in so many ways. If we talk about rigpa as it is used in explaining Dzogchen, for example, we find: essential rigpa, *ngowöi rigpa*; rigpa of the ground, *shyii rigpa*; effulgent rigpa, *tsal gyi rigpa*,[93] and so on. Also a term 'rigpa' is used to denote the essential aspect of the analysis of the mind. Then 'rigpa' also appears when a contrast is drawn between *rigpa* and *marigpa*—awareness and ignorance, or between *sem* and *rigpa*—the ordinary mind and the transcendent mind.

The term *yeshé*, often translated as 'primordial wisdom', has many different connotations. One finds a reference, for example, to this term in Maitreya's *Sublime Continuum*, where it says that this wisdom is something that is very basic, and inherent within all living creatures. So the interpretation of wisdom also differs according to the context. Because of this variety of meanings, or different levels of meaning, or contexts of teaching and practice, it is all the more important to develop a good understanding of the entire Buddhist framework as a whole.

Here I would like to tell you a short story. In Tibet there was a man who was generally regarded as being rather stupid. He was due to visit a certain family, and was anxious to impress them and to make them understand that, far from being stupid, he was a person of some intelligence. So his parents gave him very clear instructions: "As you go into the house you'll see that in the doorway is a wooden threshold. The wood that it is made from is called oak. As soon as you see the threshold, point to it and say 'That's *oak*'".

Their son went off to visit the family and everything seemed to go well. He spotted the threshold and pointed to it and said, "This is oak!" At once everyone began to think that after all he really was quite intelligent. It was then that he started pointing at all the furniture, and every bit of wood he could see in the house, announcing again and again: "This is oak. That is oak..."

So even though the context may appear to be similar, we cannot assume that a particular term will always retain the same meaning, wherever it occurs. I have found it is essential to have a proper understanding of the different shades of meaning of these terms, and of the way in which they can vary according to the context. I believe it is essential, in fact, for all serious practitioners. In any case, it is beneficial, and important too, to have a good knowledge of the different approaches of the various spiritual traditions within Tibetan Buddhism, including all the afore-mentioned traditions. For example, according to my own experience and observation, I have found the different explanations given in Dzogchen about the pristine awareness of rigpa to be extremely useful in understanding the deeper meaning, and ultimate import, of the term 'fundamental innate mind of clear light' used in the new translation schools of tantra. I have also found the explanations of the new translation schools of tantra helpful in understanding certain terms that come up in Dzogchen practice, such as 'inner radiance' and 'display'—*tsal* and *rolpa*. This kind of non-sectarian approach is one that I have found very beneficial.

Question: *What is the best way to practise, or what technique or attitude can be used, to deepen the heart connection with Padmasambhava?*

HHDL: Serious practice is the only way. For example, for a practitioner of Dzogchen meditation, the best way to make that heart connection with Padmasambhava is through meditation. But then the definition of meditation is quite specific in the context of Dzogchen practice. It is unlike other kinds of meditation where we use 'the mind'. These types of meditation involve using our faculty of mind to its full, and with exertion. In Dzogchen meditation, the practice is done in a non-dualistic manner, in the sense that there is no objectivity involved. Rather, the meditation is undertaken at a level where the mind is returned to a primordial and natural state. So in this kind of meditation there is no sense of subject and object, there is nothing to hold on to, and it is not influenced by any sense of grasping. Again, we find that the meaning of meditation will change according to the context.

Question: *How does an understanding of emptiness help you to realize compassion and loving kindness?*

HHDL: Let alone a true knowledge of emptiness, even an intellectual understanding of emptiness will enable you to perceive the possibility of the cessation of suffering, along with the delusions which lie at its root. Then, once you have realized this, and if your conviction is strong enough, your compassion towards other sentient beings caught up in the confusion of this cycle of existence will be all the greater and more powerful.

Question: *What if we feel an unbearable compassion for the suffering of other beings—especially animals, because it is often more obvious—yet we have not developed the wisdom to deal with it properly?*

HHDL: This is all the more reason why, now that you have developed that feeling of 'unbearable' compassion toward others, you should try to increase your wisdom, and intelligence, in order to deal with the actual situation. This is why practitioners on the bodhisattva path are encouraged not to be satisfied with just an idealistic idea of compassion, but to put that ideal into practice immediately. So I believe that when you follow the bodhisattva's way of life, it is possible to match your compassion, at whatever level it may be, with an active kind of interaction with others.

Question: *How can Dzogchen help us in our daily jobs and careers?*

HHDL: In the first place, it is quite difficult to have an experience of Dzogchen. But once you do have that experience, it can be extremely beneficial in dealing with your day to day life, your job, and your career. This is because that kind of experience will give you the ability to prevent yourself from being overwhelmed by circumstances, good or bad. You will not fall into extreme states of mind: you will not get over-excited or depressed. Your attitude toward circumstances and events will be as if you were someone observing the mind, without being drawn away by circumstances.

For example, when you see a reflection of a form in a mirror, the reflection appears within the mirror but it is not projected from within. In the same way, when you confront the situations of life, or deal with others, your attitude too will be mirror-like.

Also, when a reflection appears in the mirror, the mirror does not have to go after the object that is reflected: it simply reflects, spontaneously, on the surface. The same with you: since there is no attachment or agitation at having these 'reflections' in your mind, you will feel tremendous ease and relief. You are not preoccupied by what arises in the mind, nor does it cause you any distress. You are free from conceptuality or any form of objectifying. And so it really does help you, in allowing you to be free from being caught up in the play of emotions like hatred, attachment, and the like.

Question: *Is the fundamental innate mind of clear light dependent on causes and conditions? If it is not dependent, how can it be empty of independent existence?*

HHDL: This is a very good question. Often in the texts we find mention of the fundamental innate mind of clear light being not produced by causes and conditions. Now here it is important to understand that in general when we use the term 'produced phenomena' there are different connotations. Something can be called 'produced' because it is a production of delusions and the actions they induce. Again, it may also refer to a production by causes and conditions. And there is also a sense of 'produced' as being caused by conceptual thought processes.

Certain texts speak of the activities of the Buddha as permanent and non-produced in the sense that they are continuous, and that as long as there are sentient beings, the activities of the buddhas will remain without interruption. So, from the point of view of their continuity, these activities are sometimes called permanent.[94]

In the same manner, the fundamental innate mind of clear light, in terms of its continuity, is beginningless, and also endless. This continuum will always be there, and so from that specific point of view, it is also called 'non-produced'. Besides, the fundamental innate mind of clear light is not a circumstantial or adventitious state of mind, for it does not come into being as a result of the circumstantial interaction of causes and conditions. Rather, it is an ever-abiding continuum of mind, which is inherent within us. So from that viewpoint, it is called 'non-produced'.

However, although this is the case, we still have to maintain that, because it possesses this continuity, the present fundamental innate mind—this present instant of consciousness—comes from its earlier moments. The same holds true of the wisdom of Buddha—the omniscient mind of Buddha—which perceives the two truths directly and simultaneously, and which is also a state of awareness or consciousness. Since it is a state of awareness, the factor which will eventually turn into that kind of wisdom, namely the fundamental innate nature of clear light, will also have to be maintained to be a state of awareness. For it is impossible for anything which is not by nature awareness to turn into a state of awareness. So from this second point of view, the fundamental innate mind of clear light *is* causally produced.

Question: *The lojong* Training the Mind in Seven Points *teaches relative, conventional bodhicitta and absolute, ultimate bodhicitta. How does Samantabhadra or primordial awareness fit into this teaching?*

HHDL: Generally speaking, the practices explained in the type of training called *lojong*—'training the mind'—are explained mainly

from the point of view of the common approach of the paths of
sūtra and tantra. Therefore the view of emptiness taught in that text,
Training the Mind in Seven Points,[95] is not presented from a Dzogchen
point of view. Yet a practitioner who has the understanding and
experience of Dzogchen meditation can definitely integrate that
into their practice of lojong if they are following this text.

Take the example of Patrul Rinpoche, one of the greatest
masters of Dzogchen. His whole life revolved around the
Bodhicaryāvatāra, a text which outlines the principal bodhisattva
practices, and mainly the training of the mind. I am quite certain
that when he followed the practices of the Bodhicaryāvatāra, Patrul
Rinpoche must have been integrating them with his experience
of Dzogchen.

Question: *Why have you chosen to complete the Dzogchen teachings with
the empowerment of Padmasambhava?*

HHDL: Generally speaking, for a genuine practitioner of
Dzogchen, there are certain prerequisites that should be met prior
to engaging intensively in Dzogchen practice. These include having
received complete empowerment into any of the deities of Highest
Yoga Tantra, and also having engaged in both the common and
uncommon preliminary practices of Dzogchen. This must then be
followed by receiving a direct transmission or blessing for the
practice of Dzogchen from a living master, through receiving
instruction on a text such as the *Yeshé Lama*.[96]

The empowerment being given tomorrow is based on
Padmasambhava, and this is in fact a practice similar to the Guru
Yoga practice, of which there are a number of different kinds. In
order to practise Dzogchen, first of all you need to receive the
blessing of a transmission that comes down through an uninterrupted lineage. The lineage here stems from the primordial buddha
Samantabhadra and has been passed down through a succession of
lineage masters, one of whom was Guru Padmasambhava. This
practice of Dzogchen is a practice specific to Guru Padmasambhava's
lineage, and because of the significance of this, I am giving the

empowerment of Padmasambhava as a conclusion to the teaching on Dzogchen.

Question: *Certain Nyingma masters have expounded* shyentong— *emptiness of other—as the view of Dzogchen. Do you agree with them? Why is* shyentong *such a controversial view among Tibetan Buddhist philosophers?*

HHDL: If we read the writings of the great scholar Mipham, especially his commentary on the *Sublime Continuum,* we find that he explicitly mentions the importance of understanding the Dzogchen view, in which one is able to combine the teachings of emptiness, as expounded in the wisdom sūtras of the second turning of the wheel of Dharma, with the sūtras belonging to the third turning of the wheel of Dharma, particularly the *Essence of Buddhahood Sūtra.*[97] The understanding developed through a combination of the views expounded in both turnings of the wheel of Dharma will enable us to appreciate what in Dzogchen terminology are called: primordial purity, which is the main subject matter of the second turning, and spontaneous presence, which is the main subject matter of the third turning of the wheel of Dharma.

However, this does not mean that the emptiness spoken of in the second turning, that is in the wisdom sūtras, is exactly the same as what in Dzogchen terminology is called primordial purity. But one thing which is clear is that without an understanding of emptiness as expounded in the wisdom sūtras, and without taking that understanding as a basis, there is no way that you can understand primordial purity in the context of Dzogchen.

As for the question of whether spontaneous presence in Dzogchen is synonymous with what is called the *tathāgatagarbha*— the essence of buddhahood or innate mind of clear light—in the third turning of the wheel of Dharma, especially in the *Essence of Buddhahood Sūtra,* there do seem to be divergent views on that, even among Nyingma meditators and scholars.

One view is that, although there is a difference, the eventual reference for the innate mind of clear light spoken of in Maitreya's

Sublime Continuum or the *Essence of Buddhahood Sūtra* is definitely rigpa, or the spontaneous presence that is spoken of in Dzogchen. But that does not mean that the explicit mention of the two terms refers to the same thing. An example here is that in Yoga Tantra, especially in the tantra of Vairocanābhisaṃbodhi,[98] there is a mention of the rainbow body. Now although we cannot say that this rainbow body is totally synonymous with what is spoken of as the illusory body in Highest Yoga Tantra, yet eventually that reference to the rainbow body, if understood at its deepest level, will come down to the illusory body.

As I explained earlier, in the writings of the Nyingma masters Longchen Rabjam, the omniscient Jikmé Lingpa, and Mipham, there may be mention of the term 'emptiness of other', but here the reference is mainly to the fundamental innate mind, that is, to rigpa. This innate mind is 'empty of other' in that it is devoid of circumstantial conceptual thought processes. Therefore these types of emptiness of other are totally different from the emptiness of other which was refuted by many Tibetan masters in the past.[99]

There is a tradition of making a distinction between two different perspectives on the nature of emptiness: one is when emptiness is presented within a philosophical analysis of the ultimate reality of things, in which case it ought to be understood in terms of a non-affirming negative phenomena. On the other hand, when it is discussed from the point of view of experience, it should be understood more in terms of an affirming negation.

I think the reason for this statement is that when setting out your philosophical position and view of emptiness, you have to do so while taking into account the common viewpoints of sūtra and tantra on the teaching of emptiness. But when speaking from an experiential point of view, you do so more from your understanding of emptiness in terms of the perspective of Highest Yoga Tantra.

Another reason for this difference is, I think, that in the practice of sūtra and the three lower classes of tantra, the wisdom derived through special insight into emptiness is always a contemplative, analytical state of mind, and it is never a state of mental absorption, whereas in Highest Yoga Tantra a special insight into emptiness could be also a state of absorption. This is possible because in Highest Yoga Tantra the subjective mind employed in perceiving emptiness has the nature of a spontaneous experience of great bliss, and it is that faculty of great bliss which serves the purpose of analysis.

In Dzogchen practice, no effort is made to generate bliss through utilizing the channels, vital energy and essences, as is the case in the new translation school tantras. Rather, the nature of rigpa is directly introduced, and that view is what is maintained. But this is not an analytical process, because analysis means that mind would be sullied by ordinary consciousness. Rigpa is utterly relaxed, although the term *thamal gyi shépa*—'ordinary awareness', is not actually used here. Within this state of completely relaxed awareness, there is no focusing of the attention; consciousness simply rests without engaging in any kind of analysis. Should analysis set in, the experience would be sullied by ordinary consciousness; it would be mind-made, and this falls into 'the view of intellectual speculation.'

Question: *Can you relate any examples of the experience of clear light?*

HHDL: There are various types of experience, associated with different degrees of subtlety in your experience of clear light. Generally speaking, Dzogchen terminology distinguishes between two situations:

— dissolution due to the influence of liberation, and
— dissolution due to the influence of confusion.[100]

Given that there is a distinction between the ground and the appearances of the ground, when the appearances of the ground dissolve, it can happen in one of these two ways: dissolution due to the influence of liberation, or dissolution due to the influence of confusion. The former refers to dissolution through the power of yoga practised on the path, whereby coarser and subtle levels of consciousness are dissolved, and the latter refers to the dissolution that takes place automatically at the time of death. In this regard, depending on the extent to which the dissolution process has taken place, there can be different degrees to the experience of clear light. In any case, for us the whole point is to arrive, through practice, at the ultimate experience of clear light.

When that ultimate experience of clear light takes place, all the other types of consciousness, the coarse levels of mind—sensory faculties, sensory consciousnesses and the coarse levels of mental consciousness—are all dissolved, and the breathing process ceases. But one question which is not settled or certain yet is whether or not a very subtle functioning of the brain might still be present in that state. This is something we still have to discover, and I have discussed it with a number of brain scientists. Given the premise of neuroscience, that consciousness, awareness, or psychological states are states of the brain, we have to find out whether or not at that point of clear light the brain still retains some function.[101]

Question: *Do sentient beings have free will?*

HHDL: According to Buddhism, individuals are masters of their own destiny. And all living beings are believed to possess the nature of the Primordial Buddha Samantabhadra, the potential or seed of enlightenment, within them. So our future is in our own hands. What greater free will do we need?

4. "THE NATURE OF MIND IS CLEAR LIGHT"

So according to the approach of the Nyingma tradition, the teachings of tantra are divided into: the outer tantras, which are the three classes of lower tantra, and the inner tantras, which are Mahāyoga, Anuyoga, and Atiyoga. The teachings in these three inner tantras emphasize the practice of the ultimate, clear light nature of mind, and so expound the practice as embodied in the second line of the quotation to which I referred at the beginning of the teaching:

For the nature of mind is clear light.

When speaking about the clear light nature of mind, we can understand it at two levels: according to the teachings of the sūtra system, and in the context of the tantric teachings, especially Highest Yoga Tantra. Now, when the clear light nature of mind is understood in terms common to both sūtra and tantra, there can be two distinct references. One is to the emptiness of the mind, which is the objective clear light, and the other is to the essential clarity and awareness of the nature of the mind, which is the subjective experience of clear light.

For instance, in Dharmakīrti's *Commentary on 'Valid Cognition'*, an important text on Buddhist logic and epistemology, there are passages which describe how the qualities that depend upon the mind, that is to say that are mental, are stable and firmly rooted. He states this point as part of his argument for the possibility of attaining omniscience, one of the central thrusts of which is that the basis of these qualities, namely the mindstream, is stable and uninterrupted. The meaning of mind being firmly rooted and stable here should be understood in terms of the essential nature of mind, that of clarity and awareness.[102]

That aspect of clarity and awareness—the clear light nature of mind—is also defined in Maitreya's *Sublime Continuum*, and in Nāgārjuna's *Collection of Praises*, especially in his *In Praise of the Dharmadhātu*. On account of this, there emerged a viewpoint that the view of emptiness as expounded in Nāgārjuna's *Collection on Reasoning* is that of the second turning of the wheel of the Dharma and the wisdom sūtras, whereas his *Collection of Praises* presents the view of emptiness according to the teachings of the third turning of the wheel of the Dharma, especially the Tathāgatagarbha sūtra.

CLEAR LIGHT IN THE HIGHEST YOGA TANTRA

However, it is in the scriptures of Highest Yoga Tantra that an explicit emphasis is placed on developing and exploring the clear light nature of the mind. In order to appreciate the full import of the Highest Yoga Tantra teachings, it is crucial to understand that in Highest Yoga Tantra a distinction is made between two levels of mind. One is the level at which the eighty types of conceptual-ization function, which include the three phases of appearance, increase and attainment.[103] The other level is a very subtle one, that of 'the four empties', which unfold once the eighty types of conceptualization and their vital energies have dissolved.[104] These 'four empties' of this very subtle state of mind represent four degrees in the experience of emptiness. The first, second and third are called 'empty', 'very empty' and 'great empty'. Having passed through these three, you arrive at the fourth degree of emptiness, 'all-empty', which is identified as the ultimate clear light. [105]

Now, as for the techniques used to bring about that experience of subtle clear light, and cause it to manifest within the mind, different approaches are found in different tantras. In the father tantras, such as Guhyasamāja, the main emphasis is placed on the yoga of prāṇa, that is, the vital energies within the subtle channels. On the other hand, in the mother tantras, such as Heruka, the main emphasis is placed on visualizing subtle essences or 'tiklé'[106] at certain vital points within the channels, and then inducing the experience of the four joys.[107] In both of these cases the common feature is that the experience of clear light is brought about through utilizing the coarse levels of mind.

Another tantra of the new translation schools is the Kālacakra Tantra. Although again it emphasizes the practice of bringing about a manifest experience of clear light, there is one aspect that is unique to this tantra. What I am referring to is the practice of 'empty form',[108] which engenders the experience not only of clear light, but specifically of the appearing aspect of clear light. Though comparable to the practice of the illusory body found in tantras like Guhyasamāja, this feature is in fact quite different.

Some masters in the Nyingma tradition maintain that, although the appearing aspect of empty form in the Kālacakra Tantra, and the appearing aspect of tögal experience in Dzogchen practice, are both similar in being appearances of empty forms or empty bodies, the difference is that in the case of the Kālacakra Tantra, this is an aspect of the mind, whereas in tögal it is not an aspect of mind at all, but an aspect of primordial awareness or wisdom.

Even among scholars of the Kālacakra Tantra there are two principal opinions on what this empty form may be. One is that it is an inner experience, which must arise naturally from within, and so it is an experiential state, quite similar to the experience of tögal. The other maintains that this empty body is something that can also be created and manifested externally, in which case there would be a difference between the experience of tögal and the empty form as explained in the Kālacakra Tantra.

In the writings of the new translation schools of tantra there is also explicit mention of how practitioners, having experienced the ultimate clear light, should engage in certain kinds of conduct. The purpose of this is to help the practitioner transcend the polarities of normal ethical conventions. One of them is hunting. Now although you do find such recommendations for practitioners to engage in actions that usually would carry negative associations and be an affront to normal ethical conventions, if you had to account for the need for them only from the writings of the new translation schools, for someone like me it would be rather difficult. Here, I think an understanding the 'four chokshyak'[109]—ways of leaving things in their natural simplicity—of the Nyingma tradition of Dzogchen practice can throw some light on this, and particularly the one which relates to conduct and action, namely "Action, appearances: leave them as they are".

Among the eighty types of conceptualization, which the meditator needs to dissolve in order to lead to the experience of ultimate clear light, there are some that are virtuous states of mind. The reason why these virtuous states of mind need to be dissolved is not that they are in some way negative or neutral, but rather that they are conceptual thought processes.

The practice of tantra, as I have explained up to this point, is that of the new translation schools of Tibet, namely the Sakya, Kagyü, and Geluk or New Kadam traditions. Now let us look at each of them a little more closely.

In the practice of the Kagyü tradition, the main emphasis is on Mahāmudrā. Ultimately, the practice of Mahāmudrā also comes down to the experience of the fundamental innate mind of clear light. In the Kagyü tradition of Mahāmudrā, the entire practice is undertaken within the framework of what are known as the four yogas: one-pointedness, non-duality, one taste, and non-meditation. Sources I have seen differ slightly regarding these terms. In any case, one-pointedness and non-duality emphasize the two stages of śamatha and vipaśyana, while at the stage of the yoga of one taste you have arrived at the practice of clear light.[110] Among the texts which outline the practice of Mahāmudrā, the most elaborate is the one composed by Dakpo Tashi Namgyal.[111] In his writings he states that the Mahāmudrā approach cannot be classified as belonging either to the sūtra system, or to the tantra system, but it is a very distinct path.[112] To say 'distinct' seems to indicate that it is quite a special path, being neither sūtra nor tantra. Of course, individual scholars will have their own views, and if others merely glance over them, they can often end up feeling uncomfortable. Given that there are so many different scholars, it is inevitable that there will be a range of different points of view.

Now let us turn to the Sakya tradition and the practice of 'Lam Dré'—The Path Including Its Result. The distinguishing features of this approach are explained on the basis of what are called the 'triple tantra' or 'three continuums'. The first of these is the causal continuum, which is the ālaya, the basis of all, and this refers to meditation on the four maṇḍalas: the yoga of channels, essences, vital energies and syllables that are visualized at vital points of the body. The ultimate reference for this term ālaya, the causal continuum, is again the fundamental innate mind of clear light.[113]

By the way, you should not be confused by the use of this term 'ālaya'. In the sūtra system, especially in the philosophical tenets of the Cittamātra, the Mind Only school, a type of mind is asserted called the ālayavijñāna, which is the eighth consciousness, frequently translated as the 'store consciousness'.[114] In the writings of the Madhyamaka, one often finds references to emptiness as ālaya, and in the tantras, especially in the Guhyasamāja Tantra, there are frequent references to the fundamental innate mind of clear light as being the ālaya, the same as in the context of *The Path Including Its Result* in the Sakya tradition.

In Dzogchen, however, when this term ālaya is used, it does not have any of these earlier meanings. Here, the ālaya is distinguished from dharmakāya, and when this distinction is made, ālaya must be understood as referring to a neutral state of mind. Ālaya is also said to be quite calm or steady. When you recognize rigpa, this calm ālaya is dispelled, and while thoughts are not yet arising, in that gap comes a growing experience of a clear and vivid rigpa, free from any separation between 'outer' and 'inner'. So the ālaya is said to be calm, placid or undisturbed, but the term is not used in Dzogchen to refer to the fundamental innate mind of clear light.

Now we come to the Gelukpa or New Kadam tradition. Generally when we speak of the Madhyamaka teaching of emptiness—the view of the Middle Way—it should be understood in terms of the emptiness that is common to both sūtra and tantra. For even the śrāvakas and pratyekabuddhas realize this view. Therefore you cannot say that the Middle Way view *per se* is the same as the view of the indivisibility of saṃsāra and nirvāṇa or the union of clarity and emptiness in the Sakya tradition, the Mahāmudrā view of the Kagyü tradition, or the Dzogchen view of the Nyingmapas.

However, you can speak of the view of emptiness from a subjective, experiential point of view in the context of Highest Yoga Tantra. For instance in the Geluk tradition an experiential view of emptiness is realized by a state of mind that has experienced the fourth level of joy, which is called spontaneous or coemergent great bliss. That type of subjective view and all the other views spoken of above—the indivisibility of saṃsāra and nirvāṇa or union of clarity and emptiness of the Sakyapas, the Mahāmudrā view of the Kagyüpas, and the Dzogchen view of the Nyingmapas—all come down to the same thing. You could say that, if you analyse them, they all arrive at the same point.

Now when we use the term 'primordial wisdom of great bliss', we should realize that great bliss is understood causally, in the sense that you arrive at that deepest level of experience of emptiness through an experience of great bliss, which is itself induced through certain techniques. Although at this point there is no conscious experience of bliss or joy, it is through the experience of different levels of joy and bliss that you have arrived at this level of mind. Your experience of emptiness has been attained through the conscious or manifest experience of the subtlest clear light state of mind.

The beauty of this approach is that the experience of bliss is utilized in effecting the dissolution of the coarse levels of mind and energies. This results in that extremely subtle experience of clear light, which is what is called 'the primordial wisdom of great bliss'. To talk about an experience like this that ascertains emptiness—the wisdom of the non-duality of bliss and emptiness—is another way of talking about the fundamental innate mind of clear light. This is the same experience to which Mahāmudrā leads, to which Dzogchen leads, and to which the union of clarity and emptiness leads.

THE UNIQUENESS OF DZOGCHEN

Now we might ask ourselves, if these various approaches from the different traditions all arrive ultimately at the same experience or the same point, why it is said that Dzogpachenpo or Atiyoga is the pinnacle of the nine yānas?[115] The unique feature of this approach, as I mentioned already, is that in the Dzogchen system of meditation you do not employ the coarse levels of mind, such as discursive and conceptual thoughts. Rather, right from the beginning, you make the experience of clear light itself manifest, almost as if it were something tangible—a direct, bare experience of clear light.

Let me now quote from a text by Dodrupchen Jikmé Tenpé Nyima,[116] in which he says:

> In the father tantras, clear light is laid bare or mastered
> through the power of harnessing the vital energy—

prāṇa. To the extent that you have harnessed that
energy, the experience of clear light will deepen and
stabilize.

So in father tantra, it is through focusing on the key point of vital
energy that the clear light becomes evident.

In the mother tantra, you master the yoga of clear light
through the power of working with the essences, and
to the extent that your practice of tummo gains
strength, the radiance and splendour of the experience
of clear light will unfold and become more powerful.

So in these two instances, clear light is accounted for on the basis of
the yoga of subtle energy in father tantra, or the yoga of the essences
in mother tantra. Since this is the case,

However much the vital energy is gathered in, or bliss
blazes and increases, to the same extent thoughts and
concepts are cut through, and the experience of clear
light becomes steadily clearer.

With this, Dodrupchen deals with both father and mother tantras
from the new translation schools of tantra. Now:

This distinction is only on the basis of what is the
main focus or emphasis, for both features are found in
both systems.

In both father and mother tantras, there is a focus on subtle energy
and on essences, and so, apart from a question of emphasis, both
features are found in both classes of tantra. In all of them, whether
father or mother tantras, what is emphasized is the wisdom of non-
dual bliss and emptiness, and so from this point of view, all these
tantras could be said to be non-dual tantras. Now if you were to ask

what is the extraordinary and profound special feature of the Dzogchen tradition:

> In Dzogchen, on the basis of the clear light itself, the way in which the clear light abides is made vivid and certain by the aspect of rigpa or knowing. This is free from any overlay of delusion and from any corrupting effect, due to conceptual thoughts, that will inhibit the experience of clear light.

Dodrupchen makes use of the phrase "on the basis of" clear light, rather than saying "by clear light". According to him, it is "the aspect of rigpa or knowing" that either makes clear light "vivid and certain" or falls under the sway of concepts.

> It is not accomplished as something new, as a result of circumstances and conditions,

for it is already primordially present, in and of itself. Now, here what is known as 'effulgent rigpa' or 'rigpa as energy' comes into the picture. Effulgent rigpa is rigpa that arises from the ground, and as the appearance of the ground. Now the fact that I am speaking of the appearances of the ground means that I am explaining Dzogchen, but in order to explain it, at this point I shall employ the vocabulary of the new schools of tantra.

The fundamental innate mind of clear light is considered to be the nature of mind, or the ultimate root of consciousness. In the case of the five sense consciousnesses and so on—the consciousnesses that arise upon coming into contact with coarse material objects—they arise as a state which is clear and aware, in its essence. If you were to ask: "But is this created by consciousness?" the answer would be that this clear, aware essence comes about because of the fundamental innate mind of clear light. Since this is the case, the fundamental innate mind of clear light is considered to be the ground or root of all consciousness. This is the reason why, when that extremely subtle and ultimate clear light becomes evident, coarse consciousness ceases. Conversely, when coarse consciousness becomes evident, the experience of the ultimate clear light will cease. We are obliged to use the word 'cease', as in a sense it does cease, because it is no longer a direct object of your experience.

So, let us take the example of a sesame seed: it is entirely permeated by sesame oil. In the same way, as soon as there is clear and aware consciousness, it is said to be permeated by the clear light rigpa. Now this clear, aware quality is found in the experience of ālaya as well as in the appearances of the ground. At this point, more specifically, we are distinguishing between the ordinary mind and rigpa, and what is called rigpa is an extraordinary and special case of clarity and awareness.

It seems as if what we are talking about is an extraordinary quality of awareness, and one way to put this into words would be: as soon as there is a clear and aware consciousness, then this aspect of rigpa, this special and extraordinary quality, is already present. Now this aspect of rigpa, this in-dwelling clear light, is what is called 'essential rigpa'.

When coarse consciousness is functioning, the experience of the fundamental innate mind of clear light has 'ceased'. However there is still a definite quality of clarity and awareness that permeates the coarser states of consciousness. Everything in fact, from appearance, increase and attainment onwards, is permeated by clear awareness. This specific quality of rigpa is not what we would call our fundamental nature, the nature of the extraordinary unimpeded rigpa, but it is present as a quality that permeates these states. So when sensory objects are manifesting, coarse conscious-ness is already evident, and yet is always, by its very nature, clear and aware. This factor, present as an extraordinary quality of rigpa, is 'effulgent rigpa'.

Since this is so, even while coarse consciousness is evident, it is permeated by this quality of clear light rigpa. *This* is the quality of rigpa that is to be laid bare. It is a secret, which lies hidden and obscured by conceptual thinking and other factors. Yet through the blessings of the master, the force of your merit and your meditation on the pith instructions, it can be directly introduced in such a way that in the very thick of arising thoughts, you experience this extraordinary state of unimpeded, all-penetrating rigpa. This rigpa which is present in the midst of all the thoughts does not follow after outer objects or inner grasping, but is an awareness that is able to hold its own ground.

Previously, it was as though clear, aware consciousness was holding its own ground. Then you arrive at the ālaya, an unwavering state of consciousness, where consciousness remains without fluctuating, and without following after objects. Gradually your experience of this becomes deeper and deeper. The ālaya is a blank, dull, as if unconscious state. Without thoughts to follow, and so any division into inside or outside, it is unimpeded and clear, in the sense that it is unhindered and unobscured. Yet it is tainted by a quality of dullness.

Once you go beyond the ālaya, it is like someone lifting a heavy hat off his head: an extraordinary quality of rigpa comes to the fore. There is no inner and no outer, nothing like 'this' or 'that', nothing to be experienced by something experiencing it, and no duality of subject and object whatsoever. Yet it is not some unconscious state, where you do not know anything, or never think of anything at all. This rigpa does not have to be sought the way that consciousness knows an object. It is as though all objects of knowledge, outer and inner, come back to and return within it, and this is the extraordinary state of awareness that will arise.

When this aware aspect of clear light rigpa is directly introduced and recognized, it can be identified even in the very thick of arising thoughts. If what has been directly introduced is able to hold its own ground, it offers an extraordinary condition for the profound experience of clear light to arise. You do not have to invoke concepts, thoughts or anything else. This unique quality of the fundamental innate mind of clear light has been introduced, you focus on it as the key point, and, as a result, there dawns an experience unlike any other. This seems to me to be the extraordinary feature of Dzogchen.

Dodrupchen continues:

> It is not accomplished as something new, as a result of circumstances and conditions, but is present from the very outset. Clear light is brought forth by its very own subtle energy, and awakens into clarity; without allowing it to be reabsorbed and lost, you strip it bare and make it your unique focus.

When you are experiencing a coarser state than that of the clear light, one in which thoughts are proliferating and dissolving, these two factors—coarse consciousness and clear light—are blended, and so if you cannot focus on a key point of practice at this point, it is very difficult to make a distinction between thought and clear light. The secret mantra teachings of the new translation schools would approach this in their own way: thoughts, previously so active, would be cut through and radically blocked, so leading to the experience of the fundamental innate mind of clear light. In Dzogchen, by relying on the skilful pith instructions, in the very midst of thoughts themselves, the aware quality of clear light that is present is stripped bare, and you focus on this, as the key point. Consequently:

> Clear light is brought forth by its very own subtle energy, and awakens into clarity; without allowing it to be reabsorbed and lost, you strip it bare and make it your unique focus. The ultimate key point is an awareness that can clearly perceive the way in which basic space and wisdom are present. On the basis of that key point, the realization of clear light radiates in splendour, becoming clearer and clearer, like a hundred million suns.

Now if you were to ask what it is that makes this approach so unique and extraordinary:

> The process of gathering the coarse vital energy into
> the central channel, or that of the blazing and melting
> of the red and white essences, only takes place as long
> as you are practising it.

Because the experience here is one which arises through the power of your efforts, Dodrupchen says, "it only takes place as long as you are practising it". But in Dzogchen, while thoughts are active, rigpa permeates them all, so that even at the very moment when powerful thoughts like attachment and aversion are arising, there remains a pervasive quality of clear light rigpa. That rigpa is what you seek to recognize, highlight, strip bare and make into your practice.

> Here, in Dzogchen, since the clear light's natural way
> of being is like the sun and its rays, inseparable, if you
> are able, through this, to bring out the radiance of
> genuine mind, you will be able to maintain the
> experience of clear light in meditation, without it
> fluctuating, or coming and going.

Even in the 'post-meditation' state, while the six consciousnesses are actually functioning, you are introduced directly, on the basis of the clear light rigpa. Consequently, even situations such as these must be considered as meditation. In this context 'meditation' involves no split between subject and object. In any case, if rigpa is able to hold its own and remain steady, this leads to what is known as "no difference between meditation and post-meditation".[117] So there is what we might call a linkage between meditation and post-meditation. This being the case:

> You will be able to maintain the experience of clear
> light in meditation, without it fluctuating, or coming

and going. This then does not just mean being introduced to the clear light and maintaining it, *on the basis
of our present state of mind.*

This is really important. It is not a matter of resting in a state where,
at the same time as the six consciousnesses are functioning, our
present consciousness is simply not thinking about or engaging in
its objects. This is the main key point. A lot of us can say something
like, "I have achieved a state of mind at rest" or "I'm maintaining
the nature of mind", while in fact the confusion of thoughts is
merely put aside for a while and the mind is just resting. There is a
great danger that people can become confused about this. It is not
what Dodrupchen means by clear light:

> This then does not just mean being introduced to the
> clear light and maintaining it, *on the basis of our present
> state of mind.*
> Here the aware aspect of clear light or effulgent
> rigpa...

He is referring here to the effulgent rigpa, which emerges from the
essential rigpa,

> Here the aware aspect of clear light or effulgent rigpa
> is stripped bare, and you penetrate further into the
> depths of clear light to what is called 'attaining
> warmth'. This corresponds to the training in the yoga
> of clear light found in the mother tantras and other
> approaches, in which you focus on the channels, vital
> energies and essences as the key point. In Dzogchen,
> the aware aspect of clear light is such that even while
> objects seem to arise...

The appearances of objects do arise, but even as they arise, rigpa is
still present, and so...

> ...even while objects seem to arise, it is rigpa, not
> caught up by those objects, that is aroused,

That is to say, rigpa does not follow after objects of dualistic grasping, outer or inner, and is laid bare, "aroused" in the sense that it holds its own ground.

> ...and it is on the basis of this that you train. This can
> more than serve as a substitute for meditating on the
> channels, vital energies and essences.

This is what Dodrupchen Jikmé Tenpé Nyima says.

So it is at this point, with the bringing about of the experience of the fundamental innate mind of clear light, that the approach of the new translation schools of tantra and that of the old translation school of tantra ultimately converge. If you understand the distinguishing feature of the Dzogchen approach in such a manner, then you will be able to appreciate its uniqueness.

By making these observations I do not mean to imply that I have gained any great insight. But I have consulted a number of different texts, and I know that if you compare and relate them to one another, and so arrive at a certain understanding, you can really see the features that are unique. However, if I were to talk at length about what can be found in a few scattered sources, apart from your being able to say: "Well, I suppose that must be right," it would be difficult for you to gain real certainty.

The connection between lower and higher sources is such that the key points and qualities spoken of in the context of lower approaches are incorporated upward into the higher approaches. That is fine, but if you use the fact that something is simply not clearly spelled out in lower approaches as proof that it is a unique feature of higher approaches, it poses a problem. There may be something considered a positive quality in lower approaches that is incorporated into a higher approach. Equally something can be present in higher approaches which is not found in lower approaches. If there is something explained to be a wonderful quality in a lower approach that is found all the more complete in a higher approach, then that is a profound and special quality. However, if we had to consider something to be a positive quality in a higher approach solely because it is unknown in lower Buddhist approaches, where does that lead us? What would be the point, then, of even discussing the differences between non-Buddhist systems and Buddhism, let alone between Buddhist approaches? The concept of primal matter—*prakṛti*—for example, is not mentioned in Buddhist sources, but to use that to say that it therefore must be something profound will hardly do, will it?

ESSENTIAL RIGPA AND EFFULGENT RIGPA

Dodrupchen Jikmé Tenpé Nyima mentions four possible states that provide instances of essential rigpa and effulgent rigpa:[118]

— a state that is effulgent rigpa, but not essential rigpa
— a state that is essential rigpa, but not effulgent rigpa
— a state that is both
— a state that is neither of the two

1) Now the first of these—that which is only effulgent rigpa and not essential rigpa—is the aspect of rigpa we discussed earlier, which is to be identified and experienced only when coarse levels of mind and conceptual thoughts are active. At that point the type of clear light experienced is the effulgent rigpa.

2) As for what is essential rigpa, and not effulgent rigpa, this is the type of rigpa that is experienced ultimately, and it is uniquely clear light.

3) In the case of the third alternative, that which is both: if it is effulgent rigpa, that does not necessarily mean it is not essential rigpa. For in the third vision[119]—rigpa attaining its full measure—there is effulgent rigpa, in that these visions are the appearances of the ground, and yet there is also essential rigpa, in that you have taken a firm stance within the essence. So that

which is both effulgent and essential rigpa is found in the third
vision, rigpa attaining its full measure.

In fact, the first three of the four visions are experiences that arise
as a result of your having taken a firm stance in rigpa, and so they
are experiences or qualities of rigpa that are both essential rigpa and
effulgent rigpa at one and the same time.

4) Now for the fourth possible alternative: a rigpa that is neither
   the rigpa of the ground nor the rigpa of the appearances of the
   ground. If there is rigpa, must it be either the rigpa of the
   ground or the rigpa of the appearances of the ground? No, not
   necessarily. For there is a 'rigpa of all-embracing spontaneous
   presence, the dharmakāya wisdom of fruition', also called 'rigpa
   of all-embracing spontaneous presence which is the ultimate
   state of freedom', and this is neither the rigpa of the ground, nor
   the rigpa of the appearances of the ground.

On the one hand, the appearances of the ground have finished
dissolving into basic space, and so it would seem that this becomes
one with the extremely subtle clear light of the ground. But on
the other hand, there is a distinction to be made, because this
'rigpa of all-embracing spontaneous presence' is the ultimate
fruition. The term refers to the ultimate nature, and implies con-
summation.

SELF-ARISING WISDOM

In his commentary to *The Treasury of the Dharmadhātu*, Longchen
Rabjam[120] speaks of self-arising wisdom, which is in fact the rigpa
that I have been explaining:

> Self-arising wisdom is rigpa that is empty, clear and
> free from all elaboration, like an immaculate sphere of
> crystal. Its very being is such that it never explores
> objects of the senses.

This "self-arising wisdom" is rigpa, which in essence is primordially pure. Longchenpa describes it as "empty and clear". To call it empty is to refer to its essence, primordially pure. To call it clear is to speak of its nature, spontaneously present. As such, it is "free from all elaboration", and free from the elaborations of adventitious phenomena. So it is like a flawless crystal sphere, and truly "its very being is such that it never explores objects of the senses". Whatever phenomena of dualistic grasping arise, outwardly or inwardly, as Longchenpa says:

> It abides as the ground for the arising of all this, but when it comes to its own true nature, whether anything arises or not is not the issue. And so it is vivid in its natural lucidity, unimpeded in its emptiness, and pristine in its primordial purity.

He continues:

> In its true nature, rigpa is free from any elaboration, and when things arise as its energy, it does not analyse objects outwardly, examine inwardly, or interpose itself in between. By simply identifying that non-conceptual, pristine, naked rigpa, you realize there is nothing other than this true nature, free from elaboration, in all its sheer nakedness. This is non-dual self-arising wisdom.

Longchenpa now takes the example of a reflection in a mirror. When the reflection appears, it is not as though the mirror has to go out after the form reflected, since the place where those external shapes arise is back within the mirror itself. He explains:

> Like a reflection in a mirror, when objects and perceptions manifest to rigpa, that pristine and naked awareness which does not proliferate into thought is

called 'the inner power,[121] the responsiveness that is
the ground for the arising of things'.

So whatever arises as subject or object, rigpa is not bound by any
dualistic grasping whatsoever. Longchenpa continues:

> When there is no recognition, and consciousness
> streams out toward concepts, this is what is called
> 'dualistic thinking'... For a yogin who realizes the
> naked meaning of Dzogpachenpo, rigpa is fresh, pure
> and naked, and objects may manifest and appear within
> rigpa, but it does not lose itself externally to those
> objects. Dualistic grasping, the source of saṃsāra, is
> erased, rigpa resides in all its pristine, naked freshness,
> and as a sign that it is not lost in objects, there is no
> fixation on appearances, nor any urge to suppress or
> indulge them.[122]

THE THREE MODES OF LIBERATION

The teachings describe three extraordinary modes of liberation:[123]

1) Liberation through recognition of thought;
2) Liberation where the thought frees itself; and
3) Liberation of thoughts as dharmakāya, without their bringing
   either benefit or harm.

The true, and best, mode of liberation is where thoughts are liberated without benefit or harm, and this is compared to a thief
breaking into an empty house. There is nothing for the thief to steal,
nothing for an empty house to lose. Even though thought arises, it
does so within the expanse of rigpa, and owing to the energy of
rigpa. When it ceases, it ceases in and of itself.

When a thought is rising, it remains inseparable from the basic
space of rigpa. But what can happen is that we think: "Oh! A
thought has come up", or "A thought has just gone", or "Thinking's

not appropriate". The Dzogchen method of liberation is not tainted in the slightest by any such sense of grasping. In fact, the issue is not even whether thoughts arise or not. Thoughts themselves remain neither beneficial nor harmful, and in this way, they are liberated as dharmakāya.

There are one or two other points, to clarify the three modes of liberation in Dzogchen. In a sense, there is a recognition that thoughts are something to be eliminated. However, say we identify a thought as 'something to be eliminated'. This is a way of freeing thoughts after a fashion, but it is not the extraordinary mode of liberation found in the three modes.

Then again, a thought cannot stand on its own, because the whole essence of thoughts is such that moment by moment they change and they dissolve. So a thought will cease anyway, in and of itself, and, in a manner of speaking, be liberated. Yet this is a state tainted by grasping at concepts about thoughts, and so this recognition of thoughts still binds you. Again, this is not the extraordinary mode of liberation associated with the Dzogchen teachings.

The extraordinary mode of liberation, according to the Dzogchen tradition, is that thoughts have no power to benefit or harm. This is applied across the board, for each and every thought.

THE IMPORTANCE OF THE PRELIMINARY INVESTIGATION

To give an example from the tradition common to sūtras and tantras, there is a key point that we find in Āryadeva's *Four Hundred Verses on the Middle Way*[124]:

> The awareness that is the seed of existence,
> Has objects as its sphere of activity,
> When selflessness is seen in objects,
> The seed of existence is destroyed.

So according to this tradition, one common to both sūtras and tantras, the root of conditioned existence lies in our closed-mindedness and our grasping at things as truly existent. The way to

abandon this closed-mindedness and grasping at true existence is
with a mind that sees the lack of a true self or identity. This, then, is
the way to proceed that is common to both sūtras and tantras.

In a strictly tantric context, Buddhajñāna, in his *Means of
Accomplishment Entitled 'All Good'*,[125] states that the root of existence
is created by the thinking processes of ignorance, in other words it
is created by thought. This gives rise to a question: "Isn't one of the
special features of deity yoga and the development stage in tantra
that you see the lack of an identity or self? Isn't perceiving the lack
of an inherent identity a special feature of meditating on deities? In
which case, how do thoughts, as the seeds of conditioned existence,
cause harm?" This is the question raised by this whole discussion.

The term *namtok*, thought, in this case means grasping at things
as truly existent. In his commentary to the *Means of Accomplishment
Entitled 'All Good'*, Thagana[126] says that the term 'thought', as it is
used here in this text, is to be interpreted as meaning grasping at
true reality. So in any case, in both sūtras and tantras, ignorance—
marigpa—is said to be the root of saṃsāra, and in order to annihilate
this ignorance, in whichever way we are fixated on things, we refute
that fixation by seeing with a mind that has attained certainty about
the selflessness of things.

Now we come to the special feature of Dzogchen, along with all
its ramifications. From the point of view of someone like me, who
follows Dzogchen step by step, the way to examine this is as follows.
In traditions where only coarser levels of consciousness are accepted, the object to be examined is the way in which consciousness grasps at an identity or self in things, and so the only choice
you have is to meditate on a way in which to see things as devoid
of self.

Then, according to the traditions where subtler levels of
consciousness are accepted, when the fundamental innate mind of
clear light is experienced, grasping at things as true never actually
occurs. At the same time, however, virtuous states of mind can be
generated. Note that the term 'primordial wisdom'—*yeshé*—is not
used here, but rather the term 'fundamental innate mind of clear

light', and this is what is capable of generating virtuous states of mind. In the context of clear light, virtuous and positive factors can be arrived at, but non-virtue does not occur. So as soon as there is a mind that cuts through the false suppositions of mistaken thought patterns, all thoughts cease, and in the wake of the cessation of the eighty types of conceptualization, grasping at things as true simply does not arise. This is another way to proceed. In this approach then, by undermining the object of fixation which is taken as real, you are meditating on its lack of inherent identity, and so removing the entire basis on which those thoughts, which grasp at self and grasp at things as real, can arise. By undermining and removing that basis, you overcome grasping at self.

In Dzogchen, there are three factors: essence, nature and energy. Now to say, simply: "the essence is primordial purity" is not good enough; you have to have arrived at a certainty in your mind that the essence *is* primordially pure. The mere fact that it is primordially pure is not much help; you must have an experience and understanding of that essence as being primordial purity. It is the same with any phenomenon, say a vase. It is no use that it is empty, no use that it is, by nature, primordially pure, if you do not know and understand that it is.

Just so, when we speak of the three aspects of essence, nature and energy, we can go on repeating: "the essence is primordial purity", but what relevance does it have to our situation? This is what we have to understand right from the beginning. That is why at this juncture we engage in what is known as 'searching for the hidden flaw of mind', as one of the preliminary practices. In the tradition common to both sūtra and tantra, searching for the hidden flaw of mind is a stage that you cannot do without.

When Dzogchen teaches about the essence of rigpa, and it says that you meditate without engaging in any analysis, and without falling under the sway of any dualistic grasping, this is quite different from the two previous approaches. There is no following after any object that has been grasped or apprehended by the mind. For example, when you meditate on emptiness, what happens is that you meditate by using some means of conceiving of the empty nature of things, and so this is a case of ordinary consciousness following after an object. The discrepancy between Dzogchen practice and the two practices outlined above has proved quite controversial.

However, what we must not forget is that here we are talking about a preliminary phase. Let's take an example. When astronauts are launched into outer space, they arrive at a state of weightlessness. But they only experience this once they are up in space. Up until that point, weightlessness will not be part of their experience. So, we have to proceed on the basis of our specific situation, and while we are in the process of training our minds, what we have been talking about here—the preliminary investigation—is indispensable in order to proceed. There is no controversy about this.

Now there is something which Dodrupchen Jikmé Tenpé Nyima says in this regard. I consider Dodrupchen to be my teacher, and he makes a point that is very important: "In order for you to become a suitable and receptive vessel for the direct introduction to rigpa, it is explained that you must train your mind through reasoning that examines ultimate reality".[127] What he is saying is that in order to become a suitable vessel for the introduction to rigpa, you need the preliminary phase of searching for the hidden flaw of mind, whereby you train your mind through reasoning that examines ultimate reality.

Dodrupchen continues: "The teachings describe the way in which rigpa, as experienced on the path, emerges from the original ground." When you are training in the path of Dzogchen, the fundamental point is effulgent rigpa. Since the practitioner of Dzogchen has been introduced to this effulgent rigpa and is practising on the basis of it, this becomes rigpa in the context of the path.

In fact, Dodrupchen says three things: first, as a preliminary, you must engage in "reasoning that examines ultimate reality". Second, "the teachings describe the way in which rigpa, as experienced on the path, emerges from the original ground". And thirdly, "there is the usefulness of saying that rigpa has no fixed basis or origin".

He continues, "In trekchö practice, it is said that what is made evident is the inseparability of space and rigpa. So if you know this whole basis well, you will understand how to practise the union of rigpa and emptiness. Yet it would be inappropriate to speak of this without thinking, just inventing things." So, following the logic of this, it is said that you need to come to a definitive understanding of the view of Madhyamaka.

But one question still remains unanswered, and it is this: "Once you have been directly introduced to rigpa, the ground of Dzogchen, and you are maintaining it in practice, don't you use some object on which to focus? At that point, do you use some way of focusing on emptiness as the object, or not?" Since this question is raised, it needs to be given quite a lot of thought.

THE PLACE OF ANALYTICAL MEDITATION

In general, in many of the tantras of the new translation schools, there are no explicit or elaborate references to meditation on emptiness during the main practice, but rather to meditative states of great bliss. Although that is the case, still we do find emphasis on the importance of understanding emptiness prior to engaging in the practices of Highest Yoga Tantra, and the realization of emptiness is taken to be a prerequisite or indispensable factor for the successful realization of the stages of Highest Yoga Tantra. Otherwise there can be no meditation on great bliss without the understanding of emptiness.

As far as meditation on emptiness is concerned, there are two approaches: one is meditation that employs discernment and analysis, and one is meditation on the basis of settling, without analysing. Analytical meditation may support the great bliss of the Highest Yoga Tantra system, but in general, in the Highest Yoga Tantra of the new translation schools, meditation on emptiness consists entirely of settling meditation. It is not explained as analytical meditation, because to engage in analytical meditation inhibits the arising of great bliss and prevents the attainment of subtler states of mind. Since it has this effect, analytical meditation is not practised in this context.

However, in the vehicle of the pāramitās, analytical meditation is something that must be practised. The reason why analytical meditation is practised in levels up to and including the lower tantras, is that it is said to be necessary in order to gain certainty about any given object. Consciousness attains certainty about its object and becomes more and more subtle with the progressive dissolution of the vital energy; through the power of such a training, the object is experienced with ever greater clarity. Therefore analytical meditation in the pāramitā yāna leads to certainty about the objects of consciousness, through the progressive refinement of mind into increasing states of subtlety. And the certainty to which this meditation leads has the capacity to develop a hundred or a thousand fold—to an exceptional degree.

Why then is analytical meditation to be avoided in Highest Yoga Tantra? If you embark on analysis, there is the risk that the subtle energy you are gathering in through this practice will be scattered outwardly, and so it is a great hindrance to the whole purpose of the meditation. This is why the new translation schools of Highest Yoga Tantra explain that you should put aside analytical meditation and meditate on emptiness solely through settling meditation.

Now according to the Dzogchen teachings of the Nyingma school of Vajrayāna, once the yogin has reached a definitive experience by analysing the view of selflessness, and he or she is maintaining the state of rigpa as the main practice, no ordinary analysis is employed. Instead, consciousness itself simply rests. So there seems to be an extraordinary key point here, and Dodrupchen agrees.[128]

In his commentary to his *Treasury of the Dharmadhātu*, Longchen Rabjam writes that the way in which things appear is proof of their essential emptiness. How does he describe this? He takes the fact that things arise interdependently and infallibly as his reason, and on this basis, he arrives at his proof. And this is exactly what the Prāsaṅgika school describes as 'appearances dispelling the extreme of existence and emptiness dispelling the extreme of non-existence'. In fact, Longchen Rabjam then goes on to quote Nāgārjuna to this effect. But first he says:[129]

His Holiness the Dalai Lama at the Pagode de Vincennes, Paris 1982.

ABOVE: *Portrait statue of the 'Great Fifth' Dalai Lama, made during his lifetime.*

RIGHT TOP: *Granting the empowerment of Padmasambhava and his Eight Manifestations,* Paris 1982.

RIGHT BELOW: *During the teaching and empowerment,* Paris 1982.

© P. Dacre

© P. Lelluch

ABOVE: *During the empowerment, Sogyal Rinpoche casts his flower into the maṇḍala,* Paris 1982.

RIGHT TOP: *His Holiness giving the Dzogchen teaching in* London, 1984.

RIGHT BELOW: *During the teaching,* London 1984.

ABOVE: *His Holiness teaching in the Rosicrucian Temple,* Helsinki, 1988.

LEFT: *The Dalai Lama crosses the meridian, Greenwich Old Royal Observatory,* July 1984.

BELOW: *The Dzogchen teachings in* San Jose, 1989.

Courtesy Rigpa Fellowship USA

ABOVE: *His Holiness teaching in* San Jose, 1989.

BELOW: *His Holiness and Lamas,* San Jose 1989.

Courtesy Rigpa Fellowship USA

Therefore, since appearances manifest in all their variety, they are emptiness. *The Reverberation of Sound*[130] states:

> Furthermore, I shall explain the nature of dharmatā:
> Such a nature as this cannot be determined to be
>   any one thing,
> So however you label it, that is how it appears.
> From the basis underlying the variety of names
> Appear the elaborations of many terms.
> On account of the variety of names, in no way
>   determinate,
> The underlying meaning is empty by virtue of
>   merely being labelled.
> Since emptiness has never existed as anything
>   whatsoever,
> The nature of things manifests as though pure.

Ārya Nāgārjuna says:

> Since there are no phenomena
> That do not occur interdependently
> Therefore there are no phenomena
> That are not empty.

If, as in this case, what is stated in one source is also said in another, it is important to know how to relate higher and lower sources.

TWO WAYS OF INTRODUCING RIGPA

To return to the subject of rigpa, Longchenpa states:

> At this point, there are two ways to identify rigpa
> directly:
> *Direct introduction without relying on a key point* is where
> there is no outward elaboration or projection of mind,

no inner grasping, no attempt to place the mind in between these two, no fabrication by the ordinary mind, and no stirring of thoughts. Bare consciousness that is uninterrupted, even and all-pervading is present all the time.[131]

So this seems to be one way the introduction can take place, and it occurs through the blessings of the master. Given that the consciousness we already possess is beginningless, the aware aspect of clear light—its natural radiance—will be present at any point, just like the oil that saturates the sesame seed. And it provides the basis on which introduction can take place. So what is being described here is a direct introduction effected when outer circumstances, like intense devotion to the master, and inner circumstances come together.

Next, Longchenpa gives:

Six ways of direct introduction, which employ key points:[132]

1. Direct introduction by holding the mind's attention.

2. Direct introduction with the mind at rest, which involves introduction on the basis of the mind remaining stable, in its own place.

3. Direct introduction by getting to the root of the matter.

4. Direct introduction by getting rid of the sense of substantiality, which is to say that, after having cast out that sense of substantiality, you make a thorough examination. Longchenpa says that "when mind is lost to its object", any object that the mind follows is banished, and so eventually it is as though the mind has nowhere at all to go. This is the basis on which the introduction takes place.

5. Direct introduction in the interval between consciousness and its objects.

6. Direct introduction by causing distraction. This is like the experience when you are deeply absorbed in a conversation, and all

of a sudden someone calls your name and distracts your attention. In that moment, direct introduction takes place. A good example would be when the sound of 'phaṭ!' is uttered; in that gap between a former thought and the next, an unimpeded rigpa is introduced. At first the mind is astonished, yet within that startled state is an all-penetrating, unimpeded quality: "struck by wonder, yet all is transparently clear".[133]

The astonishment at this point is not the rigpa of Dzogchen. It is our feeling and our reaction to something sudden, where we ask ourselves: "What happened?" That state of not thinking about anything, or not recalling anything at all, is the neutral state of ālaya. It is explained as calm and steady, and at the present is sullied by a stupid dullness. Were this the introduction to Dzogchen, then it would all become rather simple. Every time you fell asleep, you would be on the point of being introduced to Dzogchen. And your whole life could just pass by in such a state.

Nevertheless if this experience occurs first, it would seem to be extremely useful as a foundation for the introduction to rigpa. Usually the mind is engaged in all kinds of thoughts—and lots of them. So you begin by removing them, in order that the mind is not doing or thinking about anything, and is, first of all, just resting. This state is not the introduction to Dzogchen, nor is it the rigpa of Dzogchen. But at a certain point, when outer and inner circumstances come together, the very nature of this unwavering state of mind is such that it is the basis on which a bare awareness can be experienced, a state unlike any other, untainted by any trace of stupid dullness, but all-penetrating and unimpeded, within and without.

In the vocabulary of Dzogchen, the conventional designation for this is 'rigpa'. One way of describing rigpa is to say it is all-penetratingly clear and unimpeded. It has no trace of the stupid, dull quality, but is naturally relaxed, pristine and limpid. This is the kind of experience that will come. As for how you meditate when such an experience arises, it involves what is called 'primordially present mindfulness'. When rigpa is introduced, then this primordially present mindfulness comes with it naturally, just as the rays shine from the sun. We have no need to resort to a mindfulness created through effort, as rigpa itself holds its own ground through this natural kind of mindfulness.

Then you continue to meditate, and as meditation progresses there are the *four chokshyak*, ways of leaving things in their natural simplicity:

> View, like a mountain: leave it as it is
> Meditation, like the ocean: leave it as it is
> Action, appearances: leave them as they are
> Fruition, rigpa: leave it as it is

Then, as a support for these four, we find the three samādhis:[134]

> Samādhi of the all-pervasive seal;
> Samādhi of great, natural abiding;
> Samādhi of supreme immediacy.

Dodrupchen says that all phenomena are quite definitely such that they arise as rigpa's energy or rigpa's display.[135] From the point of view of the new schools of tantra, everything that appears arises as the display of great bliss, and the display of emptiness. In the terminology of Dzogchen whatever manifests arises as the display of rigpa, and that is certain. So the agent responsible for all of this—as well as the space and ground for it all—is the single state of clear light. Everything, in fact, is the display or array of clear light, and the conceptual approach of the Prāsaṅgikas too would seem to prepare you for this extraordinary understanding.

Such experiences of clear light will arise, and when they do, you are left without any fear of falling into saṃsāra; you are left without any hope of attaining nirvāṇa; you are left without any hope or fear whatsoever. All experiences and all feelings, be they good or bad, karma, its results, birth and death and change: all of this manifests as the magical display of clear light.

This is what the 'Twelve Kinds of Vajra Laughter'[136] are pointing to. When we grasp at something in the external world, swept away by its seeming solidity, we are convinced it is so real and so true, and something must be done about it. If it is something painful, we think: "What can I do to get rid of this pain?" If we see something attractive that we like and want, we will think: "That I must have!" When our minds are full of such tight and rigid grasping, this is what the 'Twelve Kinds of Vajra Laughter' are talking about.

Now there is one more point to cover from the commentary to *The Treasury of the Dharmadhātu.* When experiences like these arise, there are also spiritual traps, which are said to be "the greatest ways in which rigpa is bound".[137] There are countless variations of these spiritual traps, but Longchen Rabjam summarizes them as a group of ten. They are:

1. The trap of being bound by concepts;
2. The trap of being bound in non-conceptual states;
3. The trap of being caught up in effort;
4. The trap of grasping at appearances as true;
5. The trap of seeking elsewhere for ultimate truth;
6. The trap of grasping at empty forms as having characteristics;
7. The trap of the view of emptiness that loses sight of the true nature;
8. The trap of aimlessly chattering about your 'realization' of Dzogchen;
9. The trap of 'meditation' on 'voidness', as futile as throwing a stone in the dark;
10. The trap of enduring suffering because you are missing the key points.

There are other topics, but this brief explanation covers what I know about Dzogchen. The Dzogchen sources and scriptures deal with an enormous range of themes. There are, for example, the category of mind *Semdé*, the category of space *Longdé*, and the category of pith instructions *Mengakdé*. Even within the category of pith instructions, there are also four cycles: outer, inner, secret and innermost secret unexcelled. So there are many topics, and there are said to be many hundreds of thousands of tantras associated with them. There is also a large number of teaching manuals, but they do not differ so much from one another, as they are the kind of manuals that parallel the great scriptural sources. There is another approach, the style of which does not so much reproduce these great sources as give direct instructions to yogic practitioners. These are the bases on which the teachings take place.

In general then, there is one method of instruction that follows the scholar's or paṇḍita's tradition, and one that follows the yogin's or kusuli's tradition. When we talk about the scholar's method of instruction, this encompasses *The Seven Treasuries* of Longchen Rabjam, especially *The Treasury of the Supreme Vehicle* and *The Treasury of the Dharmadhātu*. Because such texts discuss such a huge number of topics, in considerable detail, with the aim of establishing certainty, they constitute the method of instruction according to the scholar's tradition. In collections like the *Nyingtik Yabshyi*, the treatment is much more concise, because they are taught according to the yogin's method of instruction. So there is a teaching that explains the scriptural sources, and a teaching that follows the tradition of the pith instructions.

The underpinnings of my teachings here have been the writings of Longchen Rabjam, and I have spoken selectively, basing my comments on the commentary to the *Treasury of the Dharmadhātu*. I have enjoyed myself over the last two days, and would like to thank all of you here who have been listening with such great interest. What I have taught so far should be taken simply as a key, a basis or a source, which should be complemented later on by further reading, meditation and practice. Only then will what I have taught here become beneficial and helpful.

For an actual practitioner of Dzogchen, what is of vital importance is to maintain a continuous effort in your practice. As I remarked yesterday, and I would like to reiterate: to have a real experience and realization of an advanced level of the path, it is crucial to lay a very firm foundation and grounding in the common paths. This is why in the Dzogchen system great emphasis is placed on the preliminary practices, or *ngöndro*. In the Dzogchen approach, the common ngöndro or preliminary practices include the practices of taking refuge, generating bodhicitta, the Vajrasattva meditation and recitation, maṇḍala offering, prostrations and guru yoga. The complete preliminary practices are explained systematically in great detail in a text called 'The Words of My Perfect Teacher'—*Kunzang Lamé Shyalung*, composed by Dza Patrul Rinpoche, as notes taken at a teaching given by his teacher Jikmé Gyalwé Nyugu. This text has been translated and is available in English.

So if you maintain a sustained effort, without losing your hope or your courage, you will make progress along your spiritual path, and that is certain.

PARTING ADVICE

His Holiness's closing words, after being thanked on behalf of Rigpa and all those present:

I am deeply touched by your words of thanks. As I always say, everyone has a responsibility, so we must seize that responsibility and try to contribute our own individual share. Let us try to have a better world, a happier world, with happier human beings. What I usually call my nirvāṇa—permanent cessation of negative emotional thoughts—that is my private business, my private nirvāṇa. What we really need is nirvāṇa for society—a happier human community, a society filled with loving-kindness. That's what we want, and we can build it. And for this, everyone has a responsibility. My own nirvāṇa, I can pursue by myself; that's my business. Thank you, thank you very much.

AFTERWORD

A GIFT TO THE WORLD

A TEACHING GIVEN BY

NYOSHUL KHENPO JAMYANG DORJE

ON OCTOBER 8, 1989 IN SAN JOSE

Nyoshul Khenpo was born in 1932 in the Derge region of Kham. He studied under twenty-five great masters, among whom was Shedrup Tenpé Nyima, the reincarnation of Nyoshul Lungtok. From him, he received the teachings of Longchen Nyingtik and particularly the Great Oral Lineage of Pith Instructions (*Mengak Nyengyü Chenmo*) of Dzogpachenpo. This became Khenpo's special lineage, a lineage which passed back to the Primordial Buddha, in an unbroken line, through such extraordinary masters as Khenpo Ngakchung, Nyoshul Lungtok, Patrul Rinpoche, Jikmé Lingpa, Longchenpa, Vimalamitra, and Padmasambhava. Khenpo passed these teachings on to a few close disciples, as well as to a number of the greatest masters and lineage holders of his time. He wrote a definitive *History of the Dzogchen Nyingtik*, containing the biographies of the lineage masters, and a remarkable collection of poetic songs of realization. Nyoshul Khenpo was such a consummate master of Dzogchen, and such an authority on the teachings of Longchenpa, that his disciples regarded him as Longchenpa in the flesh. He was the teacher of many of the younger generation of lamas, as well as a number of western Buddhist teachers. He passed away in France in August 1999. No one who met him can ever forget his extraordinary presence or the spirit in which he taught, which embodied so perfectly the fathomless ease and vastness of Dzogpachenpo.

Nyoshul Khenpo was one of Sogyal Rinpoche's most beloved masters, and was present and taught at many Rigpa retreats and gatherings in the period 1984-1996. One of these occasions was during His Holiness the Dalai Lama's teachings at San Jose, where he gave this teaching in the evening of 8 October, after His Holiness's session. The translator was Richard Barron (Chökyi Nyima).

A GIFT TO THE WORLD

How fortunate we are, all of us, to have had this opportunity to gather in the presence of His Holiness the Dalai Lama and receive this profound teaching of Dzogpachenpo, the Great Perfection. His Holiness is no ordinary teacher: he is universally regarded and accepted as an emanation of Avalokiteśvara, the bodhisattva who embodies the compassion of all the buddhas. To receive such a profound teaching from such an authentic and realized teacher makes this a very holy occasion.

At this point I would also like to express my appreciation to Sogyal Rinpoche, who himself, it might be noted, is recognized as the incarnation of one of the close students of Padmasambhava, the eighth century master called Nanam Dorje Dudjom. I am particularly impressed by the energy that Sogyal Rinpoche has displayed in his activities in seeking to bring the Dharma to the west, and to establish and spread the teachings of the Buddha here, so that they may once again shine like the sun, this time in the lands of the west. I would like to express my appreciation and thanks to him for all the preparations that went into this gathering, and for the work he has done in establishing the connections with all of you that brought you to this event.

When we refer to the Buddhadharma, we are speaking of a tradition that stretches back two and a half thousand years, to the time when Buddha Śākyamuni appeared in India and first taught the teachings that we now know as Buddhism. It is this event—the appearance of Buddha Śākyamuni in India—which is compared in the teachings to the rising of the sun. In the same way that the sun dispels darkness in the world, the appearance of the Buddha dispels the darkness that lies in the hearts of all beings.

Once this sun had risen, once these teachings had appeared in the world, there developed a tradition where, generation after generation, people followed these teachings, realized the point of them and became models of conduct and practice for others. Thousands upon thousands of individuals attained the fruit of these practices according to the various levels and vehicles of Buddhadharma: the stage of arhat through the practice of the Fundamental Vehicle; the stages of the great bodhisattvas through Mahāyāna practice; and the stage of siddha or realized saint through the Vajrayāna or tantric path. Through the work of these practitioners and scholars, one generation after another—thousands upon thousands of people, practising, studying and realizing the teachings—the tradition of Buddhism came to spread throughout the whole of the east, influencing to some extent virtually every culture in Asia.

Roughly a thousand years ago, this tradition of Buddhism came to Tibet, during the reign of King Trisong Detsen, who is honoured by the Tibetans for his enlightened vision as a ruler of the Tibetan people. Nowadays we are accustomed to thinking of the function of government as being largely that of amassing weaponry and spending a great deal of money on force and aggression. King Trisong Detsen, however, saw his rule of the country of Tibet as a means by which he could establish the tradition of Dharma, and so establish a spiritual tradition that would bring great benefit to his people. During his reign he set about putting this vision into action and making it a reality. He invited scholars and teachers, not only from India, the birthplace of the Buddhadharma, but also from China and other areas surrounding the Tibetan plateau where Buddhism had already spread. He spared no effort in bringing scholars and teachers from all parts of the Buddhist world to Tibet, where they could meet and engage in the task of translating the whole heritage of Buddhism into the Tibetan language. The introduction of Buddhism into Tibet ushered in a millennium of peace and benefit for the Tibetan people, a thousand years during which the entire emphasis was on harmony, on building peace, on creating co-operation, and on bringing benefit to all beings in that part of the world.

It was during this millennium of peace in Tibet that great teachers such as Milarepa attained complete enlightenment through their diligent practice of the teachings of Buddhism. It was during this millennium of peace that great scholars and meditators such as Longchenpa attained the ultimate fruition of the rainbow body, the total transformation of the physical body into light at the moment of death, through the practice of these teachings. Over this period of roughly one thousand years many people, through their practice, attained such levels of realization and very dramatic states of transformation. We must mention also the great Tsongkhapa, the founder of the Gelukpa tradition, and Sakya Paṇḍita of the Sakya order. All of these great teachers of the various traditions appeared during this thousand-year period of peace and prosperity that unfolded in Tibet, and was principally due to the influence of Buddhism on the culture.

The geographical situation of Tibet, on the roof of the world, surrounded by an almost impenetrable barrier of snow mountains, offered an environment in which for a thousand years this spiritual tradition was practised, studied, taught, meditated on, and realized by thousands and thousands of people. And the role of the rulers and government was, by and large, one of supporting and encouraging the development of this spiritual tradition. There are even cases in Tibetan history of rulers who gave up their very lives in order to invite teachers to spread these precious teachings.

The entire body of Buddhist teachings that was developed in Tibet remains intact to the present day. Its foundation has not been undermined, nor has its pinnacle been destroyed. We think of our tradition of Buddhism as a gift we have to offer the world. And all that we, the teachers of the Tibetan Buddhist tradition, would ask is that you accept our offering, enjoy it, make use of it, and benefit from it.

You might be thinking: "What is this gift, what is this Dharma you are talking about?" It is nothing more or less than our own mind. There is no Dharma beyond our own mind. This mind which we all experience when we say "my mind", or we think "I have a mind", this thing we call 'mind' has never had a point of origin throughout beginningless time. There was never a point in time when it began. Rather, there has been a thread of consciousness, a continuum, moment after moment, up to the present instant and on into the future. Even during the short span of this life, from the moment we emerged from our mother's womb, our mind has been continuously busy, continuously thinking.

The way we experience mind at present is as a continuous flow of thoughts, ideas and emotions. Some of these are tinged with desire and attachment, some with pride, some with aggression and anger, and some with jealousy, envy or hatred. But there is this continuous turmoil of thoughts, concepts and emotions churning away in our minds, moment after moment, day and night.

In a way, how we experience our mind in the waking state is very similar to how we experience dreams. Just as some dreams are fruitful and have a meaning, while others are not, some of the things we think with our waking consciousness are useful and bear fruit, while others are simply a waste of time. Whatever the case, on and on goes this relentless activity in the mind. At a certain point we simply get tired of it all. Our mind becomes exhausted. Many of us feel this sense of exhaustion with the non-stop churning and turbulence in our minds. People can even go crazy because of it. They get so tired of so much turmoil in their minds, that finally something cracks and they lose their sanity.

In any case, perhaps the greatest fundamental cause of our suffering, the on-going pain, suffering, and frustration we feel day in, day out, is the unrelenting activity of our mind. So we should begin by addressing the fundamental question of pain and suffering: why do we suffer? This brings us right back to the practice of

Dharma. For this is precisely what Dharma is for: to dispel the suffering we experience as a result of the uncontrolled, relentless activity of our minds. There is this fundamental connection between the Dharma and our mind; for as long as there is a mind to speak of, there is Dharma.

Look at the conflict, chaos and disharmony in the world around us. On a national and international level we see war, invasions and the exploitation of one country by another, all due to nationalistic pride or aggression. Then on a domestic level there are quarrels and disharmony in our own families, where husbands and wives, parents and children, continually disagree with each other and fail to get along. Regardless of what level we look at, all the strife and disharmony in the world comes back to the fact that our own minds are in turmoil. Because of this inner discord, there arise all the external manifestations—inter-personal, domestic, national and international.

All of us seek a state in which our mind abides in peace, however what we actually find is a state of violence and turmoil. Our mind, far from being peaceful, is often very wrathful and constantly obsessed. Now, from the point of view of the teachings of Buddhism, there is a discussion in Buddhist cosmology of the six states or classes of beings in saṃsāric existence. To take one example, the hell realms are described as realms of intense torment and suffering. Beings in the state of hell experience extreme agony on account of the intense heat or cold. The Buddhist teachings point out that the direct cause of such a rebirth is anger in our own mind.

In a way, there is a connection that we can see. Whenever you get angry with someone, you feel hot all over. Your temperature rises. You go red in the face, and you can even give yourself a headache. In the short term, there are very disturbing effects to anger. When that becomes such a habitual pattern that it produces rebirth in hell, the being there experiences, as a result of that pattern, an environment that is on fire, an environment that is totally destructive and totally hostile. We should not consider this as an external place to which people are sent as a punishment. It is the distorted appearance or projection in the minds of beings in those states, caused by their karmic patterns.

So from the point of view of our own mental conditioning, and how we will experience things in the future, we have good reason to learn how to calm our minds and cultivate a state of tranquillity where the mind can simply rest and abide in a state of peace. This is where Buddhism can be of such great help, in providing the means by which we can discipline ourselves to train and transform our own mind. The fact is that no one else can do this for us.

It does not matter how many friends try to help us, or how much we try to rely on things outside of ourselves. Unfortunately, to date, there is no medicine for the mind. There are, it is true, medicines to control the mood, and diminish the awareness or consciousness, but there do not exist medicines for the mind in the same way that there are for the body. We cannot cure the mind that easily, especially by relying on some external situation, person or substance. In order to cure and restore balance to our minds we need to follow a spiritual path, and this is what Buddhism primarily provides.

Otherwise we find ourselves very helpless when we experience personal suffering, which we all do. When some tragedy befalls us— say one of our parents, or our partner, or our lover dies—we have nothing to fall back upon, no mental balance, no state of calmness on which we can depend to deal with such a personal tragedy. Instead we resort to strategies which are self-destructive, like drinking ourselves into oblivion. Yet if you were to ask people who are substance-abusers, why they drink or take drugs so much, it is unlikely that they would reply that it is a really good thing to do, or that they find something inherently valuable in getting blind drunk. That is not the point. People do this to themselves in order to try to stop thinking. Whether they are conscious of it or not, what they are trying to do is block out thoughts that they do not want to think, and they have no other means of doing it. This is what can drive people to take their own lives, as the ultimate way of trying to escape their pain. They find themselves in a state of total despair, because they have nowhere else to turn. No one outside of them-selves, nothing they can ingest, no external situation they can put themselves in, is going to be of any ultimate help, and so in utter desperation they turn to suicide.

The whole purpose of the Buddhist teachings is to provide an alternative to this rather bleak picture, to give someone who has nothing to rely on something that is truly reliable—namely their own personal cultivation, through their own effort, of a state of mind which abides in calm. What we all need is for our mind to reside in a state of peace. The last thing we need is more mental turmoil.

At this point, let me give you a very brief overview of the Buddhist teachings, as I understand them. We hear a great deal of reference to what seem to be three different approaches: Madhyamaka, Mahāmudrā, and Mahāsandhi or Dzogchen. First and foremost, we should understand that all of these have a common root, what we might call the root yāna or Fundamental Vehicle. This involves a recognition on the part of the practitioner that all the suffering we experience as an individual, all the suffering that is integral to this cycle of existence, has its root in the mind, in the mind of the individual being that experiences that suffering. Perhaps the greatest stumbling block to true happiness is our misperception, our insistence on perceiving in terms of self or ego, where we take the mind, or body, or the mind-body complex, to be a single, eternal entity in and of itself.

When we begin to examine that fixation, both intellectually and through the practice of meditation, we can determine that the body, which we misperceive as having a self-nature of its own, is in fact composed of smaller elements. We can trace this right down to the sub-atomic level. We can begin to see how our mind-body aggreg-ate is just that, an aggregate, a compound of different elements, rather than some definite entity in itself. Then, rather than relying on some naive assumption of selfhood, we begin to understand the physical *body* as something composite, impermanent, and lacking any self-nature of its own.

When we begin to examine our *minds*, as the other element in our make-up, we can again determine, both intellectually and eventually through direct experience, that mind *per se* is not a thing in and of itself. We are not discussing some single entity when we discuss mind. What we are discussing has no origin, no cessation, and cannot be localized or described in ordinary conceptual terms. This examination, this kind of analysis, is known as the cultivation of *prajñā* or wisdom, and aims to arrive at a deeper insight and wisdom into the nature of reality. Linked with this, though not quite the same, is the cultivation of *samādhi*, a deep state of meditative absorption where, as mentioned earlier, mind can settle into a state of calm. Then as a supportive element in our practice, there is the training in *śīla*—ethics, morality and discipline. Take the example of a gardener planting a bush. If the gardener wants the bush to grow healthy and strong, he or she will place a fence or barrier around the bush to protect it from damage. In the same way, the various levels of ordination, all the moral codes, disciplines and ethical systems of Buddhism, provide the protective and supportive environment for our wisdom and meditation to develop. These three higher trainings of wisdom, meditation and ethics constitute the Fundamental Vehicle of Buddhism and underlie all of the different approaches and yānas of Buddhism.

When we examine all the different elements of our experience, all the phenomena in the world around us, we can determine, both through intellectual analysis and through meditation, that not only does the individual personality lack any true self-nature, but in the same way each and every entity or phenomenon we encounter lacks a self-nature. And so we arrive at the conclusion that all phenomena are empty. Emptiness pervades not only our own individual ego or sense of self, but the whole of reality. This is what is referred to as the Madhyamaka approach or philosophy of the Middle Way.

Above and beyond that, there is the understanding that not only are all phenomena in saṃsāra and nirvāṇa essentially empty or devoid of self-nature, but also the root of all these phenomena, the

source from which they all spring, is the mind. This ties in more
with the Mahāmudrā approach, and it is slightly more profound.
Madhyamaka and Mahāmudrā are examining the same thing from
different points of view, and the Mahāmudrā approach tends to go
one step further.

The next, and final, step after that is to determine where that
mind comes from—the ground of being from which the ordinary,
saṃsāric mind emerges, the mother that gives birth to the child of
ordinary mind. This discovery of a self-arising state of primordial
awareness, one that goes beyond ordinary, conceptual thought, is
that with which the approach of Mahāsandhi or Dzogchen is concerned. It is on this basis, the glimpse or realization of this, that true
Dzogchen practice takes place. This is why Dzogchen is often referred to as the consummate result, the ultimate fruition of practice.

To summarize, the source of suffering in our experience is our
clinging to or misapprehension of mind and body in terms of some
kind or self or ego. Through practice, we arrive at the realization of
non-self, the lack of self-nature of mind and body. Then, in the
Madhyamaka approach, we realize the emptiness of all phenomena,
not just the mind and body of the individual. This completely
uproots and dissolves all the conflicting emotions that reside as
deeply ingrained patterns in the ordinary person's mind. With this
realization, all the passion and aggression, attachment and pride,
jealousy, envy, and greed, that are supported by clinging to self are
dissolved, along with that notion of self. The next step is to discover
mind as the source of all these phenomena and to realize the nature
of that mind. The final step, from the Dzogchen point of view, is
to discover the ground of being from which mind arises. This
ground of being is often personified as the Primordial Buddha
Samantabhadra or Kuntuzangpo, which means 'all-good' or 'positive
in every way'. If we define the purpose of Dharma as the attainment
of the state of peace, then from the Dzogchen point of view, this is
the final or supreme state of peace that anyone can discover.

In terms of who can make this discovery, it is wide open. It does
not matter whether you are male or female, which race you belong

to, or which country you come from. None of these make any difference. The only person who can prevent you from realizing this goal is you, yourself. Each and every one of us has the potential to realize fruition. The only one who closes the door to the practice is you. It is not as though someone is going to come along and say: "Oh No! You can't practise this...you don't fit in here." Nor will anyone fling open the door to you, and say: "This is the Buddhadharma, please come in..." This is not what happens. It is you, yourself, who make the decision. It is you who open the door, and you who step inside, of your own accord. Then it is you who follow the path, right to the end.

At this point, I feel I need go no further, as I have said enough to give you an introduction and an overview of the Buddhist teachings from my point of view. However, I would like to pass on one little bit of advice I give to everyone. Relax. Just relax. Be nice to each other. As you go through your life, simply be kind to people. Try to help them rather than hurt them. Try to get along with them rather than fall out with them. With that, I will leave you, and with all my very best wishes.

COMPASSION, THE HEART OF ENLIGHTENMENT

Reflections on the Place of Compassion
at the Close of the Twentieth Century

A PUBLIC TALK BY

HIS HOLINESS THE DALAI LAMA

SANTA CRUZ, CALIFORNIA, 7 OCTOBER, 1989

This public talk by His Holiness the Dalai Lama was sponsored by Sogyal Rinpoche and Rigpa Fellowship and took place at the Santa Cruz Civic Auditorium. The translator was Geshe Thupten Jinpa. His Holiness was introduced by environmentalist and Chairperson of the Santa Cruz County Board of Supervisors, Gary Patton:

> The words Dalai Lama are a title, meaning 'Ocean of Wisdom'. The Dalai Lama, whose name is Tenzin Gyatso, describes himself as a simple Buddhist monk. He is, I believe, that. He is also a learned scholar and a scientist. He has great patience. He is the foremost teacher of Buddhism in the world. He is the spiritual and temporal leader of the Tibetan people, six million Tibetans whose nation has been occupied for over thirty years by China. Over a million Tibetans have lost their lives because of that occupation and the oppression that has attended upon it.
>
> This simple Buddhist monk is the head of a Government-in-Exile, including an elected democratic parliament, which carries out its governmental functions for the people of Tibet, even though the Government is separated at this time from Tibet itself. He is a great spiritual leader and teacher, a great political leader and

head of state, and as such he has travelled extensively throughout the world, and he is travelling here to Santa Cruz today. He has met with people who are leaders of state, heads of government, and with ordinary men and women like you and me.

He is profoundly committed to the cause of the restoration and preservation of the fragile environment of this beautiful planet. He is one of the great environmental leaders of this world. He is also dedicated to bringing an end to the spectre of nuclear war; he is dedicated to non-violence, a spokesperson for religious pluralism, international understanding, and world peace. And as we all know, the Dalai Lama has just been honoured by being named the Laureate of the Nobel Peace Prize.

HIS HOLINESS THE DALAI LAMA

Brothers, Sisters...

It always gives me the greatest satisfaction and joy to meet other people, and share our experiences in a spirit of altruism. So I am extremely happy to be here with you today. Whenever I come to give a talk like this, I do so firstly as just another human being. In that regard, I feel that of the greatest importance are the good human qualities of love and compassion. Essentially, every human being has the potential to awaken these qualities; the only question is whether we really take them seriously or not. Even in the cruellest person, deep down, there still lie the seeds of compassion and love. The sign of this is that even they appreciate it, quite naturally, when someone shows them affection. It makes them happy, because deep inside them love and compassion, the very nature of a human being, are present.

If we look at human beings, we find that when we begin our lives, the main factor which nurtures and sustains our existence is compassion or love. Scientists maintain that during the period the unborn child spends in its mother's womb, the calmness of her mind is crucial for its development. And then immediately after birth and over the next few weeks, which is the period critical for the development of the brain, the mother's touch on her child's body is vital for the healthy development of its brain. This demonstrates how the very nature of human beings is such that they need some kind of affection, even on a physical plane. Then our first action on our first day is to take our mother's milk. So as a human being, our very earliest activities are intimately bound up with affection.

Basically a human being is a social animal. We have to live together, whether we like it or not. That is a fact. That is reality. As this is the case, somewhere in nature, things are arranged to allow for it. It is up to us to have a sense of responsibility towards that. Let's look at very small creatures. Take bees, for example. I am quite fond of honey, so naturally I'm more curious about bees. I consider that bees are very kind to me, for as time goes by, year after year, I have consumed a large amount of honey, which means that many, many, thousands of bees have worked in order to produce it. These tiny insects have no religion, no teacher, no training. Simply as a fact of nature, because of the way they exist, they have to live together as social animals, and so they have an instinctive sense of responsibility.

Sometimes I feel that, although our intelligence is much sharper, and the human heart much greater, in certain respects we human beings are poorer than these tiny insects. They bear their sense of responsibility very faithfully. Of course sometimes they may fight, but overall, as a result of their individual sense of responsibility, their whole colony survives and continues.

Our human nature is essentially the same. If it were different, as with some other species of animal which apart from mating lead single, isolated lives, then here on this planet of ours these great towns and cities would never have appeared. Human nature is such that we have to live together. Yet at the same time our sense of responsibility is wanting, and our attitude towards our other fellow human beings, I feel, leaves a lot to be desired.

As a result, there may be millions upon millions of people in those huge cities of ours, yet there are so many individuals who suffer from loneliness. There is no one to whom you can turn, to help you share your deepest feelings. So instead of a feeling of friendship, you can end up with an agitated feeling towards everyone you see. How tragic this is!

We have to ask ourselves the question: what is wrong? Is there something amiss at a material level? Definitely not. Is there something wrong with the machinery we have, or with science and technology? I don't think so. Of course, it is undeniable that industrialization has changed our way of life. But finally the answer to this question is related intimately to our own mental attitude. Over the last few days I have been meeting scientists, mainly specialists on the brain, as well as psychologists and psychotherapists. According to one scientist's figures, the percentage of people in this country who suffer from some kind of mental illness is quite high—twelve or thirteen percent. I was quite surprised when I heard this. The percentage is so high, after all, that even we might be among them! Although we feel our mind is quite perfect, in a deeper sense there may be something wrong, even with us.

Over these few days of discussion, each individual scientist put his or her own view and offered different explanations, but the majority of them agreed on the key cause of the mental unrest so prevalent today. It became clear that the principal source of mental unrest and depression is lack of sympathy and affection.

I think you might find the following story quite interesting. A few weeks ago I met someone whose mind, I was told, is severely disturbed. At the beginning, I used all of my reasoning to encourage him, explaining that, as a human being, there was no need for him to be discouraged, because we have such a good human brain and intelligence. I pointed out how, with determination, we can solve all our human problems and overcome all obstacles, and so there is no reason to worry or be discouraged or depressed. Personally, I always find this kind of reasoning quite effective, but this time it failed. He was not impressed by this line of thinking. On the contrary, instead of showing any appreciation, he developed a rather contrary attitude. After listening to what I had to say, he became even more agitated, and asked me, "Why are you concerned about my problem? How do I know if your attitude is sincere or not?" I felt really sad. I was quite moved as well, and as I was explaining something or other, my hand reached out and caressed his arm. It was a natural gesture, a sincere expression of how I felt. Gradually, his mood altered; I could see his face beginning to change, and finally a smile began to appear. Then as I gained confidence, I increased that expression of affection. At last a big smile spread right across his face.

I told him, "Please consider me as an old friend. Any time, you can come to see me. Whatever I can do to help you, I am ready to do. I am at your service." When I said this, then his mood, it was clear, became very happy and joyful. The following day he came to see me again. When he arrived, he already had a happy air about him, but nevertheless he was trying to pretend otherwise and was not smiling. Anyway, what this incident really gave me was another confirmation of how powerful genuine compassion, love, or altruism can be, to affect other people's minds. And how they can remove fear and suspicion, and alleviate feelings of insecurity and mistrust.

So I always consider compassion as the key, not only for achieving and maintaining our own mental calmness, stability and happiness, but also as something extraordinarily useful for creating a healthy human society. By that I mean a happier and less harmful human society. Therefore—whether it be in individual cases, on a family level, a national level, or an international level—altruism, love and compassion are the basis for success, for happiness, and for a happy environment.

We have seen how crucial these good human qualities are for a human being, from before birth and afterwards. The only question now is whether we take them seriously, and care about them or not. This does not necessarily mean becoming a religious person or a 'believer'. It is not necessary to subscribe to some system of beliefs. You can remain a non-believer. At the same time, though, for as long as we are human beings, we need love and compassion. This is why I consider altruism so essential.

Then there is the question of the future of humanity. That means those who at the moment are young children, and who hold the key to the future of the human race. Again, an atmosphere of friendship, harmony and compassion is of prime importance for the healthy development of their minds and bodies. We can see quite clearly that those children who have very caring parents, and who grow up in a compassionate atmosphere, enjoy a much healthier mental and physical development. They are much happier. On the other hand, when families are divided, constantly quarrelling, and lack a happy atmosphere, it has a tremendous effect on the children's minds. So it is evident that when we talk about the future, compassion and altruism again have a key role.

This brings us to the subject of world peace. How do we achieve peace in the world? It is not through anger, through hatred, or through rampant competition. Of course, nuclear missiles may have worked as a deterrent, but they are only a temporary solution, and in the long term they are unwise. In any case, at a time when we have an economic crisis on our hands, this issue becomes highly complicated. On the one hand, governments are spending billions and billions on armaments, and on the other, nobody wants to have a real war or to use these weapons. So much money, so much energy, and so much human intelligence is spent on arms that, from that point of view, it would be better to use them! But nobody wants to, because no one can afford to take such a risk. So while we strive to develop more and more powerful and destructive weapons, at the same time we don't want to use them. All this money and energy are just squandered, and the only thing they bring is fear.

True world peace can only be achieved through peace of mind. And peace of mind springs from a genuine realization that all human beings are brothers and sisters. Different ideologies and different political or economic systems are only secondary; the most important point is that we are all the same human beings, living on one small planet. For our very survival, we need other continents and other people; we depend on the cooperation of other human beings. It is quite clear: only by developing inner peace first is there any real hope or chance of keeping a lasting world peace.

Everything on this planet functions according to the law of nature. Particles come together, and on the basis of their co-operation everything around us, our whole environment, can develop and be sustained. Our own body too has the same structure. Different cells come together and work together in co-operation, and as a result, human life is sustained. In a human community, the same law and principle of co-operation applies. Even for an aeroplane to fly, or for a single machine to work, it can only do so by depending on many other factors, and with their co-operation. Without them it is impossible. Just so, to sustain everyday life in human society, we need co-operation.

So the path to genuine co-operation is again through sincere compassion and love. Sometimes we misunderstand compassion as being nothing more than a feeling of pity. Compassion is much, much more. It embraces not only a feeling of closeness, but also a sense of responsibility. When you develop compassion, it will help you enormously to generate inner strength and self-confidence, and to reduce your feelings of fear and insecurity. So compassion and love, embodied in an attitude of altruism, are qualities that are of tremendous importance for the individual, as well as for society and the community at large.

The greatest obstacles in the way of compassion and love are anger and hatred. So in order to develop compassion, first of all it is vitally important to be able to handle and tackle your anger. If you are unable to apply remedies to overcome your anger, it will be quite difficult to cultivate and develop love and compassion. The usual method we apply to reduce anger goes along the following lines. First, we try to investigate, and ask ourselves: What is the benefit of anger? Does it have any value at all?

What we notice is that when we face some problem or a taxing situation, anger does give us extra energy. Often in such predicaments we feel discouraged or afraid, but then anger will arise, as our helper, and provide us with some kind of energy. That seems to be the only value of anger.

But then we have to examine this very carefully. Yes, anger does bring us some sort of additional energy, but upon closer examination we can see that it is almost a blind energy, and so a dangerous one. The reason is quite clear. When anger arises, swells, and dominates our whole mind, at that moment the best part of the human brain is not functioning properly. When anger reaches its full peak, a person becomes almost mad. At that point many wrong decisions can be taken. For example, sometimes in anger we will use very harsh words towards someone, but when our anger has disappeared, we feel very shy about meeting him or her again. This is basically because we never wanted to use that kind of language, but once our mind was dominated by anger, we no longer had any control. All these negative reactions, none of which we want, come about because we act impulsively, and swerve out of control.

So the energy brought by anger is not so reliable, and not so useful after all. It is an energy, but there is no guarantee which way it will go. Actions taken out of anger's blind energy may hit the target or they may not; it is never very sure, is it? So, when we take the only positive quality or benefit that we can possibly associate with anger, the energy it brings along with it, we find it is extremely questionable whether it is useful or not.

On the other hand, the same energy can be channelled, by means of a thorough examination of our situation. Say we have some problem, but while we remain sincere and humble, someone else takes advantage of us. Now we should study the situation. What we may find is that, if we do not take counter-measures, that person becomes even more aggressive, and performs more activities that are essentially unjust. Simply consider the interest of the person who attacks you. If you let him carry on unjustly taking such advantage, ultimately it may be more harmful to him, let alone to you. So we realize the full implications, and our sense of responsibility is still present. In order to stop the long-term consequences for that person, we take action, but without a trace of anger or ill feeling.

Counter-measures which are taken without anger, but which are based upon a thorough examination of the whole situation, are much more effective.

Meanwhile, of course, it could not be clearer that anger destroys your mental peace, and in that respect it is extremely harmful to your health. From my own little experience, I have observed that health and mental stability have a very close link. Everybody needs to take care of their own health, and if I could tell you one 'secret' point, it is this: let your mind simply remain calm, and in an atmosphere of altruism. This has a tremendous effect on our body.

In order to reduce and minimize the force of anger, it is very important to practise forgiveness and tolerance. Often people consider tolerance and patience as tantamount to signs of weakness. However, I believe that in reality, anger rises less readily in someone who is guided by reason and by truth, while people with less reason and less self-confidence fall prey to anger much more easily. What this shows is that anger is a sign of weakness, and tolerance and patience are signs of inner strength.

Tolerance and patience are extremely important for the balance of our mind. How do we practise them? Simply to think that they are noble principles is not enough. It is when we actually hit difficulties that the real opportunity to practise patience comes along. Who is it then that can create that kind of opportunity? Our enemy. In this sense, our enemy is like a teacher, one who is sincerely teaching us patience and tolerance. For a person who believes in the importance of compassion and love, the practice of patience and tolerance is essential. And the only factor that provides us with the opportunity to practise patience is our enemy. If we can only reflect along these lines, whatever strong negative attitude or ill feelings we have towards our enemy will naturally reduce.

On the surface altruism, compassion and love seem to be actions associated with selflessness. But I feel that if we are truly 'selfish', then we will take care of other people, help other people, serve other people, be more concerned about others' welfare, make more friends, and generate more smiles. Then we will find that when we need help there will be plenty of helpers. If we have no concern for others, we neglect them and we do not care about their well-being, then in the long-term we will be the losers.

One thing is quite clear here: as a human being we need friends, and friends are not won through quarrels, anger or jealousy. The only quality that attracts genuine friendship is affection. Sometimes we might have the impression that if we had money or power, then friends would automatically arrive. But that kind of notion does not stand up to careful examination. Those who appear with big smiles when you have power and money are not true friends of you as an individual, but friends of money or friends of power. This is self-evident. As long as you have power or wealth, these friends are always there. Even if you push them away, they will come back, whereas when you have no money and no power then there is no trace of these so-called 'friends'. It can be hard to find out even where they are. If you try to telephone them, you may get no answer—or at best only a very short one!

Now these friends, in a nutshell, think only of money and power. And when is it that we need a friend most? When we are prosperous and things go well for us, friends are not so necessary; we can manage by ourselves. It is when our fortunes decline that we need a friend. Then that former kind of friend is really useless.

A genuine friend will come if the attitude of your mind is sincere and genuinely altruistic. Usually people will say how much they love a smile. But they need to be genuine smiles. Some smiles have something very artificial about them, and instead of bringing satisfaction, they just raise suspicion. Artificial smiles are no use. However, I consider a genuine smile to be something unique to human beings.

If you have this attitude of altruism, or a genuine respect for others, it is a basis upon which you can have the feeling that all others are brothers and sisters. There are no barriers, in fact, between us. When I give public talks in different countries around the world, some of the faces I know, but the majority are new. Yet, to my mind, basically we are all the same human beings, and so from my own inner experience as a human being, I can tell that you want happiness and do not want suffering. A human being is designated as such on the basis of the combination of a human body and a human mind. This body is a human body, this voice is a human voice, and there is a certain energy, which you can call the human mind or the human brain. Beside that, even if we investigate to find out what a real human being is, we cannot find it.

As human beings, we are all the same. So there is no need to build some kind of artificial barrier between us. At least my own experience is that if you have this kind of attitude, there is no barrier. Whatever I feel, I can express; I can call you 'my old friend'. There is nothing to hide, and no need to say things in a way that is not straightforward. So this gives me a kind of space in my mind, with the result that I do not have to be suspicious of others all the time. And this really gives me inner satisfaction, and inner peace.

So I call this feeling a 'genuine realization of the oneness of the whole of humanity'. We are all members of one human family. I think that this understanding is very important, especially now that the world is becoming smaller and smaller. In ancient times, even in a small village, people were able to exist more or less independently. There was not so much need for others' co-operation. These days, the economic structure has completely changed, so that modern economies, relying on industry, are totally different. We are heavily dependent on one another, and also as a result of mass communication, the barriers of the past are greatly reduced. Today, because of the complexity of interdependence, every crisis on this planet is essentially related with every other, like a chain reaction. Consequently it is worthwhile taking every crisis as a global one. Here barriers such as 'this nation' or 'that nation', 'this continent', or 'that continent' are simply obstacles. Therefore today, for the future of the human race, it is more important than ever before that we develop a genuine sense of brotherhood and sisterhood. I usually call this a sense of 'universal responsibility'.

This is the first point I wish to make. Wherever I go, I usually speak about this. If you find something interesting or useful in what

I have said, then please experiment with it in your daily life. If it proves useful, all well and good; if you find it is of no use, and of no interest, then forget it.

Now we come to the second issue I wish to address. As a Buddhist monk I am always seeking to encourage a better understanding between the different religions. Religion is, after all, supposed to be the one remedy for reducing mental tension. Yet unfortunately sometimes religion itself becomes yet another factor for creating divisions, quarrels and conflict among human beings. This is quite tragic. So a close dialogue and harmony between the different religions is something which I see as essential, and I am always trying to look for ways towards arriving at a better understanding.

Of course, there are differences between the faiths, and some of them are fundamental ones. For example, followers of Buddhism and Jainism do not accept the theory of God or a Creator. Many other religions, such as Christianity, Judaism and Islam, find their fundamental faith in God, the Creator. I tend to look at these differences from another point of view. How is it that two such very different teachings coexist? I believe that because there are countless different mentalities among human beings, one particular teaching will inevitably be more effective and suitable for certain people. For others, another religion will be more appropriate and more effective. For instance, look at all the different kinds of food we eat. Compared to the human mind, the human body is less sophisticated, but even so, there are so many varieties of taste, and different people are fond of different dishes. The mind is that much more sophisticated, and so there are many different varieties of mentality. One religion simply could not satisfy all human beings, and so to have different teachings and philosophies is, I believe, of greater use to a wider variety of people.

The most important insight comes, however, when we look at the results. We can find good human beings, very warm-hearted people, as a result of the practice of each of these different religions. This shows that no matter what the differences in philosophy or teachings, they are all equally effective in producing good human beings. Therefore there is no point in disrespecting one religion or another. This deserves thorough and careful examination, for the understanding it brings can help to develop genuine respect towards all the different religions.

So there is scope for coming together, working together, and trying to make a common effort for world peace, by cultivating peace in the family and peace in the individual mind. That is the purpose of religion, not to build churches or temples or cathedrals. The main aim of different religions is to cultivate positive feelings and increase positive human qualities, and to reduce the negative ones. Therefore every major religion teaches us love, compassion, forgiveness and a sense of brotherhood and sisterhood. Although there are different explanations and different shades of meaning given to love and compassion, broadly speaking every faith teaches the same essential thing. And so far, I have found along with some friends of mine who belong to other religions, that through dialogue and through constantly exchanging our views and ex-periences, we can develop mutual respect and mutual learning. This learning is so helpful for enriching our own practice. Some of my Christian friends already practise certain Buddhist methods, and likewise there are many things we Buddhists can learn from our Christian brothers and sisters. This approach is as useful as it is important.

I am quite satisfied with the progress in this field, and sometimes I even feel some small sense of achievement in the contribution that I have made. In general, over recent years, the dialogue between different religions has been increasing and improving.

Thirdly, as a Tibetan, and as a Dalai Lama, I would like to express my deep thanks to those people who take such an interest in our Tibetan culture, including Tibetan Buddhism, and who show such sympathy for the Tibetan cause. I appreciate this very much. We are only six million Tibetan people, but our cultural heritage is unique. We have a recorded history of more than two thousand years. From the archaeological record, some believe that the roots of Tibetan culture may stretch back six or even eight thousand years. At any rate, Tibet is one of the ancient cultures of the world. Today there is every danger that this civilization will be eliminated, entirely. So this is really a crucial era. At such a time, when people, acting as our human brothers and sisters, show us so much concern, we are very encouraged. So I want to thank you, and through you, your friends who are taking such a keen interest, and who support the Tibetan cause.

Thank you very much.

NOTES

PREFACE

1   *The Meaning of Life*, p. 99.
2   rdo grub chen, in *rdzogs chen skor*, 8b/1, new edition, p. 554.

GROUND, PATH AND FRUITION

3   In Dudjom Rinpoche: *History of the Nyingma School in The Nyingma School of Tibetan Buddhism, Its Fundamentals and History*, pp. 821-824.
4   A number of very important Nyingma and Dzogchen masters figure in the life of the fifth Dalai Lama. He received teachings from Khönton Paljor Lhundrup (1561-1637), who was an important teacher in the transmission of the Guhyagarbha Tantra and Dzogchen. His closest student was Zurchen Chöying Rangdrol (1604-1657 or 1669), who studied with him from the age of seventeen, and to whom he gave teachings on the Guhyagarbha Tantra and on Nyingtik. A very powerful master, who was much sought after for protection, Zurchen Chöying Rangdrol gave many teachings to the 'Great Fifth', including Vajrakīlaya, Kagyé and Nyingtik. He recognized Rigdzin Pema Trinlé (1641-1717), one of the close disciples of the fifth Dalai Lama, as the fourth reincarnation of the great tertön Rigdzin Gödemchen (1337-1408), and enthroned him at the monastery of Dorje Drak, founded in 1610 by his predecessor Rigdzin Ngak gi Wangpo (1580-1639). The most important master during this period for the transmission of the Nyingma and Dzogchen teachings was the great tertön Terdak Lingpa, Minling Terchen Gyurmé Dorje (1646-1714). He was the son of Nyötön Sangdak Trinlé Lhundrup (1611-62), a master who was particularly significant in the transmission of the Do Gongpa Düpa, and who received teachings on the Guhyagarbha Tantra from the fifth Dalai Lama. Terdak Lingpa studied under his father and the fifth Dalai Lama. He established the great monastery of Orgyen Mindroling, and accomplished tremendous work in revitalizing the

ancient tradition of the Nyingmapas. His outer, inner and secret biographies exist, detailing his discovery of a large number of termas and his profound realization. Among his great disciples were the fifth Dalai Lama himself, Dési Sangyé Gyatso and Lochen Dharmaśrī. The younger brother of Terdak Lingpa, Lochen Dharmaśrī (1654-1717) was ordained by the fifth Dalai Lama. He studied under his brother, becoming extraordinarily learned. His collected works number eighteen volumes, wherein are to be found his famous commentaries on the Guhyagarbha Tantra and the Three Vows. Terdak Lingpa and Lochen Dharmaśrī were regarded as the incarnations of Vairocana and Yudra Nyingpo. See Dudjom Rinpoche, pp. 825-834; 683-4 and 679-683 especially.

5   Tashi Topgyal, master of the Northern Treasures, born in c.1557, was a tertön and reincarnation of Ngari Panchen. His son Rigdzin Ngak gi Wangpo was the third incarnation of Rigdzin Gödemchen, revealer of the 'Northern Treasures', and blessed the fifth Dalai Lama in the year of his birth.

6   Cf. Dudjom Rinpoche, pp. 822-3.

7   See *Secret Visions of the Fifth Dalai Lama*, Samten Karmay, London: Serindia, 1988. Especially pp. 20-21.

8   Guru Rinpoche and his Eight Manifestations appear in the empowerment as: the master Padma Thötreng, the vidyādhara Padmajungné, the bhikṣu Padmasambhava, the scholar Loden Choksé, the majestic and overpowering Padma Gyalpo, the yogin Nyima Özer, the bhagavān Śākya Senge, the great wrathful Senge Dradok and the crazy Dorje Drolö.

9   A condensed translation was made on the spot by Ven. Georges Dreyfus. This teaching was re-translated for this book in its entirety by Richard Barron (Chökyi Nyima).

10   Taktra Rinpoche (stag brag rin po che ngag dbang gsung rab) served as tutor to His Holiness the Dalai Lama, and gave him his vows as a novice monk. He accepted the regentship of Tibet in 1941, resigning in 1950, aged 75, when the Dalai Lama was offered full authority over Tibet. In *Tibet: A Political History*, by W.D. Shakabpa, New York: Potala, 1984, p. 286.

11   His Holiness is referring to the two types of svābhāvikakāya: "The definition of a nature body is an ultimate sphere possessing two purities. The two purities are purity from the object of negation, inherent existence, and purity from the adventitious defilements. According to these two purities, the nature body can be categorized into two types. The first is the naturally pure nature body (rang bzhin rnam dag gi ngo bo nyid sku) and the second is the 'pure of adventitious' nature body (glo bur rnam dag gi ngo bo nyid sku). The naturally pure nature body is the Buddha's ultimate truth, the emptiness of inherent existence of the Buddha's omniscient mind. The 'pure of adventitious' nature body is the Buddha's cessation in that it is the complete and final cessation of the adventitious defilements." *The Fundamental Potential for Enlightenment*, Geshe Acharya Thubten Loden, Melbourne: Tushita, 1996, p. 155

12   *Mūlamadhyamakakārikā*, XXIV, verse 8.

13   *Madhyamakāvatāra*, VI, verse 89. The verse continues "Buddha taught that

living beings all arise from karma, and so without mind, there could be no karma".

14   He deals with this in *Madhyamakāvatāra*, VI, verses 84-90. In refuting the Cittamātrin viewpoint, Candrakīrti points out that Buddha, in the sūtra, is not denying external forms, and that "mind only" in the quotation should be understood as meaning that mind is the primary factor, and nothing else is as important. See *On the Interpretation of the Mahāyāna Sūtras*, Donald S. Lopez, Jr., in *Buddhist Hermeneutics*, Honolulu: University of Hawaii Press, 1988, pp. 53-6.

15   On the four reliances, see *The Central Philosophy of Tibet*, RAF Thurman, Princeton: Princeton University Press, 1984, pp. 113-30.

16   B. Alan Wallace writes: "This verse, often quoted in Tibetan Buddhist literature, is cited from the Vimalaprabha commentary on the Kālacakra, although it appears in the Pali canon as well. The Sanskrit occurs as a quotation in Tattvasamgraha, ed. D. Shastri, Varanasi: Bauddhabharati, 1968, K.3587". See *Consciousness at the Crossroads*, p. 183.

HITTING THE ESSENCE IN THREE WORDS

17   *Takdrol* is one of the 'five methods that lead to liberation without the need for meditation'. These are sometimes given as: liberation through seeing (cakras); liberation on hearing (mantra); liberation by tasting (nectar); liberation by touch (mudrā or takdrol); and liberation by recollection or thinking (phowa). Numerous kinds of *takdrol* exist: many are mantras in diagrams related to the Dzogchen teachings, and others belong to the tantras. The takdrol can form part of a more detailed empowerment, or it can be given independently as a simple empowerment on its own. Sometimes a text of a tantra is used as a takdrol and worn, for example, in a locket on the top of the head. (Information kindly given by Tulku Thondup Rinpoche).

18   Though *Hitting the Essence in Three Words* is one popular translation of the title, the 'words' in question are more a case of 'statements', 'verses', or 'lines'. On the importance of these verses, see Namkhai Norbu Rinpoche's Foreword in John Reynolds, *Golden Letters*, pp. 11-19.

19   See Tulku Thondup, *Masters of Meditation and Miracles*, pp. 59-60, and John Reynolds, *Golden Letters*, pp. 179-189, who gives the life story of Garab Dorje from the *Logyu Chenmo*, "The Great History", in the *Vima Nyingtik*.

20   For Patrul Rinpoche's life story, see *Masters of Meditation and Miracles*, pp. 201-210; *Heart Treasure of the Enlightened Ones*, pp. 231-237; *The Words of My Perfect Teacher*, pp. xxxii-xxxv; *Golden Letters*, pp. 297-305.

21   Zenkar Rinpoche (Thub bstan nyi ma): *rdza dpal sprul rin po che'i rnam thar mdor bsdus* in *khams khul mkhas dbang rnams kyi snyan ngag dper brjod phyogs sgrig*, published by si khron mi rigs dpe skrun khang, 1987, pp. 10-16. This also appears in *sher phyin mngon rtogs rgyan rtsa 'grel* by the same publisher, 1997, pp. 1-8.

22   "For those who have not yet generated bodhicitta, the first three chapters of

the *Bodhicaryāvatāra* explain how to do so.Then, to prevent bodhicitta from declining, there follow the instructions in the chapters on carefulness, attentiveness, and patience.After this, the chapters on endeavour, meditative concentration and wisdom describe how bodhicitta can be continuously developed. Finally, the tenth and concluding chapter discusses how to share and dedicate this bodhicitta that has been generated, protected from decline, and increasingly developed." *A Flash of Lightning in the Dark of Night*,Tenzin Gyatso, Boston: Shambhala, 1994, p. 17.

23   In *Tant que durera l'espace*, Dalai Lama, traduit du tibétain sous la direction de Dagpo Rimpotche par Marie-Stella Boussemart, Paris: Albin Michel, 1996, pp. 21-2.

24   Its full title reads: 'The Heart Treasure of the Enlightened Ones,The practice of View, Meditation and Action: A Discourse Virtuous in the Beginning, Middle and End.' See Dilgo Khyentse, *The Heart Treasure of the Enlightened Ones*, Boston: Shambhala, 1992.

25   Dodrupchen Jikmé Tenpé Nyima's biography of Patrul Rinpoche explains: "For many years, when he taught on the *Bodhicaryāvatāra*, large numbers of flowers called *Serchen*, with between thirty to fifty petals, would suddenly blossom, and they became known as *bodhicaryāvatāra* flowers." People had never seen such huge flowers before: orange in colour and looking like sunflowers, they were offered in the *Bodhicaryāvatāra* offering ceremonies. (From information kindly given by Tulku Thondup Rinpoche) Dodrupchen Jikmé Tenpé Nyima, *Collected Works*,Vol. Nga, page 113, folio 7a/3. Zenkar Rinpoche in his *Concise Biography of Patrul Rinpoche* mentions that this took place in the vicinity of the Śrī Singha College at Dzogchen monastery.

26   See note 5 above.

27   The Northern Ter tradition centres around the terma revelations of Rigdzin Gödem Ngödrup Gyaltsen (1337-1409).The main seat and source of this tradition is the monastery of Thubten Dorje Drak, built in 1632 by the third Rigdzin Chenmo Ngak gi Wangpo.The reincarnations of Rigdzin Gödem, known as the Rigdzin Chenmos, are still the heads of the Changter tradition, as well as of Dorje Drak.At Dartsedo (Kanding, in Eastern Kham), there is a monastery called Do Dorje Drak, as one of the Rigdzin Chenmos was born in the family of Chagla Kings of Dartsedo.There are also a few monasteries in the Golok area, but most of the Changter monasteries are to be found in Western Tibet, the provinces of Tsang and Töd or Ngari, and the Himalayan areas of India, Nepal and Ladakh.Among the most important of Rigdzin Gödem's many terma revelations are the *Kagyé Rangjung Rangshar* and the *Dzogpachenpo Kunzang Gongpa Zangthal*. Extremely popular in the Nyingma world is the *Le'u Dünma*, the 'Prayer in Seven Chapters' to Guru Rinpoche. Many of the termas were discovered in Zangzang Lhadrak in Tsang,Western Tibet. It was because this area was considered to be 'north' and also perhaps because it lay to the north of Samyé, that this tradition got its name.

28   In this context, *dhāraṇīs*, in Tibetan *gzungs*, are mantra-like mnemonic formulae.A common division of mantras is into: secret mantras, knowledge mantras, and *dhāraṇī* mantras.

29   His Holiness explained this on the previous day, Friday 6 July; see *The Meaning of Life*, p. 98.

30   "As Dodrupchen Jik-may Denbay-nyi-ma says, all of the texts of Highest Yoga Tantra in all of the New Translation and Old Translation Schools teach just the practice of the fundamental innate mind of clear light." *The Meaning of Life*, pp. 97-8.

31   For example, in *rdzogs chen thor bu*, p. 194; p. 555 new edition. "In the Dzogchen approach, even in the midst of concepts, clear light resides just as sesame oil permeates the seed, and in that very situation you can recognize rigpa directly and maintain awareness of it..."

32   The six collections of consciousness are: the five sense consciousnesses (sight, hearing, smell, taste, touch), plus mind consciousness.

33   See *rdzogs chen skor*, p. 295, new edition, p. 659.

34   See below in His Holiness's 1989 teaching, p. 196.

35   As the Dalai Lama explained: "There are different ways of visualizing the deity, depending on whether you follow the methods of Mahāyoga, Anuyoga, or Atiyoga. Here, in the Dzogchen tradition of Atiyoga, the deity is visualized in a single instant of total recall."

36   His Holiness deals with the same question of permanence in his *Union of the Old and New Schools*, in *Kindness, Clarity and Insight*, p. 210-11: "It is considered 'permanent' in the sense of abiding forever and thus is presented as a permanent mind. It is permanent not in the sense of not disintegrating moment by moment but in the sense that its continuum is not interrupted—this being analogous to the statement in Maitreya's *Ornament for Clear Realization* that a Buddha's exalted activities are considered permanent in that they are inexhaustible. It is also non-produced in the sense that it is not adventitiously and newly produced by causes and conditions [since its continuum has always existed]." The quotation from Maitreya's *Abhisamayālaṃkāra* is verse 11, chapter 8.

37   In his *Union of the Old and New Schools*, His Holiness says: "In the same vein, the Geluk scholar and adept Norsang Gyatso (1423-1513) says that whatever exists is necessarily compounded (*saṃskṛta, 'dus byas*), though his referent is more general than the usual meaning of 'compounded'. He is not asserting that all phenomena, including permanent phenomena are produced upon the aggregations of causes and conditions, but that all phenomena exist conditionally, in dependence both on their parts and on a conceptual consciousness that designates them. Similarly because this basic mind of Nyingma is not *newly* produced in dependence on causes and conditions, it is called 'non-produced', the reference being to a broader sense of the term." *Kindness, Clarity and Insight*, p. 211.

38   The *Vajrapañjaratantra*. This is the source of the famous verse that follows.

39   Within the Dzogchen teachings, the terms *tantras*, *āgamas* and *upadeśas*, in Tibetan *rgyud*, *lung* and *man ngag*, take on a particular significance. See for example Chögyal Namkhai Norbu in *Primordial Experience*, Mañjuśrīmitra, translated by Namkhai Norbu and Kennard Lipman, Boston: Shambhala, 1987, pp. xii-xiv.

40 "In Sanskrit", His Holiness added, "'A' is a syllable of negation".

41 In Tibetan: *rig pa mig la gtad/mig nam mkha' la gtad.*

42 From this point, Patrul Rinpoche's text will be indented. The verses of the root text appear first, followed by the commentary in which the root verses are embedded. This translation of *The Special Teaching of the Wise and Glorious King* was collated by Patrick Gaffney, from an original by Sogyal Rinpoche, as mentioned in the Preface. Please see the Bibliography for translations by Erik Pema Kunsang, Sarah Harding and John Reynolds.

43 *Lung* means scriptures; *rig* is reasoning.

44 Mangtö Ludrup Gyatso (1523-96) was a prominent scholar in the Sakya school. His Holiness quoted him on the previous day while referring to the Sakyapa view of the causal continuum that is the ālaya, which Mangtö Ludrup Gyatso identifies as the fundamental innate mind of clear light. "According to the thought of Mangtö Ludrup Gyatso, all of the phenomena of cyclic existence and nirvāṇa are to be viewed as the sport or reflection of the fundamental innate mind of clear light, in that they are all of the same taste in the sphere of clear light. This is the view of the undifferentiability of cyclic existence and nirvāṇa." *Meaning of Life*, pp. 95-6. His Holiness also invoked the views of both Jamyang Khyentse Wangchuk (1524-68) and Mangtö Ludrup Gyatso on the two truths during his teaching at Dzogchen monastery in 1992.

45 In London in April 1988, His Holiness referred to "a passage from the Sakya literature, which says that between the arising of different moments of conceptual thought, the clear light nature of mind occurs uninterruptedly." *The World of Tibetan Buddhism*, p.151. This is attributed to Sakya Paṇḍita.

46 His Holiness has quoted this statement by Dodrupchen Jikmé Tenpé Nyima on a number of occasions. "Dodrupchen says that when we are able to ascertain all appearing and occurring objects of knowledge as the sport of the basic mind, we perforce understand even better the position of the Consequence School that these exist only through the power of conceptuality." *Kindness, Clarity and Insight*, p. 214. See also *The World of Tibetan Buddhism*, p. 120, and *The Gelug/Kagyü Tradition of Mahāmudrā*, pp. 225-6.

47 Otherwise, "searching for the hidden flaw of mind" is one of the preliminaries in the path of Dzogchen. See below, pp. 140 and 190.

48 One of Milarepa's songs was to a young woman disciple, Paldarbum: "If you felt fine in meditating on the sky, so be it with the clouds. Clouds are but the manifestation of the sky; therefore, rest right in the sphere of the sky." Garma CC Chang, *The Hundred Thousand Songs of Milarepa*, Abridged edition, New York: Harper, 1962, pp. 50-62.

49 See below, pp. 176-7, 181, 183-4 and 190.

50 His Holiness explains the Tibetan word *phyal ba* to mean "always unchanging".

51 Patrul Rinpoche attributes this saying to Dzogchen Guru Shyiwa and explains it in his *Pith Instruction on the Supreme Vehicle of Ati, A Clear Explanation of the Natural State*, in his Collected Works, volume 4, pp. 709-735. This reference is given in *The Lion's Gaze*, p. 89.

52   *Uttaratantra*, ch.1, v.51.

53   His Holiness discusses this at greater length in Part Four of this book.

54   The title of the text *The Special Teaching of the Wise and Glorious King* also incorporates a reference to its author. 'Glorious', which appears in the title as the Sanskrit 'Śrī', is in Tibetan 'Pal', the first syllable of Patrul Rinpoche's name.

55   Dodrupchen, in *rdzogs chen skor*. Published by Dodrupchen Rinpoche, Gangtok, Collected Works, Vol. cha, p. 207, f. 4a; new edition, vol. ka, p. 586.

DZOGCHEN AND THE BUDDHADHARMA

56   He recorded his exploits in: *Across Asia, From East to West in 1906-1908*, parts I-II, Helsinki, Société Finno-Ougrienne 1940. Part I, pp. 687-695. Mannerheim's report to the Czar about his meeting with the Dalai Lama is recorded in *The Memoirs of Marshal Mannerheim*, translated by Count Eric Lewenhaupt, New York: Dutton, 1954, pp. 71-2. See also: *Mannerheim, The Years of Preparation*, J.E.O. Screen, London: Hurst, 1993, p. 58.

57   In the teaching which appeared as *The Four Noble Truths*, His Holiness quotes Maitreya in the *Sublime Continuum*: "Just as the disease needs to be diagnosed, its cause eliminated, a healthy state achieved and the remedy implemented, so also should suffering, its causes, its cessation and the path be known, removed, attained and undertaken." p. 37.

58   Cf. *The Four Noble Truths*, p. 54.

59   ibid. p. 54 . His Holiness adds: "The reason it is called the suffering of conditioning is because this state of existence serves as the basis not only for painful experiences in this life, but also for the causes and conditions of suffering in the future."

60   Cf. *The World of Tibetan Buddhism*, p. 99, where this union of method and wisdom is discussed at greater length.

61   Or 'innate unenlightenment.' See *Buddha Mind*, where Tulku Thondup quotes Longchenpa: "Synonyms for the universal ground of traces are: innate unenlightenment,…" p. 220. "At the time of distraction into delusions, the aspect of one's not realizing the wisdom which dwells in oneself is called innate unenlightenment." p. 252.

THE PINNACLE OF ALL YĀNAS

62   A number of these conferences have been published, in: *Gentle Bridges*, edited by Jeremy Hayward and Francisco Varela, Boston: Shambhala, 1993 (Mind and Life I, 1987); *Consciousness at the Crossroads*, Ed. Zara Houshmand, Robert B. Livingston and B. Alan Wallace, Ithaca: Snow Lion, 1999 (Mind and Life II, 1989); *Healing Emotions*, edited by Daniel Goleman, Boulder: Shambhala, 1997 (Mind and Life III, 1991); *Sleeping, Dreaming and Dying*, edited by Francisco Varela, Ph.D., Boston: Wisdom Publications, 1997 (Mind and Life IV, 1992).

63   Published as *Worlds in Harmony, Dialogues on Compassionate Action*, Berkeley: Parallax Press, 1992.
64   This appears in *Kindness, Clarity and Insight*, pp. 200-232.
65   *Kindness, Clarity and Insight*, p. 222, and p. 208. See *The World of Tibetan Buddhism*, pp. 128-9 on the same theme.
66   Quoted in *Dzogchen and Padmasambhava*, Sogyal Rinpoche, Santa Cruz: Rigpa, 1989, p. 85, and *Natural Great Perfection*, Nyoshul Khenpo, translated by Surya Das, Ithaca: Snow Lion, 1995, p. 158.
67   He also adds: "It is also important to study Kunkhyen Jikmé Lingpa's text "Treasury of Enlightened Attributes" (*Yönten Dzö*), at the end of which you will find an explanation of Dzogchen practice." *The World of Tibetan Buddhism*, pp. 144-145.
68   *Kindness, Clarity and Insight*, pp. 220-221.
69   For commentaries on 'The Eight Verses of Training the Mind' by H.H. the Dalai Lama see *Transforming the Mind*, His Holiness the Dalai Lama, translated by Geshe Thupten Jinpa, edited by Dominique Side, London: Thorsons, 2000, also *Kindness, Clarity, and Insight*, The Fourteenth Dalai Lama, Ithaca: Snow Lion, 1984, pp. 100-15, and in *Four Essential Buddhist Commentaries*, H.H. the XIVth Dalai Lama, Dharamsala: LTWA, 1982, pp. 89-120. Other teachings on this famous text are: *Compassion, The Key to Great Awakening*, by Geshe Tsultim Gyeltsen, Boston: Wisdom Publications, 1997, pp. 25-43, and *The Essence of Mahāyāna Lojong Practice*, Sermey Khensur Lobsang Tharchin, Howell, NJ: Mahāyāna Sutra and Tantra Press, 1998.
70   *Chos dbyings rin po che'i mdzod*, vol. ga (3) in Dodrupchen Rinpoche's reprint of the *Seven Treasuries* in Gangtok.
71   Khenpo Ngakchung, Kathok Khenpo Ngawang Palzang (1879-1941) was an emanation of Vimalamitra, and a key figure in the transmission of the Longchen Nyingtik. He was the most gifted student of Nyoshul Lungtok Tenpé Nyima (1829-1901/2), who gave him Patrul Rinpoche's oral lineage of pith instructions. Khenpo Ngakchung's disciples included Jamyang Khyentse Chökyi Lodrö, Shedrup Tenpé Nyima (the root master of Nyoshul Khenpo Jamyang Dorje) and Chadral Rinpoche.
72   From the 8,000 verse Prajñāpāramitā: *Aṣṭasāhasrikāprajñāpāramitā*, 'phags pa shes rab kyi pha rol tu phyin pa brgyad stong pa. See *The Perfection of Wisdom in 8,000 lines and Its Verse Summary*, E. Conze, Delhi: Sri Satguru Publications, 1994, p. 84 (The same theme occurs in the Pali scriptures, in Aṅguttara Nikāya I (10) quoted in *Buddhist Texts Throughout the Ages*, ed. by Conze, Horner, Snellgrove and Waley, Oxford, 1954, p. 33, no. 6.)
73   For example Dodrupchen says: "The genuine rigpa and the clear light vajra mind have one and the same meaning" and "The main point is that the rigpa taught in the Dzogchen approach and the wisdom of clear light are one and the same" in *rdzogs chen thor bu* p. 194 (p. 555, new edition) and p. 198 (p. 559 new edition). He adds: "As for the position that rigpa is the fundamental clear light of Highest Yoga Tantra, there are countless indisputable sources in Dzogchen that identify the clear light of death as rigpa," in *rdzogs chen skor* p. 292 (p. 656, new edition). See also *The Meaning of Life*, especially pp. 97-8,

and *The World of Tibetan Buddhism*, pp. 128-9, where His Holiness quotes Dodrupchen again.

74   For an extensive discussion on Buddhist epistemology see Lati Rinpoche and Elizabeth Napper: *Mind in Tibetan Buddhism*, Ithaca: Snow Lion, 1980. Also *Mipham's Beacon of Certainity*, pp. 57-60.

75   'Apperception' or 'reflexive awareness' is regarded as being accepted by the Sautrāntika, Cittamātra and Yogacāra Svātantrika schools, but refuted by Vaibhāṣika, Sautrāntika Svātantrika and Prāsaṅgika. Śāntideva refutes its existence in the *Bodhicaryāvatāra*, chapter nine, verses 17-25. See also *Mipham's Beacon of Certainity*, pp. 497-8.

76   The twelve links of dependent origination are ignorance, karmic formations, consciousness, name and form, the six bases of consciousness, contact, feeling, desire, attachment, becoming, birth, and old age and death. See The *Meaning of Life*, passim; Jeffrey Hopkins, *Meditation on Emptiness*, pp. 275-83, 707-11; and Steven D. Goodman, *Situational Patterning*, in Crystal Mirror III, Emeryville: Dharma Publishing, 1974, pp. 93-101.

77   Buddha taught the twelve links in detail in *The Rice Seedling Sūtra*; see *The Meaning of Life*, p. 7, and *The World of Tibetan Buddhism*, p. 162.

78   Longchenpa discusses the Prāsaṅgika Madhyamaka in his *The Treasury of Wish-Fulfilment*, p. 536, calling it the highest system of dialectical philosophy. He confirms this in his *The Treasury of Tenets*, p. 201-12, and *The Treasury of the Supreme Vehicle*, p. 91. In his commentary to chapter eight of *The Treasury of the Dharmadhātu*, he writes "Most of the methods of comprehending the freedom of extremes, and so on, of Natural Great Perfection are similar to Prāsaṅgika Madhyamaka. However, Madhyamaka regards the emptiness as the important thing. Dzogpachenpo, relying on the primordially pure and naked intrinsic awareness (rigpa) which is just non-existent and unceasing, comprehends it and all the phenomena arisen from it as free from extremes like space." Tulku Thondup, *Buddha Mind*, p. 104. *Lung gi gter mdzod*, p. 76b/1. Mipham writes in his *Beacon of Certainty*: "In cutting through to primordial purity, one needs to perfect the Prāsaṅgika view." (Derge edition, vol. 9 of Mipham's *Collected Works*, folio 9b6, or page 119, folio 25a/6 of Mipham Sungbum vol. Shri, Chengdu edition.) For the references to Longchenpa, see *Mipham's Beacon of Certainity*, pp. 92-97, and 486-7, and Mipham on p. 209, and pp. 310-311.

79   For a comprehensive discussion of this Madhyamaka reasoning, see Jeffrey Hopkins, *Meditation on Emptiness*, pp. 131-50, London: Wisdom, 1983. See also *Mipham's Theory of Interpretation*, Matthew Kapstein, in *Buddhist Hermeneutics*, edited by Donald S. Lopez, Jr., Honolulu: University of Hawaii Press, 1988, pp. 156, and 170-1.

80   His Holiness refers again to this chapter of *The Treasury of Wish-Fulfilment* in his teaching in France in 1997, where he says: "Longchen Rabjam proposes numerous methods of classifying the two fundamental truths, and among them one where the fundamental or innate refers to ultimate truth, and the adventitious to conventional truth. So he asserts the ultimate truth of the fundamental, innate nature, devoid of adventitious phenomena, and he

establishes the ultimate truth of the fundamental innate mind of clear light."
See *Pacifier l'esprit*, Dalaï Lama, transcrit par Jigmé Khyentsé Rinpoché et
traduit du tibétain par Patrick Carré, Paris: Albin Michel, 1999, p. 144. See
also *The Gelug/Kagyü Tradition of Mahāmudrā*, p. 207. Kyabjé Dudjom
Rinpoche refers to *The Treasury of Wish-Fulfilment* in "The Two Truths
According to Great Madhyamaka", in *Fundamentals of the Nyingma School*,
pp. 209ff.

81   Four types of nirmāṇakāya or emanation body are given by Maitreya in his
      Ornament for the Mahāyāna Sūtras: artisan emanation body, birth emanation
      body, great enlightenment emanation body and supreme emanation body.
      Buddha Śākyamuni is an example of the supreme emanation body. See *The
      Fundamental Potential for Enlightenment*, pp. 179ff.

82   In his *Union of the Old and New Schools*, His Holiness also points to different
      uses of the term ultimate. He elaborates on the quotation from Maitreya,
      explaining "the *objective* ultimate is emptiness, the *practical* ultimate is the
      wisdom consciousness of meditative equipoise; and the *attained* ultimate is
      nirvāṇa." *Kindness, Clarity and Insight*, p. 210. He refers to it again in *The
      Gelug/Kagyü Tradition of Mahāmudrā*, p. 207. The verse is from
      Madhyāntavibhaṅga, dbus dang mtha' rnam par 'byed pa, P5522, vol. 108,
      ch. 3, verse 11.

83   Cf. *Kindness, Clarity and Insight*, p. 209. Uttaratantra, ch. 1, verses 20-21.

84   His Holiness discusses shyentong at length in *The Gelug/Kagyü Tradition of
      Mahāmudrā*, in the context of his commentary on the First Panchen Lama's
      'Root Text for the Precious Gelug/Kagyü Tradition of Mahāmudrā: The
      Main Road of the Triumphant Ones'. His analysis hinges on whether the
      shyentong view combines the second and third turnings of the wheel of
      Dharma. See pp. 234-9.

85   Vasubandhu's *Abhidharmakośakārikā*, Chos mgon pa'i mdzod kyi tshig le'ur
      byas pa, P5590, vol. 115. There is an English translation from the French of
      Louis de la Vallée Poussin by Leo Pruden: *Abhidharmakośabhāṣyam*, four vols.
      Freemont: Asian Humanities Press 1988-9.

86   On their realization of emptiness see *Mipham's Beacon of Certainty*,
      pp. 278-9.

87   Ch. 1, verse 2.

88   Cf. *The World of Tibetan Buddhism*, p. 99.

89   Given in Tsepak Rigdzin, *Tibetan-English Dictionary of Buddhist Terms*,
      Dharamsala: Library of Tibetan Works and Archives, 1993, as: action seal,
      samaya seal, dharma seal and great seal or seal of emptiness.

90   So called because "they advocate certain physical penances, such as fasting,
      maintaining special diets and so on". *The World of Tibetan Buddhism*, p. 104.

91   The three inner tantras are also known as the vehicles of overpowering
      means "because they contain methods for manifesting the subtlest level of
      mind by dissolving the gross levels of mind and energies, by which the
      practitioner brings his mental state to a deep level beyond the polarities of
      discriminating between good and bad, dirty or clean, and so on, and is thus
      able to transcend the worldly conventions governed by such polarities." *The*

World of Tibetan Buddhism, p.104.This division of the nine yānas into vehicles from the direction of the origin of suffering, vehicles of gaining awareness through austerities, and vehicles of overpowering means is said by Kyabjé Dudjom Rinpoche to derive from *The General Sūtra which Gather All Intentions*. See his *The Nyingma School of Tibetan Buddhism*, translated and edited by Gyurmé Dorje and Matthew Kapstein, Boston: Wisdom, 1992, vol.1, p. 81.

92   His Holiness discusses these three divisions within Highest Yoga Tantra in *The World of Tibetan Buddhism*, p. 105, and *The Gelug/Kagyü Tradition of Mahāmudrā*, pp. 242-4. For a more elaborate account of the four classes of tantra, see The Thirteenth Dalai Lama in *Path of the Bodhisattva Warrior*, The Thirteenth Dalai Lama and Glenn Mullin, Ithaca: Snow Lion, 1988, pp. 275-306, also Tsongkhapa, et al: *Tantra in Tibet*, pp. 151-64, London: George Allen and Unwin, 1977, and *Kalacakra Tantra*, Tenzin Gyatso, the Dalai Lama, edited, translated and introduced by Jeffrey Hopkins, London: Wisdom, 1989, pp. 62-7.

93   In the fourth Mind and Life dialogue, His Holiness described different kinds of rigpa: "There are three types of pristine awareness. *Basic pristine awareness* (Tib. *gzhi'i rig pa*) acts as the basis for all of saṃsāra and nirvāṇa, and is identical to the subtle clear light. This is the pristine awareness one experiences at the time of death, but not during the ordinary waking state. It is from this awareness that the foundation consciousness arises. Then, through meditative practice, after the experience of foundation consciousness you can experience a second kind of pristine awareness, namely *effulgent awareness* (Tib. *rtsal gyi rig pa*). The third kind of pristine awareness is called *natural pristine awareness* (Tib. *rang bzhin gyi rig pa*). Where does this natural awareness come in? As a result of meditative practice it is possible to gain direct experience of the subtle clear light, and the subtle clear light so experienced is said to be the natural clear light, as distinguished from the basic clear light. The basic clear light can be experienced only at the time of death." *Sleeping, Dreaming and Dying*, p. 122.

94   See above, pp. 52-3.

95   There are a number of teachings and commentaries on this lojong instruction, such as: His Holiness the Dalai Lama, *Awakening the Heart, Lightening the Mind*, San Francisco: Harper, 1995; Gyalwa Gendun Druppa the First Dalai Lama, *Training the Mind in the Great Way*, Ithaca: Snow Lion, 1993; Jamgön Kongtrul, *The Great Path of Awakening*, Boston: Shambhala, 1987; Chögyam Trungpa, *Training the Mind and Cultivating Loving Kindness*, Boston: Shambhala, 1993; Geshe Rabten and Geshe Ngawang Dhargyey, *Advice From a Spiritual Friend*, New Delhi: Wisdom Culture, 1977; Gomo Tulku, *Becoming a Child of the Buddhas*, Boston: Wisdom, 1998; Sermey Khensur Lobsang Tharchin, *Achieving Bodhicitta*, Howell: Mahayana Sutra and Tantra Press, 1999; Pema Chödrön, *Start Where You Are*, Boston: Shambhala, 1994; and B. Alan Wallace, *A Passage from Solitude*, Ithaca: Snow Lion, 1992.

96   The *Triyik Yeshé Lama* was composed by Jikmé Lingpa (1730-98), and as Tulku Thondup Rinpoche observes "has become the most comprehensive

manual of Dzogpachenpo meditation in the Nyingma tradition." Based on the innermost, unexcelled cycle of the category of pith instructions, it incorporates the essence of the Dzogchen tantras, and presents primarily the practical instructions for trekchö and tögal, along with instructions for liberation in the bardo states, and liberation in pure nirmāṇakāya realms.

97   Or *Tathāgata Essence Sūtra: Tathāgatagarbhasūtra*, de bzhin gshegs pa'i snying po'i mdo, P. 924, vol. 36; Toh. 258.

98   Cf. *The World of Tibetan Buddhism*, pp. 125 and 123, where it is designated the most popular deity of Performance Tantra. See also Stephen Hodge, *Mahā Vairocana Abhisaṃbhodi Tantra*, with the commentary by Buddhaguhya, to be published in September 2000 by Curzon Press.

99   See John Whitney Pettit, *Mipham's Beacon of Certainty*, esp. pp. 111ff. Also Cyrus Stearns, *The Buddha from Dolpo*, SUNY: Albany, 1999, and Paul Williams, *Mahāyāna Buddhism*, New York: Routledge, 1989, pp. 105-9.

100   Cf. Dodrupchen, *rdzogs chen dris lan*, folio 4a, question 10, p. 569 (new edition).

101   See *Consciousness at the Crossroads*, Conversations with the Dalai Lama on Brain Sciences and Buddhism, ed. by Zara Houshmand, Robert B. Livingston and B. Alan Wallace, Ithaca: Snow Lion, 1999. Also *Sleeping, Dreaming and Dying*, The Dalai Lama, Wisdom, ed. by Francisco J. Varela, Boston: Wisdom Publications, 1997.

102   In *The Meaning of Life*, His Holiness comments: "It is said that the qualities that depend on the mind have a stable basis—the reason for this being that consciousness has no beginning and no end." p. 57.

103   See *Highest Yoga Tantra*, Daniel Cozort, Ithaca: Snow Lion, 1986, p. 73-6.

104   See *Sleeping, Dreaming and Dying*, where His Holiness explains: "The eighty types of conceptualization are various emotional and cognitive states that are elements of the mind...In Nāgārjuna's writings it is said that there are eighty types of conceptualization, which indicate various levels of energy activity, and these are associated with various states of emotions and thought. They are divided into three groups based on the level of energy activity: highest, medium and lowest, respectively. The first group has thirty-three, the second has forty and the third has seven types of conceptualization." pp. 168-9. For a complete enumeration of the eighty conceptions and their relation to the three 'appearances'—i.e. white appearance, red increase, and black attainment—see *Buddhist Ethics*, Jamgön Kongtrul Lodrö Tayé, translated and edited by The International Translation Committee founded by Kalu Rinpoche, Ithaca: Snow Lion, 1998, pp. 507-9, and *The Mirror of Mindfulness*, Tsele Natsok Rangdrol, translated by Erik Pema Kunzang, Boston: Shambhala, 1987, pp. 32-4.

105   On the four empties, see *Highest Yoga Tantra*, p. 73.

106   Tiklé (*thig le*) in Sanskrit 'bindus' are often translated as 'drops' or 'essences'. There are said to be two types, red and white, gross and subtle, which reside within the channels; their melting and flowing through the channels give rise to the experience of bliss.

107   The four joys are: joy, supreme joy, special joy and innate joy. See *Highest Yoga Tantra*, p. 76.

108 See *Highest Yoga Tantra*, pp. 121-131.

109 See below, p. 196.

110 "The first two are said to be in common with the Sūtra path; through one-pointed yoga, calm abiding of the mind is achieved, and through non-elaborative yoga, special insight into emptiness is achieved. Through one-taste yoga, an extraordinary special insight is achieved in which all appearing and occurring phenomena are seen as of one taste in the sphere of the fundamental innate mind of clear light. When this path, which is unique to Mantra, increases in strength, it becomes non-meditative yoga." *The Meaning of Life*, p. 96.

111 Takpo Tashi Namgyal, *Mahāmudrā, The Quintessence of Mind and Meditation*, Delhi: Motilal Banarsidass, 1993.

112 For example, see *Mahāmudrā, The Quintessence of Mind and Meditation*, pp. 109-16.

113 H.H. Sakya Trizin explains: "the causal continuum or ālaya refers to the continuity of the seed for attaining Buddhahood—the buddha nature which is in all of us."

114 The 'foundation' or 'storehouse consciousness' is the most subtle of the eight consciousnesses defined in this school. Imprints created by actions induced by negative emotions are stored in the ālayavijñāna, until such time as the conditions for their appearance arise. His Holiness discusses this in *Sleeping, Dreaming and Dying*. pp. 86-7.

115 Longchenpa in his commentary to *The Treasury of the Dharmadhātu* says: "Ati, vehicle of the vajra essence, is said to be the summit, exalted above all other vehicles like the king of mountains towering, supreme, above the four continents that surround it. *The Tantra of the Great Naturally Arising Awareness* says: 'The pinnacle of all views is explained as Ati, the Dzogpachenpo'." *Lung gi gter mdzod*, Chapter 7, p. 64b in Dodrupchen Rinpoche's edition; p. 1066 in the edition published by Dharma Publishing.

116 In *rdzogs chen skor*, in his Collected Works, volume cha, pp. 231-2, new edition, volume ka, pp. 606-7, published by Dodrupchen Rinpoche, Gangtok, Sikkim.

117 His Holiness is quoting from *The Special Teaching of the Wise and Glorious King*. See page 75.

118 His Holiness is essentializing and quoting Dodrupchen's essay on the ground and appearances of the ground in his collection on Dzogchen: *rdzogs chen skor*, in his Collected Works, vol. cha, pp. 227-8, folios 14a5-15a3, or vol. ka, pp. 602-3 in the new edition.

119 The four visions are: manifest intrinsic reality, increasing of experience, rigpa attaining its full measure, and exhaustion of phenomena, beyond the mind.

120 In the *lung gi gter mdzod*, folios 51a-52b, Adzom Chögar edition, published by Dodrupchen Rinpoche, Gangtok, Sikkim; Dharma Publishing edition, p. 1023.

121 The term *rtsal* is translated as energy or inner power. *Lung gi gter mdzod*, folio 54a; p. 1032.

122 *Lung gi gter mdzod*, folios 54a and 55a; pp. 1033 and 1035.

123 See below, pp. 83-4.

124 *Yogacaracatuḥśataka*, rnal 'byor spyod pa'i bzhi brgya pa: chap. 14, verse 25.
     See *Yogic Deeds of Bodhisattvas, Gyel-tsap on Aryadeva's Four Hundred*,
     commentary by Geshe Sonam Rinchen, translated and edited by Ruth
     Sonam, Ithaca: Snow Lion, 1994, p. 275.

125 The *Samantabhadranāmasādhana*, kun tu bzang po zhes bya ba'i sgrub pa'i
     thabs, by Buddhaśrījñāna, appears in the Tengyur: bstan 'gyur rgyud 'grel,
     Ti 33b-42b. See *A Complete Catalogue of the Tibetan Buddhist Canons*, edited
     by Prof. Hakuju Ui, entry #1855.

126 *Śrī-samantabhadra-sādhana-vṛtti*, dpal kun tu bzang po'i sgrub thabs kyi 'grel
     pa, by Thagana, in bstan 'gyur rgyud 'grel, Ti, pp. 224a-274b. See *A Complete
     Catalogue of the Tibetan Buddhist Canons*, edited by Prof. Hakuju Ui,
     entry #1868.

127 *rdzogs chen skor*, p. 299; new edition, p. 662. See also *rdzogs chen thor bu*,
     pp. 194-5; 555-6.

128 For example, in his Introduction to *The Precious Treasury of the Way of Abiding*,
     Tulku Thondup Rinpoche quotes Dodrupchen from his *rdzogs chen skor*,
     folio 7b/4; p. 592: "Use intrinsic awareness as the way [meditation]. Maintain
     only that awareness. Do not employ any concepts, since concepts are mind
     [and not the nature of mind]. Meditate [on intrinsic awareness after] having
     distinguished between mind and intrinsic awareness." Also, cf. *rdzogs chen thor
     bu*, pp. 194-5; new edition, pp. 555-6.

129 Chap 12, folio 178b; pp. 1438-9. The verse from Nāgārjuna's
     Madhyamakamūlakārikā is Chap. 24, verse 19.

130 *The Reverberation of Sound*—sgra thal 'gyur rtsa ba'i rgyud—is the 'root tantra'
     among the seventeen tantras of the most secret unexcelled cycle of pith
     instructions in Dzogchen.

131 *Lung gi gter mdzod*, Chapter 9, Folio 83a; p. 1126.

132 *Lung gi gter mdzod*, Chapter 9, Folio 83b; p. 1126.

133 See page 67.

134 *Lung gi gter mdzod*, Chapter 10, 107b, 112a-117a.

135 For example, in *rdzogs chen skor*, p. 229; 662.

136 The source of The Twelve Kinds of Vajra Laughter quoted by Longchenpa
     is *The Heaped Jewel Tantra* (rin chen spuns pa'i rgyud) *Lung gi gter mdzod*,
     Chap. 12, 161a-161b.

137 *Lung gi gter mdzod*, Chap. 12, p. 167a; 1400-1.

GLOSSARY OF TERMS

Some of the terms that appear in this book are listed below. Those marked with an asterisk have more than one English equivalent.

affirming negative phemonena	*ma yin dgag*
affirming phenomena	*sgrub pa*
afflictive emotion★	*nyon mongs pa*
ālaya	*kun gzhi*
all-penetrating★	*zang thal*
all pervading vajra space	*mkha'khyab mkha'i rdo rje*
analytical meditation	*dpyad sgom*
appearance	*snang ba*
appearances/manifestations of the ground	*gzhi snang*
appearing object	*snang yul*
attachment to experience	*nyams zhen*
apperceptive nature of the mind★	*rang rig*
attainment	*thob pa*
attaining warmth	*drod 'thob*
basic space	*dbyings*
basic space of the pure state of clear light	*dag pa 'od gsal gyi dbyings*
basis of all★	*kun gzhi*
bliss, clarity and non-conceptuality	*bde gsal mi rtog*
calm, steady ālaya	*kun gzhi brtan po*
category of mind	*sems sde*
category of pith-instructions	*man ngag sde*
category of space	*klong sde*
causal continuum	*rgyu'i rgyud*
cessation	*'gog pa*
clear light	*'od gsal*
clear light of death	*'chi'i 'od gsal*
closed-mindedness	*gti mug*
coarse and subtle states of energy and mind	*phra rags kyi rlung sems*

coemergent great bliss	*lhan cig skyes pa'i bde ba*
common preliminary practice	*thun mong gi sngon 'gro*
compassionate energy★	*thugs rje*
cognitive obscurations★	*shes bya'i sgrib pa*
concentration★	*ting nge 'dzin*
consciousness	*shes pa; rnam shes*
contemplative meditation★	*'jog sgom*
contaminated	*zag bcas*
conventional truth	*kun rdzob bden pa*
cycle of existence	*'khor ba*
delusions★	*nyon mongs*
diamond slivers	*rdo rje gzegs ma*
differentiating ordinary mind and rigpa	*sems rig shan 'byed*
display	*rol pa*
dissolution due to the influence of confusion	*'khrul stobs kyis thim pa*
dissolution due to the influence of liberation	*grol stobs kyis thim pa*
dualistic thinking	*gzung 'dzin gyi rnam rtog*
eight doorways of spontaneous presence	*lhun grub kyi sgo brgyad*
eighty conceptualizations/indicative conceptions	*kun rtog brgyad bcu*
effortless yāna	*rtsol bral gyi thegpa*
effulgent awareness/rigpa★	*rtsal gyi rig pa*
emotional obscurations★	*nyon mongs pa'i sgrib pa*
emptiness	*stong pa nyid*
emptiness endowed with all the aspects of skilful means	*rnam kun mchog ldan*
emptiness of other	*gzhan stong*
empty form	*stong gzugs*
energy★	*rtsal; thugs rje*
entity, essence	*ngo bo*
essences	*thig le*
essential awareness/rigpa	*ngo bo'i rig pa*
ethical discipline	*tshul khrims*
even and all-pervasive	*phyal ba*
father tantra	*pha rgyud*
five supreme paths for buddhahood without meditation	*ma bsgom sangs rgyas chos lnga'i lam mchog*
flow	*yo langs*
formal meditation	*mnyam gzhag*
four axioms or seals of Buddhadharma	*chos kyi sdom bzhi/lta ba bka' btags kyi phyag rgya bzhi*
four empties	*stong pa bzhi*
four maṇḍalas	*rten dkyil 'khor bzhi*
four reliances	*ston pa bzhi*
four seals	*phyag rgya bzhi*
four states of imperturbable rest★	*cog bzhag bzhi*
four visions	*snang ba bzhi*

four ways of leaving things in their natural simplicity*	cog bzhag bzhi
free from elaboration	spros bral
fundamental innate mind of clear light	gnyug ma lhan cig skyes pa'i 'od gsal gyi sems
grasping at things as truly existent	bden 'dzin
great compassion	snying rje chen po
ground	gzhi
ground rigpa	gzhi'i rig pa
highest yoga tantra	sngags bla na med pa
ignorance/misknowledge	ma rig pa
illusory body	sgyu lus
imputed phenomena	btags yod
increase	mched pa
indivisibility of saṃsāra and nirvāṇa	'khor 'das dbyer med
indwelling rigpa	rig pa ngang gnas
inference	rjes dpag
inherent power of wisdom	ye shes kyi rang rtsal
innate	lhan cig skyes pa
inner lucidity	nang gsal
inner power; radiance*	rtsal
inseparability of space and rigpa	dbyings rig gnyis dbyer med
insight*	shes rab
intrinsic nature of reality; dharmatā	chos nyid
introduction	ngo sprod pa
karmic formations	'du byed kyi las
key point*	gnad
listeners' vehicle	nyan thos kyi theg pa
liberation upon arising	shar grol
liberation without being of benefit or harm	phan med gnod med du grol ba
loving-kindness; love	byams pa
mahāmudrā	phyag rgya chen po
matter	bem po
meditation	sgom pa
meditative stabilization/absorption*	ting nge 'dzin
meeting of mother and child clear light	'od gsal ma bu 'phrod pa
method of liberation	grol lugs
mind only school	sems tsam pa
mind; ordinary mind	sems
mother clear light present as the ground	gzhi gnas ma'i 'od gsal
mother tantra	ma rgyud
nakedly free/naked liberation	cer grol
natural and genuine mindfulness	rang babs gnyug ma'i dran pa
naturally inherent wisdom	rang gnas ye shes
nature	rang bzhin
negating phenomena	dgag pa

no fixed basis or origin	*gzhi med rtsa bral*
non-affirming negative phenomena	*med dgag*
non-dual tantra	*gnyis med rgyud*
non-duality★	*spros bral*
non-meditation	*sgom med*
object of apprehension	*'dzin yul*
obstructions to knowledge	*shes bya'i sgrib pa*
one-pointedness	*rtse gcig*
one taste	*ro gcig*
origins of suffering	*kun 'byung*
ordinary consciousness	*blo*
ordinary awareness	*tha mal gyi shes pa*
other-powered	*gzhan dbang can*
outer lucidity	*phyi gsal*
path clear light of practice	*nyams len lam gyi 'od gsal*
perfection vehicle	*phar phyin theg pa*
person who progresses in instantaneous leaps	*cig car ba*
person who progresses in gradual stages	*rim gyis pa*
pervasive suffering of conditioning	*khyab pa 'du byed kyi sdug bsngal*
philosophical tenets	*grub mtha'*
pith instruction	*man ngag*
post-meditation	*rjes thob*
primordial wisdom	*ye shes*
precious mind	*rin chen sems*
primal matter	*gtso bo*
primordial wisdom of great bliss★	*bde ba chen po'i ye shes*
primordially present mindfulness	*ye babs kyi dran pa*
produced phenomena	*'dus byas*
proliferation of delusion	*'khrul 'byams*
pure vision	*dag snang*
radiance	*gdangs*
reaching a definitive conclusion	*gtan la 'bebs pa*
realization	*rtogs pa*
reasoning that examines ultimate reality	*don dam dpyod pa'i rigs pa*
recognition	*ngo shes pa*
release★	*grol ba*
responsiveness★	*thugs rje*
rigpa as energy★	*rtsal gyi rig pa*
rigpa of all-embracing spontaneous presence	*lhun grub sbubs kyi rig pa*
samādhi of great, natural abiding	*rang gnas kyi ting nge 'dzin*
samādhi of supreme immediacy	*thog babs kyi ting nge 'dzin*
samādhi of the all-pervasive seal	*rgyas 'debs kyi ting nge 'dzin*
scriptural authority and reasoning	*lung rigs*
searching for mind's hidden flaw	*sems kyi mtshang btsal ba*
stupid dullness, quality of	*rmongs cha*

reflexive awareness*	rang rig
self-arising wisdom of rigpa	rang 'byung rig pa'i ye shes
self-liberation	rang grol
settling meditation*	'jog sgom
six consciousnesses	rnam shes tshogs drug
skilful means	thabs
solitary realizers' vehicle	rang sangs rgyas kyi theg pa
space particles	nam mkha'i rdul
spiritual trap	chos kyi gzeb
spontaneous presence	lhun grub
spontaneous great bliss	lhan cig skyes pa'i bde ba
śrāvakas	nyan thos
stability	brtan pa
suffering of change	'gyur ba'i sdug bsngal
suffering of suffering	sdug bsngal gyi sdug bsngal
superimposition and exaggeration	sgro skur
supreme nirmāṇakāya	mchog gi sprul sku
ten traps	gzeb bcu
the path including its result	lam 'bras
thought	rnam rtog
three higher trainings	bslab pa gsum
three immovables	mi gyo ba gsum
to be made fully evident	mgon du byed pa
training the mind	blo sbyong
transcendent wisdom of great bliss*	bde ba chen po'i ye shes
transparently clear*	zang thal
triple tantra	rgyud gsum
true cessation	'gog bden
true path	lam bden
twelve kinds of vajra laughter	rdo rje gad mo bcu gnyis
twelve links of dependent origination	rten 'brel bcu gnyis
two truths	bden pa gnyis
ultimate truth	don dam bden pa
uncommon preliminary practices	thun min gyi sngon 'gro
uncompounded	'dus ma byas pa
uncontrived	ma bcos
union of emptiness and clarity	gsal stong zung 'jug
union of rigpa and emptiness	rig stong zung 'jug
unobstructed, unimpeded*	zang thal
valid cognition	tshad ma
vehicles from the direction of the origin of suffering	kun 'byung 'dren pa'i thegpa
vehicles of gaining awareness through austerities	dka' thub rig byed kyi theg pa
vehicles of overpowering means	dbang sgyur thabs kyi theg pa
view	lta ba
vital energies	rlung

vital point*   gnad
visions of the vajrakāya   rdo rje sku'i snang ba
wisdom   ye shes; shes rab
wisdom mind; intent   dgongs pa
wisdom that comes from contemplation   bsam pa'i shes rab
wisdom that comes from listening   thos pa'i shes rab
wisdom that comes from meditation   sgom pa'i shes rab
wonderment; transfixed in wonder;
    struck by wonder   had de ba

BIBLIOGRAPHY

SOURCES

Quoted or mentioned by His Holiness:

SŪTRAS AND TANTRAS

Essence of Buddhahood Sūtra
Tathāgatagarbhasūtra
de bzhin gshegs pa'i snying po'i mdo
P924, vol. 36; Toh. 258

Rice Seedling Sūtra
Śālistambhasūtra
sa lu'i ljang po'i mdo
P876, vol. 34

Sūtra on the Ten Grounds
Daśabhūmikasūtra
mdo sde sa bcu pa
P761.31, vol. 25

Transcendent Wisdom in Eight Thousand Lines
Aṣṭasāhasrikāprajñāpāramitāsūtra
'phags pa shes rab kyi pha rol tu phyin pa brgyad stong pa'i mdo
P734, vol. 21; Toh. 12

Guhyasamāja Tantra
Guhyasamājanāmamahākalparāja
gsang ba 'dus pa zhes bya ba brtag pa'i rgyal po chen po
P81, vol. 3

Hevajra Tantra
Hevajratantrarāja
kye'i rdo rje zhes bya ba rgyud kyi rgyalpo
P10, vol. 1

Kālacakra Tantra
Śrīkālacakranāmatantrarāja
dpal dus kyi 'khor lo'i rgyud kyi rgyal po
P4, vol.1

Reverberation of Sound Root Tantra
sgra thal 'gyur rtsa ba'i rgyud
NGB vol. 10, no. 155

Vajra Tent Tantra
Ḍākinīvajrapañjaramahātantrarājakalpa
mkha' 'gro ma rdo rje gur zhes bya ba'i rgyud kyi rgyal po chen po'i brtag pa
P11, vol.1

TREATISES AND COMMENTARIES

Āryadeva
Four Hundred Verses on the Middle Way
Catuḥśatakaśāstrakārikā
bstan bcos bzhi brgya pa zhes bya ba'i tshig le'ur byas pa
P5246, vol. 95

Buddhajñāna
Means of Accomplishment entitled 'All Good'
Samantabhadranāmasādhana
kun tu bzang po zhes bya ba'i sgrub pa'i thabs
bstan 'gyur, 65 rgyud 'grel 39, No. 2718, Ti, 33b–42b

Candrakīrti
Entering the Middle Way
Madhyamākavatāra
dbu ma la 'jug pa
P5261, vol. 98; P5262, vol. 98; Toh. 3861

Dharmakīrti
Commentary on 'Valid Cognition'
Pramāṇavārttikakārikā
tshad ma rnam 'grel gyi tshig le'ur byas pa
P5709, vol. 130; Toh. 4210

Maitreya
Sublime Continuum of the Great Vehicle
Mahāyanā-uttaratantraśāstra
theg pa chen po rgyud bla ma'i bstan bcos
P5525, vol. 108; Toh. 4020

Discriminating the Middle from the Extremes
Madhyāntavibhāga
dbus dang mtha' rnam par 'byed pa
P5522, vol. 108

Ornament of Clear Realization
Abhisamayālaṃkāra(nāmaprajñāpāramitopadeśaśāstra)
mngon par rtogs pa'i rgyan
Dg. T. Shes phyin, vol. ka; Toh. 4020

Nāgārjuna
Fundamental Treatise on the Middle Way
Mūlamadhayamakākarikā
dbu ma rtsa ba'i tshig le'ur byas pa
P5524, vol. 95

Śāntideva
The Way of the Bodhisattva
Bodhicaryāvatāra
byang chub sems dpa'i spyod pa la 'jug pa
P5272, vol. 99

Thagana
Commentary on the Means of Accomplishment of Glorious 'All Good'
Śrīsamantabhadrasādhanavṛtti
dpal kun tu bzang po'i sgrub thabs kyi 'grel pa
bstan 'gyur, 65 rgyud 'grel 39, No. , Ti, 224a–274b

Vasubandhu
Treasury of Knowledge
Abhidharmakośakārikā
chos mngon pa'i mdzod kyi tshig le'ur byas pa
P5590, vol. 115; Toh. 4089

WORKS BY TIBETAN AUTHORS

Dakpo Tashi Namgyal
Light of the Moon
nges don phyag rgya chen po'i bsgom rim gsal bar byed pa'i legs bshad zla ba'i 'od zer

Dodrupchen, Jikmé Tenpé Nyima
From The Collected Works of Dodrupchen Jikmé Tenpé Nyima Pal Zangpo
rdo grub chen 'jigs med bstan pa'i nyi ma dpal bzang po'i bka 'bum
Published at Chorten Monastery, Deorali, Gangtok, Sikkim, by Dodrupchen
Rinpoche:

On Dzogchen
rdzogs chen skor
Vol. cha, pp. 201-314; new edition, vol. ka, pp. 581-675

Dzogchen Miscellany
rdzogs chen thor bu
Vol. cha, pp. 179-200; new edition, vol. ka, pp. 539-561

Questions and Answers on Dzogchen
rdzogs chen dris lan
Vol. cha, pp. 493-513; new edition, vol. ka, pp. 563-579

Jikmé Lingpa
The Treasury of Enlightened Attributes
yon tan rin po che'i mdzod
Collected Works, 'jigs gling bka' 'bum (Adzom), vol. ka: yon tan mdzod and bden
gnyis shing rta; vol. kha, rnam mkhyen shing rta
Published for Dodrupchen Rinpoche by Pema Thinley, Sikkim, 1985

Longchen Rabjam
From *The Seven Treasuries*
mdzod bdun
Edited by Dodrupchen Rinpoche, Gangtok, Sikkim

The Treasury of the Dharmadhātu
chos dbyings rin po che'i mdzod
1964, pp. 1-26

The Treasury of Scriptural Transmission
lung gi gter mdzod
212 folios

The Treasury of Wish-Fulfilment
yid bzhin rin po che'i mdzod
44 folia, numbered pp. 1-87
White Lotus, pad ma dkar po (commentary to source verses) in two volumes: vol. I,
250 folios, numbered pp. 89-589; vol. II, 196 folios, numbered pp. 1-391.

Milarepa
Hundred Thousand Songs
mi la'i mgur 'bum : the collected songs of spiritual experience of Jétsun Milarepa,
edited by Tsang Nyön Heruka. Reproduced from the 1980 Kokonor edition.
Gangtok: Sherab Gyaltsen, 1983, pp. 874.

Mipham
Commentary on the Sublime Continuum
theg pa chen po rgyud bla ma'i bstan bcos kyi mchan 'grel mi pham zhal lung
Collected Works, sde dge mgon chen edition, edited by Dilgo Khyentse
Rinpoche, Kathmandu: Dilgo Khyentse, 1990, vol. pa.

Patrul Rinpoche
The Special Teaching of the Wise and Glorious King, with its Commentary
mkhas pa sri rgyal po'i khyad chos 'grel pa dang bcas pa
Collected Works, dpal sprul bka' 'bum, published in five volumes by Szechuan
Minority Nationalities Institute, Tibetan section, 1984, volume 4, pp. 737-753.
Also in the volumes of his collected works published by si khron mi rigs dpe
skrun khang, from 1987-8.

Selected Bibliography

By His Holiness the Dalai Lama

The World of Tibetan Buddhism, The Dalai Lama, translated, edited and annotated
by Geshe Thupten Jinpa, Boston: Wisdom, 1995

The Gelug/Kagyü Tradition of Mahāmudrā, H.H. the Dalai Lama and Alexander
Berzin, Ithaca: Snow Lion, 1997

Kindness, Clarity and Insight, The Fourteenth Dalai Lama, translated and edited by
Jeffrey Hopkins and Elizabeth Napper, Ithaca: Snow Lion, 1984

The Dalai Lama at Harvard, His Holiness the Dalai Lama of Tibet, translated and
edited by Jeffrey Hopkins, Ithaca: Snow Lion, 1988

The Meaning of Life, The Dalai Lama, translated and edited by Jeffrey Hopkins,
Boston: Wisdom, 1992

The Kālachakra Tantra, The Dalai Lama and Jeffrey Hopkins, Boston: Wisdom, 1989

Flash of Lightning in the Dark of Night, Tenzin Gyatso, Boston: Shambhala, 1994

Tant que durera l'espace, Dalaï Lama, traduit du tibétain sous la direction de Dagpo Rimpotché par Marie-Stella Boussemart, Paris: Albin Michel, 1996

Pacifier l'esprit, Dalaï Lama, transcrit par Jigmé Khyentsé Rinpoché et traduit du tibétain par Patrick Carré, Paris: Albin Michel, 1999

The Four Noble Truths, His Holiness the Dalai Lama, translated by Geshe Thupten Jinpa and edited by Dominique Side, London: Thorsons, 1997

Transforming the Mind, His Holiness the Dalai Lama, translated by Geshe Thupten Jinpa and edited by Dominique Side and Geshe Thupten Jinpa, London: Thorsons, 2000

ON DZOGCHEN

Chökyi Nyima Rinpoche, *The Union of Mahamudra and Dzogchen,* translated by Erik Pema Kunsang, edited by Marcia B. Schmidt, Hong Kong: Rangjung Yeshe, 1989

Drubwang Tsoknyi Rinpoche, *Carefree Dignity,* compiled and translated by Erik Pema Kunsang and Marcia Binder Schmidt, edited by Kerry Moran, Boudhanath: Rangjung Yeshe, 1998

Dudjom Rinpoche, *The Nyingma School of Tibetan Buddhism,* translated and edited by Gyurme Dorje, with the collaboration of Matthew Kapstein, Boston: Wisdom, 1991

Khenpos Palden Sherab and Tsewang Dongyal, *The Lion's Gaze,* translated by Sarah Harding, Boca Raton: Sky Dancer, 1998

Longchen Rabjam, *The Precious Treasury of the Way of Abiding,* translated under the direction of H.E. Chagdud Tulku Rinpoche by Richard Barron (Chökyi Nyima) and edited by Padma Translation Committee, Junction City: Padma Publishing, 1998

Namkhai Norbu, Dzogchen, *The Self-Perfected State,* edited by Adriano Clemente, translated from the Italian by John Shane, London: Arkana, 1989

Nyoshul Khenpo, *Natural Great Perfection,* translated by Lama Surya Das, Ithaca: Snow Lion, 1995

Padmasambhava, *Advice from the Lotus Born,* translated by Erik Pema Kunsang, Boudhanath: Rangjung Yeshe, 1994

Patrul Rinpoche, *The Heart Treasure of the Enlightened Ones*, with commentary by Dilgo Khyentse, translated by The Padmakara Translation Group, Boston: Shambhala, 1992

Patrul Rinpoche, *The Words of My Perfect Teacher*, translated by The Padmakara Translation Group, Boston: Shambhala, 1998

John Whitney Pettit, *Mipham's Beacon of Certainty*, Boston: Wisdom, 1999

John Reynolds, *Golden Letters*, Ithaca: Snow Lion, 1996

Sogyal Rinpoche, *Dzogchen and Padmasambhava*, Santa Cruz: Rigpa, 1989

Sogyal Rinpoche, *The Tibetan Book of Living and Dying*, San Francisco: Harper, 1992

Tsele Natsok Rangdrol, *Circle of the Sun*, translated by Erik Pema Kunsang, Boudhanath: Rangjung Yeshe, 1990

Tulku Thondup, *Buddha Mind*, Ithaca: Snow Lion, 1989

Tulku Thondup, *Masters of Meditation and Miracles*, edited by Harold Talbott, Boston: Shambhala, 1996

Tulku Urgyen Rinpoche, *As It Is, Vol. 1* and *Vol. 2*, translated by Erik Pema Kunsang, Boudhanath: Rangjung Yeshe, 1999

Tulku Urgyen Rinpoche, *Rainbow Painting*, translated by Erik Pema Kunsang, Boudhanath: Rangjung Yeshe, 1995

ON BUDDHISM AND TIBETAN BUDDHISM IN GENERAL

Āryadeva, *Yogic Deeds of the Bodhisattvas*, Gyel-tsap on Āryadeva's Four Hundred, commentary by Geshe Sonam Rinchen, translated and edited by Ruth Sonam, Ithaca: Snow Lion, 1994

Daniel Cozort, *Highest Yoga Tantra*, Ithaca: Snow Lion, 1986

Deshung Rinpoche, *The Three Levels of Spiritual Perception*, translated by Jared Rhoton, Boston: Wisdom, 1995

Jeffrey Hopkins, *Meditation on Emptiness*, Boston: Wisdom, 1983

Maitreya, *Maitreya on Buddha Nature*, a new translation of Asanga's mahāyāna uttara tantra śāstra by Ken and Katia Holmes, Forres: Altea, 1999

Nāgārjuna, *The Fundamental Wisdom of the Middle Way*, Nāgārjuna's Mūlamadhyamakakārikā, translation and commentary by Jay L. Garfield, New York: Oxford University Press, 1995

Ngorchen Konchog Lhundrub, *The Beautiful Ornament of the Three Visions*, translated by Lobsang Dagpa, Ngawang Samten Chophel and Jared Rhoton, Singapore: Golden Vase, 1987; Ithaca: Snow Lion, 1991

Shantideva, *The Way of the Bodhisattva*, translated by The Padmakara Translation Group, Boston: Shambhala, 1997

Takpo Tashi Namgyal, *Mahamudra: The Quintessence of Mind and Meditation*, translated and annotated by Lobsang P. Lhalungpa, foreword by C. Trungpa, Delhi: Motilal Banarsidass, 1993

R.A.F. Thurman, *The Central Philosophy of Tibet: A Study and Translation of Jey Tsongkhapa's Essence of True Eloquence*, Princeton University Press, 1991

Tsong-ka-pa, *Tantra in Tibet*, translated and edited by Jeffrey Hopkins, London: George Allen and Unwin, 1977

THE MIND AND LIFE CONFERENCES

Gentle Bridges, edited by Jeremy Hayward and Francisco Varela, Boston: Shambhala, 1993 (Mind and Life I, 1987)

Consciousness at the Crossroads, edited by Zara Houshmand, Robert B. Livingston and B. Alan Wallace, Ithaca: Snow Lion, 1999 (Mind and Life II, 1989)

Healing Emotions, edited by Daniel Goleman, Boston: Shambhala, 1997 (Mind and Life III, 1991)

Sleeping, Dreaming and Dying, edited by Francisco Varela, Boston: Wisdom, 1997 (Mind and Life IV, 1992)

ACKNOWLEDGEMENTS

First and foremost, our gratitude goes to His Holiness the Dalai Lama for his generosity in giving these unique teachings. Next we should like to thank Sogyal Rinpoche for having invited His Holiness to give the teachings in 1982, 1984 and 1989, and for his continuing inspiration. Thanks go to Geshe Thupten Jinpa for his translation and guidance, and to Richard Barron (Chökyi Nyima) for his translation and his priceless assistance with the whole of this endeavour.

Our deep gratitude must be noted equally to Alak Zenkar Rinpoche and Tulku Thondup Rinpoche for their spontaneous kindness and expert clarification of a great number of points. For their many vital suggestions and improvements to the text, our thanks are due to E. Gene Smith and Steven D. Goodman. We would like to take this opportunity too to thank Dzogchen Rinpoche and the monks of the Dzogchen monastery in Kollegal in India for having made Tibetan transcripts of a number of teachings.

Those who played a key role in the organizing of the teachings presented in this book, and whom we should like to thank here, include, in chronological order: Tsering Dorjee, Kalön Tashi Wangdi, Phuntsog Wangyal, Kalön Tempa Tsering, Kazur Tenzin Geyche, Kazur Lodi Gyari Rinpoche, Rinchen Dharlo and Kazur Tenzin N. Tethong. For his help in facilitating the teachings in Paris, we would like to thank Dagpo Rinpoche. We would like to acknowledge the

Finnish Tibet Committee for their kind permission to include His Holiness's teaching in Helsinki, and thank Antti Tihveräinen, and the Director of the Mannerheim Museum.

A number of members of Rigpa around the world took part in the preparation of this book, directly or indirectly, notably Susie Godfrey, Sue Morrison, Jeannie McSloy, Janine Philippou, Adam Pearcey, Dominique Side, Andreas Schulz, Michael Pope, Susan Oliver, Alex Leith, Graham Price and Sebastien Reggiany. Many others played their part in organizing His Holiness's teachings in Paris, London and San Jose, and especially Claire Michaud, Babette Bridault, Philip Philippou, Sandra Pawula and Mary Ellen Kelleher. Our thanks go to Jeffrey Cox and Sidney Piburn at Snow Lion, and to Martin Schofield for his invaluable advice.

The publication of this book has been made possible through the generosity of Kris Yao and Pei-Lan Shen.

As for any inaccuracies or errors which have crept into this work, the editor reserves the right to claim them entirely as his own.

Our design in editing this book for publication has been to carry out the wishes of His Holiness the Dalai Lama, to make these teachings available, and to help them be of benefit to as many as possible.

Patrick Gaffney
Rigpa International

RIGPA

RIGPA is a Tibetan word which means 'the innermost nature of mind'. Rigpa is also an international network of Buddhist centres, founded by Sogyal Rinpoche in various countries around the world, which offers a graduated path in the study and practice of Buddhism.

— Over the years, many eminent masters from all traditions of Buddhadharma have been invited to teach at Rigpa centres and retreats. They have included Kyabjé Dudjom Rinpoche, Kyabjé Dilgo Khyentse Rinpoche, H. H. Sakya Trizin, the 16th Gyalwang Karmapa, and Kyabjé Ling Rinpoche. Rigpa has had the blessing of sponsoring many teachings and empowerments by His Holiness the Dalai Lama, in London (1981, 1984 and 1988), Paris, (1982 and 1986), Santa Cruz and San Jose (1989), Amsterdam (1999) and the south of France (2000).

— Alongside regular courses in study and practice, retreats in each country are complemented by international retreats at Lerab Ling in southern France, and longer retreats at Dzogchen Beara in south west Ireland.

— Rigpa's Spiritual Care Education and Training Programme makes the Buddhist teachings available to caregivers serving the dying and the bereaved, in the spirit of *The Tibetan Book of Living and Dying*.

— In Asia, Rigpa supports the activity of the great masters and monasteries, and has been instrumental in establishing the Dzogchen monastery in Kollegal, south India, inaugurated by His Holiness the Dalai Lama in 1992.

SOGYAL RINPOCHE received his initial training in Tibet from one of the greatest lamas of the twentieth century, Jamyang Khyentse Chökyi Lodrö. He continued his studies with Kyabjé Dudjom Rinpoche, Kyabjé Dilgo Khyentse Rinpoche and Nyoshul Khen Rinpoche. He regularly visits Rigpa centres worldwide, participates in major conferences, and teaches in Europe, North America, Australia and Asia. Author of the classic *The Tibetan Book of Living and Dying*, Rinpoche's gift of communicating the highest truths of the teachings of Buddhism to people leading busy modern lives has made him one of today's leading interpreters of Tibetan Buddhism.

For further details, please contact:

RIGPA US
449 Powell Street, Suite 200
San Francisco, CA 94102
Phone: +1-415-392 2055
Fax: +1-415-392 2056

RIGPA UK
330, Caledonian Road,
London N1 1BB
Phone: +44-207-700 0185
Fax: +44-207-609 6068

RIGPA GERMANY
Paul Gerhardt-Allee 34,
81245 Munich
Phone: +49-89-89 62 05 15
Fax: +49-89-89 62 05 58

RIGPA HOLLAND
Van Ostadestraat 300
1073 TW, Amsterdam
Phone: +31-20-470 5100
Fax: +31-20-470 4936

INTERNATIONAL RETREAT CENTRE
Lerab Ling, L'Engayresque,
34650 Roquedonde
Phone: +33-467-88 46 00
Fax: +33-467-88 46 01

RIGPA IRELAND
Dzogchen Beara
Garranes, Castletown Bere,
Co. Cork
Phone: +353-27-730 32
Fax: +353-27-731 77

INDEX